Crossroads and Cosmologies

Cultural Heritage Studies

UNIVERSITY PRESS OF FLORIDA

Florida A&M University, Tallahassee
Florida Atlantic University, Boca Raton
Florida Gulf Coast University, Ft. Myers
Florida International University, Miami
Florida State University, Tallahassee
New College of Florida, Sarasota
University of Central Florida, Orlando
University of Florida, Gainesville
University of North Florida, Jacksonville
University of South Florida, Tampa
University of West Florida, Pensacola

Cultural Heritage Studies
Edited by Paul Shackel, University of Maryland

The University Press of Florida is proud to announce the creation of a new series devoted to the study of cultural heritage. This thematic series brings together research devoted to understanding the material and behavioral characteristics of heritage. The series explores the uses of heritage and the meaning of its cultural forms as a way to interpret the present and the past. The series highlights important scholarship related to America's diverse heritage.

Books include important theoretical contributions and descriptions of significant cultural resources. Scholarship addresses questions related to culture and describes how local and national communities develop and value the past. The series includes works in public archaeology, heritage tourism, museum studies, vernacular architecture, history, American studies, and material cultural studies.

Heritage of Value, Archaeology of Renown: Reshaping Archaeological Assessment and Significance, edited by Clay Mathers, Timothy Darvill, and Barbara J. Little (2005)

Archaeology, Cultural Heritage, and the Antiquities Trade, edited by Neil Brodie, Morag M. Kersel, Christina Luke, and Kathryn Walker Tubb (2006)

Archaeological Site Museums in Latin America, edited by Helaine Silverman (2006)

Crossroads and Cosmologies: Diasporas and Ethnogenesis in the New World, by Christopher C. Fennell (2007)

Crossroads and Cosmologies

Diasporas and Ethnogenesis in the New World

Christopher C. Fennell

Foreword by Robert Farris Thompson
Editor's foreword by Paul A. Shackel, series editor

University Press of Florida
Gainesville/Tallahassee/Tampa/Boca Raton
Pensacola/Orlando/Miami/Jacksonville/Ft. Myers/Sarasota

Library of Congress Cataloging-in-Publication Data:
Fennell, Christopher.
Crossroads and cosmologies: diasporas and ethnogenesis in the new world /
Christopher C. Fennell; forewords by Paul A. Shackel and Robert Farris Thompson.
p. cm.—(Cultural heritage studies)
Includes bibliographical references and index.
ISBN 978-0-8130-3141-5 (alk. paper)
1. Blacks—America—Social life and customs. 2. Africans—America—Social life and
customs. 3. Blacks—America—Ethnic identity. 4. Africans—America—Ethnic identity.
5. African diaspora. 6. America—Social life and customs. 7. America—Ethnic relations.
8. Ethnicity—America—History. 9. Ethnohistory—America. 10. Cosmology—History.
I. Title.
E29.N3F46   2007
973.'04960739–dc22
2007005244

The University Press of Florida is the scholarly publishing agency for the State University System of Florida, comprising Florida A&M University, Florida Atlantic University, Florida Gulf Coast University, Florida International University, Florida State University, New College of Florida, University of Central Florida, University of Florida, University of North Florida, University of South Florida, and University of West Florida.

University Press of Florida
15 Northwest 15th Street
Gainesville, FL 32611-2079
http://www.upf.com

For Lee

They were the first great listeners, attuned
To interval, relationship, and scale,
The first to say above, beneath, beyond,
Conjurors with love, death, sleep, with bread and wine,
Who having uttered vanished from the world
Leaving no memory but the marvelous
Magical elements, the breathing shapes
And stops of breath we build our Babels of.

Howard Nemerov, *The Makers*

Contents

Figures

Editor's Foreword

Studies of the African diaspora involve the histories and heritage of people who were forced to leave their traditional homeland. Although it has taken archaeology several decades to become part of this exciting dialogue, the field is ripe for stimulating questions about the past and its implications for the present and the future. *Crossroads and Cosmologies* is an important part of the growing literature that examines the heritage of displaced peoples.

Historical archaeology studies of African American history began in the late 1960s, during the height of the Civil Rights Movement, when Charles Fairbanks (1974) conducted excavations of slave cabins on Kingsley Plantation in northeastern Florida. Several decades earlier, some archaeologists worked on plantation sites, but the main objective of their archaeology was the restoration of the "big house" rather than to focus on the lives of the enslaved (with the exception of the work by Bullen and Bullen 1945). Fairbanks' work is notable because his efforts helped to interpret a way of life that was neglected in the national public memory. He influenced a generation of archaeologists who performed "plantation archaeology." This work helped to provide a new dimension to the understanding of African American lifeways.

Later, Robert Schuyler (1974) and James Deetz (1996) explored issues related to free African American communities. Over the next several decades, those performing archaeology on African American sites struggled with issues of pattern recognition. Many archaeologists eventually realized that the search for patterns made it difficult to interpret African American culture, mostly because they did not pay enough attention to context and meaning (Franklin and McKee 2004; Orser 1989).

In the late twentieth century, diaspora studies became prominent in many disciplines, and I believe that the historical archaeology of African Americans was jolted into this forum because of the crisis that developed with the African Burial Ground in New York City. In 1991, archaeologists discovered the remains of more than four hundred African individuals dating to the seventeenth and eighteenth centuries during pre-construction work for a federal building. The African American community, with the help of politicians, demanded proper treatment as well as more in-depth studies of the human and cultural remains. The African diaspora became the focus of the work that followed over the next decade. This approach made contributions to understanding the roots of these displaced people and the impact of enslavement on this New York population. These people came from a number of areas, such as the Kongo, Ghana, Ashanti, Dahomey, Benin, and Yoruba, abducted within warring states driven by the slave trade and the demand for labor in the Americas and Europe. The archaeology and the biological analysis shed new light on issues of enslavement in the north, and now those living have a richer understanding of African American heritage in New York City. Jolting to the traditional public memory is the fact that the city had one of the largest enslaved populations in the country before the American Revolution (Cantwell and Wall 2001).

The African Burial Ground project stimulated and encouraged others to look at diaspora issues, and there has been a growing trend in archaeology away from the plantation and toward understanding the heritage of those who were displaced (Singleton and Bograd 1995; Weik 1997). This work has shifted from a mainly American pursuit to a more global phenomenon (see for instance Agorsah 1996; Franklin and McKee 2004; P. Mitchell 2005; Yelvington 2006).

The focus on the ways in which particular cultures and their intangible heritage survived, diminished, or continued is an important part in understanding the impact of forced migration. This work by Christopher Fennell is a significant contribution to the literature related to beliefs and expressions of particular African cultures. He argues that looking into the private spaces of individuals is an essential way of identifying cultural traditions that survived the Middle Passage and endured the brutality of plantation life.

Looking at belief systems has always been somewhat problematic for archaeologists. Rather than relying on the concept of creolization, Fennell provides us with a different and powerful way of looking at the results of cultural interactions and material culture expressions. Core symbols, he emphasizes, help express a culture's identity and cosmology. He ties this idea to the concept of ethnogenic bricolage, a creative process in which individuals from different cultural backgrounds interact in new settings. While being suppressed, emblematic expressions and core symbols are brought "underground" and continue to be part of private and individual spaces. These symbols are employed in healing, protection, prayer, and love. These are important concepts for knowing how symbolism works within a culture while also understanding the impact of the diaspora.

Fennell's work is also about understanding context. While it may be easy to interpret a particular symbol as belonging to a specific African tradition, understanding the regional context in which the artifact is found allowed him to investigate other non-African traditions. In one case he carefully developed a context for an archeological find, a sculpted human skull with four initials in a cross-line motif. While examining similar materials uncovered from other African American sites, he concluded the object is part of a German-American folk religion called hexerei. This example serves as a cautionary tale, encouraging us to understand context and meaning.

From the late fifteenth century Europeans have had contact with parts of the Americas, and by the seventeenth century the forced migration of people changed the American landscape. The study of the African diaspora is a vibrant and emerging field, and there is a clear need for understanding its past and present social and political implications. *Crossroads and Cosmologies: Diasporas and Ethnogenesis in the New World* brings a new and exciting perspective in African diaspora studies and helps us understand the role of archaeology in contributing to African American heritage.

Paul A. Shackel, series editor

Foreword

Christopher Fennell's *Crossroads and Cosmologies* opens with Howard Nemerov's poem *The Makers*.

> They were the first great listeners, attuned
> To interval, relationship, and scale,
> The first to say above, beneath, beyond,
> Conjurors with love, death, sleep, with bread and wine. . . .

In this spirit we enter a new archaeology, probing the formerly forgotten or overlooked visual traces of American vernacular women and men, in this case traditionalist African American and German-American. As he does so, Fennell transcends the earlier terms for cultural continuity, retention and survival, in favor of more sophisticated readings.

I was impressed by his section on the Kongo civilization of central Africa. To BaKongo the past is now, and they call it tradition. Key elements of their classical religion, however masked by Christianity, pass on intact into the twenty-first century. This is a given. It is abundantly attested via a critical reading of ethnohistorical accounts spanning more than four centuries.

In January 2006, I was in Mbanza Kongo, site of the ancient capital, and studied a main cemetery. When someone dies in Kongo, mourners may fashion a special archway, called a *fumba* or *lukote*. These are cosmograms. The curve of the fumba or lukote represents the blue dome of heaven, domain of God. It's a hieroglyph of spiritual transition. Dapper illustrates one at the entrance to a cemetery in the northern Kongo city of Lwangu in 1668. A late nineteenth-century explorer noted one too. When I reached the hilltop cemetery of Mbanza Kongo on January 2, 2006, there was one again, covering a grave, like a map to the Almighty, doubled for emphasis.

This leads to a discussion of the Kongo cosmogram (*dikenga*), the literature of which Fennell controls for us. Dikenga (literally, "the turning") stands for the cycling of the sun around four cardinal points: dawn, noon, sunset, and midnight when the sun is shining in the world of the dead. But it also stands for the cycling of the soul. Fennell shows how dikenga ultimately stands for the cycling of all things. He notes that the crossed lines of the cosmogram are viewed as God's writing, not to be drawn by any person without solemnity.

This lore comes in handy when we are confronted with a cosmogram in a black dwelling in Brazoria, Texas. The cardinal points include objects which strongly suggest intra-African fusions of patterns of belief; that is, the iron emblems of the Yoruba god of iron placed within the ruling obsession of the Kongo dikenga. Tentatively, the makers of this site had knowledge of *palo cruzao*, such as black Cuban mixing of the Kongo spirit Sarabanda with the Yoruba lord of iron, Ogún. Brazoria is near Houston and Galveston, ports in touch with Havana.

This is the first text on Afro-Americanist archaeology in which we are rewarded with discussion of those all-important Kongo spirits called *bisimbi* or *basimbi*. They live in the forest (*nfinda*), and they live in the water (*maza*). Bisimbi form the highest class of the dead. They led such powerful lives that when they died, they came back, died, and came back once again. Fennell elaborates: "[simbi] originated as the souls of living persons, which evolved through multiple cycles of death and rebirth as living person, then soul, then ancestor, then simbi." Honoring their power, God transforms them into immortal pools or waterfalls or mountains. Citing Laman, Fennell continues, "'As the basimbi (from simba, to hold, keep, preserve) safeguard the country, man could not exist anywhere without them.'"

Why should Americans know this? Because there are no fewer than three simbi pools in South Carolina. Two of these pools are noted in the literature, the other notice I collected from a white oral source in Charleston in the late 1980s.

In Kongo twisted roots or strangely bent branches are signs of the spirit. They stand for simbi. Across the state line in tidewater Georgia, at Sunbury in Liberty County, simbi-like lengths of twisted forest wood were put up in a black Baptist cemetery by Siras Bowen in the 1930s. He awed his neighbors with these strange, twisted forms. "I doubt I could go into the forest and find trees like that" one of his friends told a student of mine in the summer of 1967. The most simbi-looking of the sculptures was emblazoned with a cosmogram, nestled within a curve of the wood. It read simultaneously as Kongo and Christian. Fennell discusses what happens when original Kongo ideas fuse with symbols drawn from other religions, as we saw in Brazoria.

In the black barrios of Rio de Janeiro an object from the ancient Mediterranean, the figa, showing a human hand with thumb inserted between fingers, making a sign to throw back the evil eye and envy, may have fused with the simbi concept of spirit captured in dramatic torsions of wood. The Museu da Policia in Rio includes in its collection remarkable pieces of twisted forest wood, each branch ending with a carving in the shape of a figa-gesture, like a simbi tree making warding-off gestures. Siras Bowen worked in terms of one of the strong currents of Kongo visual influence in the United States, traditional black burial decorations. But we lack context, of makers and ritual, for the figa-enhanced twisted wood sculptures of black Rio de Janeiro. So we leave these exciting objects in a suspense account, pending more research.

A later chapter involves the careful glossing of a single German-American log cabin in Virginia and its visual trove. Under this house Fennell found a small figure of a skull with a cross and initials. A credulous researcher might announce, "Aha: this obviously connects with the skull figures of the late Son Thomas of black Mississippi, and certain face jugs of black South Carolina." But the cabin was the residence of frugal German-Americans. Patiently excavating and sifting all kinds of evidence, Fennell devotes an entire chapter to proving that the skull and its signs derived from German-American traditions, not Kongo or any other.

In other words, this is more than a book on recent archaeology. It is a model of research. Fennell gives us specific tests by which to measure the relative strength of a given cultural interpretation. He is correcting the literature as well as advancing it.

Robert Farris Thompson
2 February 2006
New Haven

Acknowledgments

The perseverance and creativity of people subjected to terrible adversities in the past provide heartening instances of individual and cultural accomplishments. Archaeologists are privileged to uncover and honor the material traces of those past moments. This book presents expanded analysis and interpretations of historical and archaeological evidence that I addressed to varying extents in earlier publications (Fennell 2000, 2003a, 2003b). This study presents new data and conclusions, including my proposal for a theoretical construct of "ethnogenic bricolage." I also present an interpretative framework that integrates archaeology's methods for examining stylistic patterns with the dynamics of core symbols derived from the work of symbolic anthropologists. Additional historical and anthropological data are presented, including accounts of the Afro-Cuban cultures of Santería and Palo Monte Mayombe, and folk religion practices in Germany and related areas of North America. I also provide expanded and detailed consideration of multivalent symbolism in the material culture of spiritual beliefs and practices uncovered by archaeologists at historic-period sites in the United States.

In developing the analyses of style, symbolism, group identity, and ethnogenesis that I apply in this study, I have received very helpful comments, critiques, and encouragements from Anna Agbe-Davies, Edward Ayers, Kenneth Brown, Frederick Damon, James Davidson, James Delle, Michael Dietler, Leland Ferguson, Garrett Fesler, Maria Franklin, Grey Gundaker, Jeffrey Hantman, Kenneth Kelly, Michael Klein, Mark Leone, Wyatt Mac-Gaffey, Larry McKee, Charles Perdue, Jr., Mark Warner, and Anne Yentsch, among others. I am deeply indebted to Robert Farris Thompson for his insights, advice, and encouragement, and for generously writing a foreword to this book.

I also received very helpful critiques and comments on my analysis of issues concerning folk religions, ethnicities, and stylistic communication from Mary Beaudry, the late James Deetz, Mark Groover, Audrey Horning, Randall McGuire, Paul Mullins, Charles E. Orser, Jr., Robert Schuyler, Roy Wagner, Laurie Wilkie, and Don Yoder. Erik Midelfort and the late Christopher Crocker encouraged my research on folk religion practices in Germany and related traditions in the United States.

My thanks to James Kelly, director of the Virginia Historical Society Museum in Richmond, for arranging permanent curation and exhibition of a remarkable artifact uncovered in my archaeological investigations in Loudoun County, Virginia. That artifact is now part of a permanent exhibition at the Museum, entitled "The Story of Virginia: An American Experience." I also greatly appreciate the enthusiastic support of the landowners of the site where that artifact and associated archaeological remains were recovered. Without their curiosity and hospitality, that project of archaeological and historical research would not have occurred.

I am also very grateful to my colleagues at the Department of Anthropology, University of Illinois, Urbana-Champaign, for their support while I worked on completing this project, including Stanley Ambrose, Matti Bunzl, Thomas Emerson, Paul Garber, Steve Leigh, Barry Lewis, Andy Orta, Timothy Pauketat, Helaine Silverman, Olga Soffer, and Norman Whitten. Ethel Hazard provided valuable research assistance. My sincere appreciation goes to the editors of the University Press of Florida, two peer reviewers of the manuscript, and series editor Paul Shackel for all their guidance, very helpful comments, and encouragement.

I wish to express my greatest thanks to Lee Anne Fennell for all her insights, critiques, and support throughout this project. I dedicate this book to her.

Introduction

Diasporas, Histories, and Heritage

From the beginnings of European colonial expansions in the fifteenth century onward, diverse cultures of Europeans, Africans, and Native Americans came together, interacted, and influenced one another in New World locations. How did these diverse groups construct and maintain social group identities? Archaeological and historical studies of key elements of belief systems, cultural practices, and related symbolic motifs provide highly valuable evidence for understanding the expressions of such identities over time. In addition to insights available from documentary and oral history records, the material expressions of key cultural elements offer significant indicators of social identities and the shifting contours of group boundaries.

This book examines the interactions of cultures and the ways individuals negotiated the complex terrain of intersecting social orders. I explore the challenges people faced in establishing new social relationships and ways of making sense of their experiences and surroundings as diasporas from one region and culture moved into new locations. By the term *diasporas* I mean dispersions of people to new locations due to abduction or to hostile circumstances in the lands from which they fled. These movements could distance families from the cultures to which they had previously subscribed. *Culture*, in the general sense, entails the learned beliefs, knowledge, practices, and behavior with which a people live as a group. As a central element of such a shared meaning system, a *cosmology* comprises the way a group understands the workings of the world, nature, and the cosmos. Cosmologies thus encompass what we think of as religion, physics, and philosophy in a comprehensive framework. Other facets of a culture, such as a particular belief in how one can seek the aid of spiritual forces or how one should design and build a coherent dwelling, are often referred to as *traditions* or *customs* within the culture.

A *culture group* consists of an identifiable population whose members share a particular meaning system that we call *a culture* and who employ that shared belief system to provide a cohesive way of organizing their lives and interactions with one another. Anthropologists refer to the concept of a particular culture group by various terms, including *ethnic group* or *ethnicity*, with the root of *ethnos* being derived from the Greek word for "a people." Similarly, the term *ethnogenesis* refers to the general process by which members of a population form a shared meaning system and a related social order that transform them into a new, identifiable culture group. Other terms used for ethnicities include *social group* or *social networks*, with the understanding that both are unified by the shared meaning system of a particular culture. However labeled by historians and anthropologists, the members of such culture groups experienced profound impacts when they were swept up in the large-scale developments that led to their diaspora. Those impacts propelled many people from one place and cultural configuration to new locations where they confronted adversity, opportunity, tragedy, and the challenges of persevering.

Starting in the fifteenth century, European colonial regimes created a transatlantic institution of enslavement that particularly targeted a number of societies in the west and west central regions of Africa. Operating over four centuries, the transatlantic slave trade had profound and brutal impacts upon all societies caught in its grasp. In 1993, the United Nations Educational, Scientific, and Cultural Organization (UNESCO) established the Slave Route Project to facilitate greater understanding of the causes, contours, and effects of that destructive institution (UNESCO 1993). Within this perspective, the slave trade is viewed as an early form of globalization that caused extensive social, cultural, and economic disruption to numerous African societies and lives. The UNESCO Slave Route Project seeks to promote greater knowledge, memory, and dialogue concerning the history and continuing impacts of that colonial system (UNESCO 2006a). In doing so, this UNESCO project works to overcome the "silence that has shrouded" the history of bondage (3). It further seeks to preserve and commemorate the tangible and intangible cultural heritage of the individuals and societies that confronted the adversities of the enslavement system (7).

The importance of intangible cultural heritage played out in a critical way in the movement of particular African traditions across the Atlantic Ocean during the slave trade. Captive Africans were rarely able to transport the heirlooms of their tangible cultural heritage with them to New World plantations. However, their knowledge, beliefs, and skills in performing the cultural traditions of the society from which they were abducted could be applied in locations in the Americas to create new material expressions of those legacies. European slave traders could steal their captives' tangible heirlooms, but not the intangible facets of knowledge, beliefs, and expressive skill.

In 2003, UNESCO undertook additional steps to promote and protect the diversity of cultural traditions worldwide by issuing the "Convention for the Safeguarding of the Intangible Cultural Heritage." Earlier efforts by the UN to protect the cultural heritage of diverse peoples around the globe had focused primarily on tangible expressions, such as monuments, architecture, and the built environment (Ahmad 2006; UNESCO 2003: 1–2). After a period of ratification and approval by member nations of UNESCO, the 2003 Convention took effect on April 20, 2006 (UNESCO 2006b: 24). Now begins the hard work of identifying, celebrating, and protecting such instances of intangible cultural heritage.

UNESCO defines intangible cultural heritage as "the practices, representations, expressions, knowledge, skills—as well as the instruments, objects, artefacts and cultural spaces associated therewith—that communities, groups and, in some cases, individuals recognize as part of their cultural heritage" (UNESCO 2003: art. 2.1). These elements of a community's heritage are "transmitted from generation to generation" and play a key role in providing members of that community "with a sense of identity and continuity" (art. 2.1). As people subscribe to, learn, and perform these beliefs and practices, they create and shape material culture in an interdependent process that produces instances of their *tangible* heritage (UNESCO 2003: 1). Such tangible expressions range in scale from small objects to architecture and built landscapes.

For today's communities, this recognition of the significance of intangible cultural heritage raises the importance of understanding the histories of how their belief systems and traditions developed and changed over time. The question of how intangible heritage today was shaped by the past is part of the broader dynamics addressed in this book. UNESCO's focus on intangible cultural heritage also raises questions about the permanence or transience of particular belief systems and related social practices and traditions. Studies of changes over time in such belief systems help us to understand how today's communities deal with the degrees of stability and flux in their intangible cultural heritage.

Members of UNESCO weighed a number of motivating concerns in creating a formalized method for addressing the potential dangers facing the intangible cultural heritage of particular social groups. A principal motivation was the realization that nationalist movements and the global impacts of capitalist economies have often undercut and destroyed such heritage within more "traditional" communities (UNESCO 2003: 1). Similar assaults occurred with even greater frequency in the history of European colonial impacts in the past. This book explores the ways in which particular cultures and their intangible heritage survived, diminished, or continued to develop in the face of such transatlantic colonial regimes imposed by European interests.

Implementation of UNESCO's protections for intangible cultural heritage will likely confront questions of whether the performance of certain beliefs and practices by some members of a community can be viewed as representing a coherent group's social and cultural identity. In contrast, such performances could instead be viewed as idiosyncratic and not representative of the shared culture. I explore this relationship between individual creativity and social group dynamics through detailed studies of particular African diasporas and European immigration movements. The chapters of this book examine changes over time in the developments of individual expression and social group identities within those populations.

The articulation of a people's cultural heritage involves complex processes of remembering and forgetting (see, for example, Lowenthal 1997: 32; Shackel 2001: 655–56). Scholars who have studied the formation of cultural heritage claims by particular groups have come to characterize *heritage* as a selective emphasis on elements of a people's "history" that includes instances of omission, as well as remembrance and commemoration. For example, experts working with UNESCO to develop implementation plans for protecting cultural heritage have found that a particular social group's claims for the importance of its heritage are often subject to dispute by political factions or special interests within that community (UNESCO 2006b: 29). Different constituencies within a community often emerge to offer divergent perspectives of what elements of the group's heritage should be viewed as significant, authentic, and defining of the group's collective sense of identity (Shackel 2001: 655–56; UNESCO 2006b: 29).

As historian David Lowenthal (1996: xi) put it, "History explores and explains pasts grown ever more opaque over time; heritage clarifies pasts so as to define them with present purposes." Molefi Kete Asante (1993: 139–40), an advocate of pan-African and Africa-centric intellectual and political movements, similarly contended that people tend to define their heritage in a focused and singular way, "despite the multiplicity of cultural backgrounds that go into that heritage." He observed that a group's "heritage might be composed of many backgrounds but in the end we inherit a unified field of culture, that is, one whole fabric of the past rather than split sheets or bits and pieces. Otherwise what we inherit is not very useful" (140).

Material culture expressions play a key role in these acts of performance and remembrance of a social group's heritage. This book presents detailed studies of the material culture created as part of the beliefs and practices of changing social group identities over time. These cultural developments occurred in the context of the transatlantic movement of peoples from Africa and Europe to New World locations over the past few centuries. This history reveals another process of attempted erasure. Past colonial forces subjugated enslaved Africans in part by seeking to destroy and suppress their cultural heritage. On the terrain of New World plantations, overseers sought to suppress the institutions of political organization, kinship, and group ceremonies and rituals of particular African cultures targeted by the transatlantic slave trade. Nonetheless, archaeologists and historians have uncovered increasing evidence of the ways in which Africans and their descendants carved out social spaces in the New World where they continued individualized observances and expressions of the beliefs and practices of particular African cultures. Such individualized observances in private spaces did not represent the mere shreds and patches of past cultures. Those expressions entailed vibrant and vital exercises of cultural traditions that led to further development and change of those customs and beliefs over time.

Many historical analysts find it useful and accurate to define particular cultures that existed in a past time period and geographic territory by examining the patterned and repeated expressions of beliefs and practices by members of that cultural group. Such approaches raise key questions that parallel those raised by constituent groups' competing views of the appropriate ways to define their cultural heritage. For example, as an analyst, how does one articulate the core criteria of beliefs and practices that defined a past culture group? How does an analyst define the character of beliefs and practices among people who move from one region and cultural system to new settings and new social contexts? When a number of distinct cultural systems came into contact with one another in the past, what impacts did each have upon the others?

Historians, anthropologists, and archaeologists have engaged in debates that echo the controversies over selective definitions seen in the realm of competing heritage claims (Mathers, Darvill, and Little 2005: 2–3; Segal and Handler 1995: 397; L. Smith 2005: 82–83). These are analogous types of debates, but historical analysis and heritage claims are distinct in important ways. Historical analysis typically utilizes much different methods of proof and persuasion than do particular community constituents promoting a claim of cultural heritage. As Lowenthal (1996: 121) observed, "Heritage exaggerates and omits, candidly invents and frankly forgets, and thrives on ignorance and error. Historians' pasts, too, are always altered by time and hindsight. To be taken seriously by other historians, however, these revisions must conform with accepted tenets of evidence."

Contested declarations within cultural heritage claims of whether certain traditions are vital and continuing, or were rather ephemeral and expired in the past, have been mirrored by a debate within studies of African diasporas to the New World. Scholars such as E. Franklin Frazier (1966a, 1966b) argued that the trauma and disruption of slavery and the brutal system of transporting captive Africans to the New World effectively destroyed and prevented any particular cultural traditions of African societies from becoming manifest in New World communities. In contrast, analysts such as Melville Herskovits (1941) looked within the communities of African descendants in the New World for evidence of "survivals" and "retentions" of particular cultural traditions of the African societies from which people were abducted into bondage.

Anthropologists Sidney Mintz and Richard Price (1976) again focused on the traumatic character of the institution of slavery in arguing that analysts should look for ways in which African descendants created new and dynamic cultures in locations throughout the Americas. In addition to the horrors of the Middle Passage in which captive Africans were transported in ships across the Atlantic to New World locations, Mintz and Price focused on the diversity of African cultures targeted by the slave trade. Writing three decades ago, they contended that historical evidence showed that European slave traders purposefully mixed captive Africans from different societies and different language groups together to prevent social solidarity within the captive groups when they were transported to plantations in the Americas (9–11).

In view of such circumstances, Mintz and Price (1976: 27–31) argued that it was unlikely that the particular cultural traditions of specific African societies would be retained and performed in New World settings in the way Herskovits had envisioned. Instead, they said analysts should look for the rapid creation of new cultural forms in communities of diverse captive Africans in the Americas (43–44). In the terminology of cultural heritage debates, one could translate this view into the contention that particular cultural traditions of specific African societies were often "forgotten" or "elided" in New World communities due to the traumatic impacts of the system of bondage.

Debates concerning the contours of these African diasporas continue with vigor, and new studies have turned the cycles of perspective once again. In more recent years, numerous detailed studies have been undertaken to better understand the movement of captive Africans through different coastal locations in Africa and the destinations to which they were taken in the New World (for example, Eltis 2001; Hall 2005; Thornton 1998; Walsh 2001).

These studies have resulted in expanded databases that indicate in greater detail the percentages of persons from different African societies captured and held at particular ports in Africa. Similarly, these studies provide more detailed data on the proportions of persons from different African societies taken to particular locations in the Americas.

Examining these expanded databases, a number of historical analysts have become convinced that it was much more likely than previously assumed that persons of particular African societies could find and interact with one another at New World plantations. If so, it is much more likely that captives from the same African society could find one another at particular locations in the Americas, communicate in a shared language, and continue performing some facets of the cultural beliefs and practices learned in the society from which they were abducted. In time, they could teach these beliefs and traditions to others in their New World communities and to following generations. Such cultural traditions would not be perpetuated in a static, unchanging manner, but would undergo development over time, just as they had among the past generations of the particular African society in which they were created. In the terminology of cultural heritage debates, one would view these traditions as possessing a continuing vitality which could not be extinguished by the Middle Passage and plantation brutalities.

Recent African diaspora studies have moved beyond older and simpler debates over "retentions" and "continuities" to focus on the dynamics of multilinear cultural developments. Similarly, the application of new theoretical and interpretative frameworks to increasingly robust sets of historical and archaeological data are transforming the shape of historical studies of African diasporas and the related field of historical archaeology. Archaeological investigations of African diasporas and the processes of ethnogenesis can make powerful contributions to interdisciplinary studies of ethnic, racial, and cultural dynamics in the multiple histories of the Americas.

In this study, I employ anthropological theories concerning modes of symbolic expression, the formation and maintenance of social group identities, and the roles of individual creativity and innovation within those group dynamics. I examine *core symbols* within particular cultures impacted by diasporic movements across the Atlantic. Core symbols serve within a culture to express fundamental elements of a group's cosmology and sense of identity within the world. Core symbols can be communicated through spoken words and ritual performances and are often depicted in tangible, graphic form through renderings in material culture (for example, Ortner 1973; Turner 1967, 1973). Such graphic renderings of core symbols span a continuum of expressive modes within each culture. This spectrum extends from what I refer to as *emblematic* communications, on one end of the continuum, to *instrumental* versions at the other end (see, for example, Firth 1973; Ortner 1973; Turner 1967, 1973). Emblematic versions serve to summarize the identity of a culture group as a cohesive unit and are illustrated by symbols such as a national flag, the crucifix of Christianity, or the Star of David for Judaism. Instrumental expressions of the same core symbol are abbreviated in their compositions and are used for individualized purposes. An example of such an instrumental version is seen when members of the Christian faith move their hands across heart and brow in the gesture of a cross as a sign of self-protection and individual prayer.

Core symbols within stable culture groups were deployed in a broad spectrum of expressive modes. Emblematic expressions of social group identities were typically employed in settings that involved public ceremonies celebrating group solidarity. More abbreviated and instrumental expressions of those symbols were often utilized in private settings and for individual purposes. I apply these concepts to analyze the creation and use of material expressions of core symbols within the diasporas of various cultures from Africa and Europe, such as the BaKongo, Yoruba, Fon, and Palatine German cultures, among others. I explore the divergent ways these cultural processes played out among populations at sites in North America, the Caribbean, and South America in the fifteenth through nineteenth centuries. Focusing on African diaspora cultures, I find that the use of private, instrumental symbolism was prevalent in objects reflecting BaKongo and Yoruba religious beliefs uncovered at sites in North America. This contrasted significantly with the material culture and symbolism of African descent groups in Caribbean and South American locations, such as Cuba, Haiti, and Brazil.

In those locations outside the United States, new, highly embellished symbolism was developed out of the blending of diverse African cosmologies. These embellished symbols were often displayed publicly and in ways intended to signal the formation of new culture groups and to communicate their sense of solidarity and collective cultural identity. Such new cultures formed as a result of ethnogenesis in New World locations. But how did these mechanisms of ethnogenesis work in places like Haiti and Brazil? What cultural operations contribute to the formation of such a new culture out of a diversity of antecedents and the creativity of individuals in New World settings?

Some anthropologists refer to this development as a general process of cultural admixture. Others use the term *creolization* to communicate a similar idea of indefinable cultural blending. Such analysts essentially contend that we can see evidence of the shape of diverse antecedent cultures, and we can define the patterns and contours of the new culture, but we cannot discern much of what happened in between. I propose a more specific definition of one of the primary mechanisms of ethnogenesis as observed in the histories of places like Brazil and Haiti. I call this process *ethnogenic bricolage* to distinguish it from broader concepts offered previously by historians and anthropologists.

Ethnogenic bricolage entails a creative process in which individuals raised in different cultures interact in new settings, often at the geographic crossroads of multiple diasporas. In these new locations, individuals tend to desist from displaying emblematic expressions of the core symbols of the former culture groups from which they were abducted or compelled to depart. Yet, instrumental expressions of those same core symbols continue with vigor and are employed in private, individual spaces as part of invocations for healing, self-protection, and prayers for the vitality of loved ones.

The abbreviated composition of such instrumental symbols gives them a prosaic appearance that can be recognized by members of other cultures for the basic meaning of efforts in self-determination and perseverance. Such instrumental expressions can therefore play an important role in communications across cultures and in the formation of new social relationships among individuals brought together by intersecting diasporas. In time, these social relationships can solidify into new, cohesive culture groups that articulate their own shared meaning system. From the disparate elements of varied instrumental symbols, new core symbols and emblematic designs are configured to communicate the new culture's sense of identity. I refer to this process as ethnogenic bricolage to emphasize the creative combination of diverse cultural elements into new configurations. The word *bricolage* is derived from its use by anthropologist Claude Lévi-Strauss (1966) to indicate a creative combination of elements from existing cultural systems. I explore the details of this concept in greater depth in the concluding chapter of this book and distinguish it from other concepts such as creolization.

Figure 1.1 displays locations in the New World that are discussed in this study, and figure 1.2 similarly shows the locations, cultural groups, and language areas in Africa that are addressed in the following chapters. I also examine beliefs and practices among particular groups of Europeans and European-Americans, and the ways that forms of instrumental symbolism reflected in their cultures were shaped by dynamics similar to those seen in African diasporas. Figure 1.3 displays the locations in Europe that are

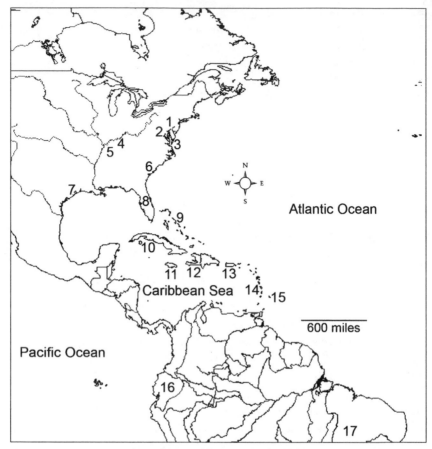

Figure 1.1. Locations in the Americas: (1) Pennsylvania; (2) Virginia—Loudoun Valley, Upper Potomac, and northern Shenandoah region, Blue Ridge, Shenandoah Valley; (3) Chesapeake—Maryland and Virginia Tidewater, Annapolis; (4) Kentucky; (5) Tennessee; (6) South Carolina coast; (7) Brazoria, Texas; (8) Florida; (9) Bahamas; (10) Cuba; (11) Jamaica; (12) Haiti, Saint Domingue; (13) Puerto Rico; (14) West Indies; (15) Barbados; (16) Ecuador; (17) Brazil. (Image by the author)

discussed in the following chapters. These independently developed beliefs and practices from Europe and Africa came to meet at the many crossroads of the New World.

The questions I pursue in this study were first motivated by my archaeological and historical investigations of a household site in the Loudoun Valley of Virginia (see fig. 1.1). Chapter 2 introduces key features of this archaeological site. The remains of a small log house, which was built in the late 1700s or early 1800s, presented me with intriguing riddles of material

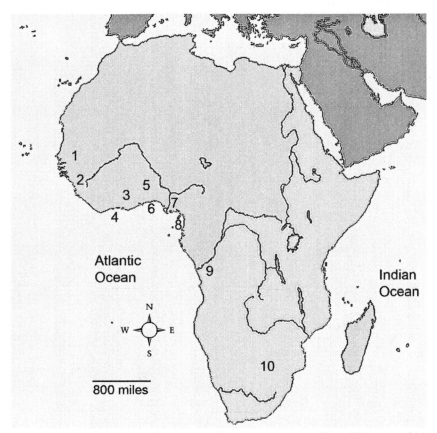

Figure 1.2. Locations, cultural groups, and language areas in Africa: (1) Senegambia, Mandinga, Bambara; (2) Sierra Leone, Mande; (3) Ashanti, Asante; (4) Gold Coast, Koramantin; (5) Dahomey, Fon, Yoruba, Ewe; (6) Bight of Benin; (7) Benin, Igbo; (8) Bight of Biafra; (9) BaKongo, Kingdom of Kongo, Ndongo, Angola; and (10) Barolong boo Ratshidi, Tshidi. (Image by the author)

culture. The house stood on property that had been leased in the late 1700s and then purchased in 1811 by a family named Demory. A thorough consideration of the wills, land deeds, rent books, tax records, and census lists of the residents of this location provides a rich, contextual picture of the community inhabited by the Demory house occupants. Members of the Demory family were of German-American heritage and worked as farmers. They also owned one or two enslaved African Americans at various times in the first decades of the nineteenth century.

Various forms of material culture at that site raised questions of the degree to which objects and dwellings can be distinctly shaped by symbolic

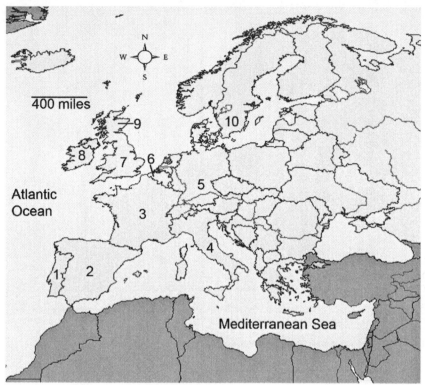

Figure 1.3. Locations in Europe: (1) Portugal; (2) Spain; (3) France; (4) Italy, Pompeii site; (5) Germany, Palatine region; (6) Belgium; (7) England, Cirencester site; (8) Ireland; (9) Scotland; and (10) Sweden. (Image by the author)

and stylistic traditions associated with particular ethnic groups. In my first excavations at the site I uncovered a small, sculpted figure from beneath the house floor that was associated with other artifacts dating within the period of 1780 to 1860. This object was sculpted in the form of a human skull and bore inscriptions of four initials and a cross-line motif that indicated it was likely created pursuant to a system of religious and cosmological beliefs.

This very local puzzle fit into a broader subject reaching to other sites in the Americas and to a transatlantic diaspora of particular African traditions. The attributes of that sculpted figure initially suggested that an African American person who lived or worked at this site may have created this object, composing its design pursuant to beliefs and practices derived from the BaKongo culture of west central Africa (see fig. 1.2). Key attributes of the object were similar to those found on artifacts uncovered at other African

American sites in North America dating from the eighteenth and nineteenth centuries.

The sculpted object found among the archaeological remains of the Demory house site opens an engaging lens for analysis. In chapter 3, I begin to examine an array of artifacts similar to that object, each of which is notable for its inclusion of cross-lined motifs and placement in a covert context. These other artifacts were uncovered in African American sites in the United States that had been occupied during and after the period of the transatlantic slave trade. Chapters 3 and 4 provide an anthropological and ethnohistorical analysis of the mechanisms through which particular social group identities and memberships shifted over time.

These cultural processes included the dynamics through which individuals created new social groups and expressions of identity in locations of diasporas. Using a core symbol of the BaKongo culture in west central Africa as an example, I define a specific method for undertaking such a study. I formulate a detailed, ethnohistorical account of this culture at one stage in its history and a related predictive model of anticipated changes over time that would be wrought by the impacts of the transatlantic slave trade. This study focuses principally on the rich symbolism of cosmological beliefs within the BaKongo culture and the ways in which facets of that culture would develop in the New World. However, the general processes revealed in this analysis are also applicable to the history of other culture groups and other forms of material expressions.

Chapter 5 examines archaeological and historical evidence for the ways in which key symbols of various African cultures were expressed in New World settings. A diverse array of artifacts uncovered in Maryland, Virginia, Kentucky, Tennessee, South Carolina, and Texas exhibit instrumental symbolism derived from African cultures such as the BaKongo, Yoruba, and Fon. At sites in Cuba, Haiti, and Brazil, the instrumental symbols of a number of cultures were combined in new ways in the process I define as ethnogenic bricolage.

Returning to the Demory site in Virginia, I find that the history of instrumental symbolism derived from particular African cultures does not provide the most persuasive basis for interpreting the meaning and significance of the skull figure uncovered there. Other sources of rich cultural traditions that operated in the region surrounding the Demory house site during this time period were the beliefs and practices brought into the area by German immigrants. Chapter 6 explores this history of immigration and related cultural traditions, including the events and motivations that affected immigrants from Germany, as well as their social cohesiveness over time.

A closer examination of the extended Demory family and their neighbors, through the evidence presented in leaseholds, land deeds, estate inventories, wills, census rolls, tax ledgers, and church records, shows a strong influence of German heritage among those residents of the Loudoun Valley. The architectural form and construction techniques used in building the house on the Demorys' land also fit closely with patterns of German-American architectural traditions in this region and time period. I conclude that facets of a German-American folk religion called hexerei provide a more persuasive template for interpreting the meaning and significance of all attributes of the sculpted figure and the context in which it was uncovered at the Demory house site. I further explore the ways in which the symbolism and stylistic patterns of hexerei and German-American building traditions could have been deployed in instrumental or emblematic modes.

In the final chapter, I describe in more detail the operations of ethnogenic bricolage as a mechanism of ethnogenesis. I define this theoretical construct to provide a more useful framework for understanding the multifaceted processes of instrumental symbolism than is offered by creolization models. Through this approach, one also sees the very important role played by instrumental symbolism as a vital aspect of the cultural heritage of societies impacted by the diasporas of the past five centuries.

The mechanisms of instrumental and emblematic symbolism explored in this study could be further illustrated by examining other types of material culture, such as funerary art forms or diverse architectural traditions. The varying influences of Yoruba, Fon, BaKongo, and European belief systems and symbolism on American healing traditions called "hoodoo," "voodoo," and "cunning" practices could likewise be explored in further detail. However, I believe that the selected examples examined in these chapters serve to illustrate how the remarkable spectra of instrumental and emblematic symbolism of multiple cultures contributed to instances of ethnogenesis in New World locations. Focusing the theoretical frameworks of archaeologists and symbolic anthropologists upon the material culture of multiple African and European cultural diasporas provides new perspectives for conceptualizing cultural transformations over time.

2

From the Diminutive to the Transatlantic

My fascination with the cultural crossroads and cosmologies that would lead to this study grew, as archaeological interest often does, out of cultural remains embedded in a particular piece of the landscape. In the autumn of 1997, my attention turned to the sagging shell of an abandoned house situated on a slope looking out over the Loudoun Valley, just east of the Blue Ridge Mountains and Shenandoah River in Virginia (see fig. 1.1). Located six miles south of Harpers Ferry and the Potomac River, on a relatively isolated site halfway up the west side of Short Hill Mountain, the house is made of thick, hand-hewn logs. These timbers were laid horizontally, one over the next, and woven together at the corners with notches cut into the rich grain of the hardwood (fig. 2.1). Heavily wooded land surrounds the house at this higher level of Short Hill, in contrast to the broad expanses of cleared fields one finds on the valley floor below.

A new property owner, walking through the acres of land that he had acquired on the Loudoun Valley floor stretching up to these mountainside reaches, wondered about the house's age. Casual conversations with his new neighbors in the valley often yielded comments that such "shacks" or "cabins" were likely the past quarters for enslaved persons before the Civil War. This log cabin appeared too small and shabby, some said, to have been a residence of a European-American family. Those were odd comments, given the fact that the house is still standing long after so many frame houses of European immigrants and settlers have faded from the landscape.

Research would show that this house stands on property that was leased in the late 1700s and then purchased in 1811 by members of a family named Demory, who were of German-American heritage. Three generations of Demory families worked several neighboring farms in the valley through the late 1800s, and enslaved African Americans labored in those fields up through the Civil War. A wealth of information about these individuals and surrounding communities can be mined from deed books, leases, rent accounts, wills, estate inventories, census lists, tax rolls, voting ledgers, church records, and other documents created in the past and preserved in public archives. I have transcribed and examined these records in an earlier publi-

Figure 2.1. Late eighteenth-century house on the Demory site, Loudoun County, Virginia. (Photograph by the author)

cation for those who wish to consider the underlying evidence of this study in greater detail (Fennell 2003a).

John Demory, Sr., appears to have been the first member of that family to settle in the Loudoun Valley. In the late 1700s, he leased large tracts of land, each comprising one hundred acres or more, from the Fairfax family, who owned the expansive "Shannondale tract" that extended for 25,500 acres through northern Virginia. John's son Peter took responsibility for one of those leased tracts of land before John passed away in 1806, and Peter later purchased a number of smaller parcels within the area of those leaseholds. The Demorys and other Loudoun Valley residents often leased such tracts largely in order to use the natural resources, such as pasturage for livestock, fields for growing crops, and wooded areas for harvesting timber to sell to local sawmills or for use as firewood. John and his family lived and farmed on one tract, while working on or subletting the others (Fennell 2003a: 49–55).

When John died in 1806, he left very little to Peter, and instead conveyed the bulk of his estate to his eldest son, John Demory, Jr. He bequeathed sums of 15 pounds "Virginia Currency" each to his children Peter and Elizabeth (Fennell 2003a: 55–56). Using currency conversion equations, and assuming a rough equivalence between British pounds and Virginia currency at that time, the 15 pounds conveyed to Peter in 1806 would roughly equate to £619 British, or $940, in the year 2000 (see McCusker 2001). A probate inventory of all of John Demory, Sr.'s, personal property placed values on those possessions that totaled to 292 pounds, 1 shilling, and 2 pence (Fennell 2003a:56). That sum in 1806 would equate roughly to £12,043, or $18,303, in the year 2000 (McCusker 2001). Perhaps John, Sr., thought Peter was already such an enterprising individual that he did not need more aid than a modest gift of 15 pounds. If so, John was not mistaken.

Peter was thirty-eight years old when his father died. Peter and his wife, Mary, had married sometime in the 1780s and raised a large family, including sons William, Mahlon, John, and Enos, and daughters Elizabeth, Louisa, Margaretha, Catharina, and Maria. By the time of his father's death, Peter had been running his own farm on a 120-acre tract leased from the Fairfax family. Peter apparently made his first purchase of land in 1804, buying from the Fairfax family a large parcel that was located downhill from the location of the log house I visited in 1997 (Fennell 2003a: 56). He and Mary made this larger tract on the valley floor their principal residence, and they developed and expanded their house and farmstead on this property until Peter's death in 1843. In 1811, Peter purchased a smaller parcel of twenty-two acres from the Fairfax family. This smaller property was situated immediately uphill from his main farmstead and contained the site on which the log house stands today (56–57).

Starting from relatively modest beginnings, Peter built up a sizable estate in his lifetime. In addition to the neighboring tracts of 146 acres and 22 acres, he purchased an additional 15-acre timber lot, located a short distance to the north of the 22-acre parcel. Over time he acquired other farm properties in the Loudoun Valley, which he later bequeathed to two of his adult children as part of his estate. Just before his death in 1843, Peter executed a last will and testament, which described and distributed his real estate holdings and place of residence. These sums and real estate holdings represented a considerable expansion over the amount of resources Peter had inherited from his father. Starting from the "15 pounds Virginia Currency" that John Demory, Sr., had given his youngest son, Peter amassed sufficient wealth to distribute several farmsteads and $14,100 in cash gifts through his 1843 will (Fennell 2003a: 58–59). Those cash bequests alone would equal the purchasing power of $335,567 today. Peter's total estate of land and personal property was valued at $17,901 in 1843, which would be equal in purchasing power to $426,027 today (McCusker 2001).

Peter had accumulated these assets through his investments in real estate and from the income produced by operating a farm. In the course of these activities over the years, he worked in coordination with many of the neighboring farms and commercial enterprises in the Loudoun Valley. The 1843 inventory of his estate lists thirty-four promissory notes, executed between him and various relatives, neighboring farmers, or other business concerns in the valley over the years, representing a total value of $4,774 in debts payable to Demory. That investment comprised 27 percent of the total value of his estate. His land was valued at $7,780 in 1843, amounting to another 43 percent of his total estate (Fennell 2003a: 58–59). The promissory notes likely reflected credits due to Demory for crops he had delivered, lands he had made available to others for tillage or pasturage, or labor he had supplied to others (see Hahn 1985: 181–83; Henretta 1978: 14–19).

In addition to his several children and the workers he could hire from the neighboring farms in the valley, Peter relied upon the labor of enslaved African Americans in running his farm operations. The 1843 inventory of his estate lists two enslaved adults, named Joseph and Henry. In addition, the county records of personal property taxes show that Peter owned one or two adult enslaved persons at the time each tax was recorded over the years 1802 through 1843. Peter's adult sons Mahlon and William also owned one or two enslaved laborers each when census records were recorded in 1840, 1850, and 1860 (Fennell 2003a: 61, 170–76).

One might view the number of slaves owned by the Demorys as being notably low. But among Virginia residents who owned enslaved laborers in this period, the ownership of one to two enslaved persons was in fact more common than the possession of greater numbers. For example, in 1860, federal census surveys found that there were a total of 52,128 slave-owning households in Virginia. Households were surveyed and categorized by the number of enslaved persons they owned. Of that total, 17,074 households, or 33 percent of the total, owned only one or two enslaved persons, a far larger percentage than each of the remaining categories of households that owned greater numbers. Similarly, in Loudoun County at that time, there were a total of 670 slave-owning households, of which 208, or 31 percent, owned only one or two slaves (ICPSR 1992).

This prevalence of ownership of only one or two laborers casts doubt on one possible interpretation of the Demorys' pattern of slave ownership: that it was designed to effect manumission. One might speculate that the Demorys were purchasing only one or two enslaved persons at a time in order to later grant them freedom in a safe and guarded manner (see Stevenson 1996: 174, 261–70). The Virginia legislature had taken action in 1806 to discourage slave owners from granting manumission to their enslaved African Americans. Legislation mandated that newly freed slaves had to leave the state within one year of their date of emancipation or risk being returned to bondage (264). The existence of that statute could have motivated some persons to acquire slaves in border counties such as Loudoun with a plan to grant their slaves freedom and sponsor their emigration to nearby Pennsylvania or Maryland. Indeed, Loudoun's position along the border with Maryland prompted formation of "stations" in the Underground Railroad along the Potomac River to aid escaping slaves (252–53). In practice, however, the 1806 statute was seldom enforced, and newly freed slaves could often stay in their Virginia county of residence after emancipation (269–70).

Overall, the Demorys' ownership of captive African Americans likely was not part of a manumission strategy, and instead fit the larger pattern of small-scale employment of enslaved laborers on Virginia farms. An additional indication that this was the case was seen in 1861. When the vote on proposed secession of Virginia from the Union was held in Loudoun County, William Demory voted in favor of secession. Mahlon apparently did not cast a vote, while many of the Demorys' German-American neighbors voted in favor of the Union (Chamberlin 2003: 10, 23–29).

While Peter had maintained his primary residence on a 146-acre tract on the Loudoun Valley floor, he had set his adult children up on neighboring farmsteads in the valley (Fennell 2003a: 58–59, 165–73). The family of one of Peter's adult sons may have been the residents of the small log house on the upland site that I began examining in 1997. Archaeological remains and architectural features of this house showed that the structure was built in the late 1700s or very early 1800s. The house was most likely constructed by a family of German-American heritage—either another family who lived on the land before the Demorys or the Demory family themselves (192–214). This log house could have provided a residence for some of the Demory family members or for their enslaved laborers.

It would be notable if the Demory family permitted enslaved persons to live at this upland house on their own. This dwelling was located a fair distance from Peter's main house on the Loudoun Valley floor. In this period in Virginia, slave owners often subscribed to views concerning appropriate methods for utilizing enslaved laborers that emphasized close supervision of those persons at all times (see, for example, Morgan 1998).

I undertook archaeological investigations of this house site on the old Demory tract for the purpose of addressing a number of research questions. My knowledge of the site and growing interest in it were first prompted by a request from the landowners. They asked that I examine the log house and assess for them its approximate age and whether it was unusual or unique in any way. I started that task by visiting the house and taking detailed measurements and photographs of its architectural features. I also dug a few

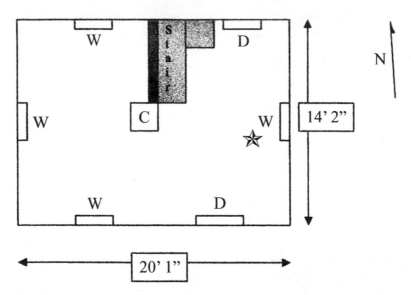

Figure 2.2. Demory site house plan with locations of clay figure (marked by the star), windows (W), doorways (D), and chimney (C). (Image by the author)

"shovel test pits"—holes one foot in diameter and usually one to two feet deep—around the house perimeter and in the dirt under the decayed planks that once covered the hand-hewn joists of the first floor. This is a fairly simple method for gaining a preliminary sample of the types and date ranges of objects that were once created, used, and discarded at a site. Those few test pits dug in 1997 revealed a number of mundane artifacts, including wrought iron nails, cut iron nails, and fragments of ceramic dishware that dated roughly to the early 1800s (Fennell 2003a: 65, 653–55). They also contained something else.

The fourth shovel test pit I dug probed into the dirt underlying the exposed sleeper joists of the house, where the floorboards had rotted away, roughly halfway between the north and south doorways (see fig. 2.2). Six inches below the soil surface, along with old nails, animal bones, and ceramic pieces, I uncovered an artifact that was likely created and used as a material component of a malevolent curse. Such objects, which were typically created and deployed in secret, are rarely uncovered. The item in question is a small clay figure of a human skull (fig. 2.3), three-quarters of an inch tall, that was sculpted by skilled hands using the red-yellow clay available from the subsoil of the area surrounding the house (see USGS 1960).

The anatomical features of the skull are very well defined and proportioned. On the upper back of the skull is a raised figure of crossed lines or a

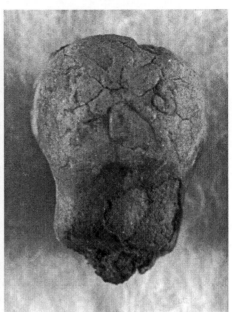

Above left: Figure 2.3. Front view of clay figure of a skull uncovered at the Demory site, Loudoun County, Virginia. This object dates to circa 1830–1860, and is 0.75 inches high. (Photograph by the author)
Above right: Figure 2.4. Rear view of clay figure of a skull uncovered at the Demory site, showing inscriptions on sculpted surface. (Photograph by the author)
Right: Figure 2.5. Diagram of inscriptions on the back of the skull figure uncovered at the Demory site. (Image by the author)

large X. The initials R, M, S, and D appear in raised clay between the arms of the X (figs. 2.4 and 2.5). The initial M is more eroded than the others and could be an H. X-rays reveal that the object has a small loop of iron wire as an internal core. The person who made this figure likely used the wire as a base to hold the clay, sculpting the material when it was partially hardened. This artisan shaped the single form of the skull with its raised inscription by hand, and then fired the unglazed figure at a relatively low temperature. The object was not made in a physical mold. However, its complex design was likely influenced and shaped by particular religious beliefs and practices. Such artifacts are often referred to as objects of conjuration by archaeologists, folklorists, and historians. This term is used to indicate that the composition of the object, and the context in which it appears to have been used, involved individualized and private invocations of spiritual forces, rather than the public display of group exercises of the associated belief system.

However, an initial question is whether this skull can be interpreted as something other than an artifact of religious expression. One possibility is that this skull was a clay toy or gaming piece. Historical archaeologist Ivor Noël Hume found a variety of remarkably well-formed toy "[f]igurines made in two-piece molds from colored clay [that] were popular in the seventeenth century" among English settlers in Virginia. However, he found no toys of this type from the eighteenth century or later (Noël Hume 1970: 314–15). The likelihood that this handmade skull figurine was a toy is undermined by the detailed inscriptions of the X insignia and initials, for which it is difficult to posit a function on a toy form. The insignias and sculpted details on this item also do not show the degree of surface wear from handling that one would expect if it were used as a toy or gaming piece (Klingelhofer 1987: 116). Catalogues of toy pieces from colonial and nineteenth-century America reveal no attributes related to the form and details of this artifact.

This skull could also be an icon of a family's coat of arms. The skull and crossbones figures could be features of an armorial design, and the initials R, M, S, and D could correspond to a family name or motto. The cross could also be a figure of St. Andrew's cross, which typically signifies a unification of different realms, such as heavenly and earthly domains or neighboring territories (Cirlot 1962: 66). I tested this possibility by examining a collection of 112,600 coats of arms from Great Britain and Europe known to exist up through the nineteenth century (Rietstap 1953). This collection revealed only three family crests that used a skull-and-crossbones motif: a family of Dalmatia with the unfortunate name of Morte, the Motte family of Bohemia, and the Schrickel family of Gorlitz. None of these coats of arms has an accompanying motto or other terms which would correspond with the initials R, M (or H), S, and D. Nor are these family names recorded in extensive lists of those who emigrated from the districts of Germany to the American colonies (for example, Yoder 1953). I also examined catalogues of armorial mottoes and found no motto that corresponds directly to these four initials.

A similar possibility is that the skull was an icon representative of a guild society or similar association, such as the Freemasons, Odd Fellows, or Knights of Pythias (Yoder 1965: 52). For example, late nineteenth-century medallions and watch charms sold at retail included skull and crossbones motifs for the Knights of Pythias and the Odd Fellows (Israel 1968: 421–22; Weber 1971: 629). However, historical information on these groups and examples of their memorabilia show no use of the combined motifs and initials corresponding to the Demory site artifact.

The skull could also have been a form of memento mori, similar to small amulets and medallions produced throughout Europe over the past few centuries. These objects typically commemorated the death of particular individuals and provided general invocations of the inevitability of death and the wisdom of living with humility in the face of such mortality. They were also often worn as protective charms against epidemic diseases (for example, Weber 1971: 2–4, 605–6). Skeletons, grim reapers, skulls, bones, and cherubs were frequent components in the designs of these small objects. However, an examination of Frederick Weber's (1971) extensive survey of memento mori revealed none with design, motifs, and initials directly corresponding to the attributes of the Demory site artifact. For example, the initials R, M, S, and D do not correspond with known mottoes on such items, even if the M and D (or H and D) were taken to be the initials of the deceased.

Thus, possible interpretations other than conjuration prove unpersuasive. The next question is whether the skull was the product of a folk religion associated with one or more ethnic groups in the relevant region and time period. Fairly extensive evidence is available from oral histories, slave narratives, and other studies in folklore and archaeology to support the interpretation that this skull was produced in accordance with African American traditions of folk religion.

Twentieth-century interviews with former slaves and free African Americans report the use of an X insignia as an invocation sign within past conjuration traditions known to the interviewees (Franklin 1997: 251; Georgia Writers' Project 1940: 135; Steiner 1901: 173; Young 1997: 21–22). The X insignia might also be of similar derivation and significance as the BaKongo cosmogram etchings that archaeologist Leland Ferguson found associated with African American colonoware pottery in the coastal area of South Carolina (Ferguson 1992: 111–16, 1999; Orser 1994: 38–39; see fig. 1.1).

Similarly, African American conjuration traditions included the practice of marking a conjure item with an X and identifying the targeted person by etching his or her name into the item, or writing the name on paper wrapped around the object. Those traditions also included a convention of placing a conjure item beneath the floor or steps of a door through which the target person regularly walked, or in the soil of a pathway the person used, as a way to activate the invocation (Bacon and Herron 1896: 145; Hand 1964: 105–6; Perdue, Barden, and Phillips 1976: 243–44, 263; Steiner 1901: 177). For example, to "throw off" a malevolent spell, the target of that invocation places his or her own conjure item under the doorstep of the first suspected conjurer and casts the malevolent forces back on that person (Hand 1964: 105–6; see also Wilkie 1997: 88–89).

These objects were not used as fetishes for repeated rituals of worship, but rather as individual invocations of spiritual forces to achieve a particular result (Genovese 1976: 224; Leone and Fry 1999: 383). Image magic can be worked, according to a number of African American accounts, by making an image of the target person in wax, mud, clay, beeswax, dough, or cloth, and piercing that image with pins or nails. The addition to this image of hair, fingernail or toenail trimmings, or personal possessions of the target person would strengthen the power of the conjure item (Hand 1964: 103; Puckett 1926: 244). Malevolent image magic could also be achieved by drawing a picture of the target person, hanging the picture up, and shooting it or driving nails into it (Hand 1964: 109; Puckett 1926: 245). A variety of techniques using pictures have been recorded in African American folklore studies: hang a photograph upside down, and the person depicted will die; bury a person's photograph in the graveyard, and that person will die when the image fades away; place a tintype photograph in water, and as the image fades, so will the person depicted (Hand 1964: 109; Hyatt 1965: 807, 810; Puckett 1926: 244–45).

Within such African American cultural practices, one could ward off conjurers and witches by placing an X on a Bible and keeping it in the house (Hand 1964: 128; Puckett 1926: 568; Steiner 1901: 178). The sign of the cross was also used to ward off curses (Hand 1964: 164). A similar belief held that one could capture and restrain the power of a witch in a bottle that had a stopper stuck with pins (Hand 1964: 131; Puckett 1926: 161). Similarly, African American conjure items have been found that incorporated a bottle-like vessel to contain other components, and such compositions were buried under the doorways or pathways likely traversed by the targeted persons (Hyatt 1965: 798; Samford 1996: 109; Wilkie 1997: 88–89).

The skull uncovered at the Demory site could be interpreted as a conjure item created in accordance with African American beliefs. The person who created this figure could have lived in the house at some point or had sufficient access to the dwelling to place the object there when it was a home occupied by others. The shape of the figure invoked the malevolence of death, the X invoked the curse, and the initials identified the targeted person in some way. This skull could have been buried under the floorboards to work its magic on the target as that person walked over the hidden item. The simple burying of a conjure item has the significance of invoking death as well. This may have been an initial curse or a counter-spell worked to fight back against a suspected witch. The M (or H) and D could be the initials of Mary, Mahlon, Margaretha, or Harry Demory, signifying the person targeted by this invocation of spiritual forces. However, I have found no correlates for the initials R and S in extensive documentary records related to the site.

The possible association of this skull figure, and its crossed-line motif, with African American cultural traditions is highly intriguing. If the crossed lines are similar to the X marks on colonoware pottery that Ferguson argues are derived from the BaKongo culture of west central Africa (see fig. 1.2), it is apparent that these are highly abbreviated expressions of a rich cultural tradition and symbolic repertoire. The covert placement of such a symbol-laden object raises provocative issues as well.

In the next chapter, I begin to examine an array of similar artifacts uncovered at African American sites in the Americas that had been occupied during the period of the transatlantic slave trade. These artifacts are notable for their inclusion of crossed-line motifs and placement in covert contexts. In following chapters, I provide an archaeological and ethnohistorical case study in which I analyze the processes by which social group identities and memberships shift over time and individuals create new social networks in new settings. In the course of such developments, existing material forms that symbolically communicate such identities can be continued or modified, and new forms of material communications can be created. Later, we will return to the Demory house site to consider again the likely meaning and significance of the skull figure and its insignias.

3

Shared Meanings and Culture Dynamics

Archaeologists have recovered a variety of objects that appear to have been used for religious purposes by African American occupants of sites dating from the late seventeenth through nineteenth centuries in North America. A number of those artifacts bear crossed lines and other attributes similar to the skull figure uncovered at the Demory site. Examples include pottery bowls with crosses incised on their bases; white clay marbles, coins, and pewter spoons with X marks scratched into them; and caches of quartz crystals, polished stones, pieces of chalk, ash, iron nails and bladelike fragments, bird skulls, crab claws, coins and bone disks secreted under the brick and wood floors of dwellings (for example, K. L. Brown 1994; Ferguson 1992, 1999; Franklin 1997; Galke 2000; Joseph, Hamby, and Long 2004; Leone 2005; Leone and Fry 1999; McKee 1995; Patten 1992; Samford 1996; Wilkie 1995, 1997; Young 1996, 1997; Zierden 2002).

Like the Demory site skull figure, these objects typically appear in contexts that indicate they were used in private, often surreptitious settings. The symbolic composition of these items also appears to be significantly abbreviated in comparison to key symbols of African cultures from the relevant time periods. These characteristics raise engaging issues concerning the processes of symbolic expression and the blending of cultural beliefs and practices over time.

The analysis presented here explores the ways in which symbolically composed artifacts likely served their creators and users as significant components of private religious rituals, as potential communicators of group identities, and as expressions of individual creativity in the forging of new social relationships. This study investigates the creative uses of facets of particular cultural beliefs over time and in new social settings. I first examine an array of artifacts that appear to have been created as expressions of certain beliefs within the BaKongo religion of west central Africa (see fig. 1.2), and I explore the changes over time and space in the modes of symbolic expressions derived from that belief system. Similar developments manifested in the material expressions of the Yoruba and Fon cultures of west Africa (fig. 1.2) are also addressed. This analysis is designed to avoid an assumption that homogeneous, "pan-African" religious beliefs characterized a wide variety of African cultures; these cultures were in fact quite diverse and rich in their beliefs and practices (for example, Lovejoy 2000: 16–17; Posnansky 1999: 22).

I apply an interpretative framework that assesses whether these artifacts possessed meaning and significance derived from core symbols found in African cultures such as the BaKongo. My interpretative approach illustrates the operation of three interrelated processes. *First*, a core cultural symbol of a particular social group is typically expressed across a spectrum, ranging from emblematic to instrumental modes. An emblematic form of a core symbol often serves to express a social group's collective identity. In contrast, instrumental forms of the same core symbol frequently consist of abbreviated and private expressions for personal purposes. *Second*, such a core symbol is usually expressed in its most fully complex and embellished form in the emblematic expressions of public and group rituals. When a core symbol of a cultural belief system is used for more private and personal ends, it is often expressed as an instrumental symbol that uses only selected and abbreviated components of the full array of the core symbol's composition. *Third*, such an individual and private use of abbreviated forms of core symbols can lead to stylistic innovation and the creation of new symbolic repertoires to express membership in social networks formed in new settings.

These three processes unfolded, for example, when persons who subscribed to the BaKongo religion in west central Africa were abducted into slavery and were able to continue their cultural practices only in covert, individualized settings in the slave quarters of plantations and "big houses" located in North America. In such social settings, these persons could not easily continue the group rituals and public expressions of their beliefs and associated core symbols. They focused instead on individualized and private uses of those core symbols to invoke spiritual powers for self-protection.

In this chapter, I begin constructing this theoretical framework concerning core symbols and their varied expressions by addressing a core symbol within the cosmological belief system of the BaKongo people. The challenges anthropologists face in evaluating the interaction of social groups, their shared meaning systems, and the conduct of individuals are also considered. The theoretical framework I develop provides interpretative methods for examining group and emblematic expressions of core symbols, more individual and instrumental expressions, and the varying deployment of such symbols by dominant and subordinated social groups.

In chapter 4, I employ these theoretical insights to formulate a methodology for assessing the significance of artifacts uncovered at African American domestic sites in North America dating to the late seventeenth through nineteenth centuries. I propose a predictive model that employs a detailed set of data that anthropologists often refer to as an ethnographic or ethnohistorical analogy. That predictive model is based on a rich set of ethnohistorical evidence concerning the past beliefs and practices of the BaKongo culture in west central Africa during the relevant time periods. *Ethnohistorical data* in this context means evidence based on the oral histories, writings, and material culture of the BaKongo people, and also evidence carefully compiled from critical readings of Europeans' (often biased) descriptions of the BaKongo culture in the past (compare Baerreis 1961; Carmack 1972; J. Handler and Lange 1978: 216–19). Then, applying that predictive model, I outline the patterns of symbolic expressions one would expect to see in new settings.

In chapter 5, I examine an apparent divergence in the way these processes of emblematic and instrumental expressions played out at sites in North America, the Caribbean, and South America. Private, instrumental symbolism was prevalent in the religious artifacts uncovered at African American sites in North America. I apply the predictive model to analyze, among other artifacts, the skull figure uncovered at the Demory house site. That object ostensibly fits the characteristics one might predict for an instrumental symbolic expression derived from the beliefs of the BaKongo culture. Such an explanation ultimately proves unpersuasive, however, due to the limited attributes of the object that fit such an interpretation.

With rare exceptions, there is little evidence of newly elaborated core symbols of blended African cultures emerging in the material culture of African Americans in this time period in the United States. This contrasts significantly with the material culture and symbolism of African heritage groups in Caribbean and South American locations, such as Haiti and Brazil. In those locations outside the United States, new, highly embellished symbolism was developed out of the blending of diverse African religions, including the BaKongo, Yoruba, and Dahomean belief systems. These embellished symbols were often displayed publicly and in ways likely intended to signal new social networks and group identities. This process of the creation of new emblematic symbols involved an exercise in ethnogenic bricolage, a concept I explore further in the final chapter of this book.

Core Symbols across a Continuum

Before examining an example of a core symbol from the BaKongo culture in detail, we should consider how anthropologists have observed and defined such expressions across numerous cultures they have studied. The characteristics of core symbols, which have also been referred to as *dominant,* or *key,* symbols, have been the subject of extensive analysis (for example, Geertz 1973: 126–41; Ortner 1973: 1338–39; Schneider 1980: 8, 113–14; Turner 1967: 20–31; 1973: 1101–4; Wagner 1986: 11–12). For example, Ortner analyzed key symbols within individual cultures as being manifested along a continuum of expressive modes. At one end of this spectrum are expressions of a key symbol that I refer to as *emblematic,* which are meaningful and significant as representations of group identity and solidarity. At the other end of the continuum are expressions that have a more limited, individualized, and instrumental purpose (Ortner 1973: 1339–40).

Emblematic symbols typically have the effect of "summing up, expressing" and "representing for the participants in an emotionally powerful way, what the system means to them" (1339). These emblematic expressions typically invoke "a conglomerate of ideas and feelings," and an array of metaphoric meanings communicated by the different elements composing the emblem. This type of representation is emblematic in that it stands for all those ideas, feelings, and metaphors "all at once" and "does not encourage reflection on the logical relations among these ideas, nor on the logical consequences of them as they are played out in social actuality" (1339–40). Ortner sees examples of such emblematic symbols in the American flag, the crucifix of Christianity, and the churinga of Australian Aborigine groups. Thus, emblematic symbols can be expressive of a variety of identity types, such as subscription to a particular cosmology, or membership in a nationality, ethnic group, or social network (1339–40).

In contrast, an *instrumental* symbol has a more practical and immediate purpose, and is "valued primarily because it implies clear-cut modes of action appropriate to correct and successful living" (1341). These instrumental symbols are thus "culturally valued in that they formulate the culture's basic means-ends relationships in actable forms" (Ortner 1973: 1341; Turner 1967: 32). Over time, actors may take components of an emblematic symbol and create a derivative, but more limited, instrumental symbol. In turn, that derived instrumental symbol may later become further developed and embellished so that it comes to function as a summarizing symbol for a different identity and shared meaning system in a later social setting (Firth 1973: 236–37; Ortner 1973: 1344; Wolf 1972: 150).

Among archaeologists, an objection is often raised regarding whether an analyst examining the limited evidence available in the archaeological record can reasonably comment on the expressive intentions of past social actors. For example, in individual compositions for instrumental purposes, the creator of a particular material representation will often design it to embody an array of metaphors, making the symbolic expression polysemous by design (Douglas 1975: 150; 1996: 10; Firth 1973: 207; Wagner 1975: 90, 98, 122). Anthropologists use the terms *polysemous, polyvalent,* and *multivalent* to indicate that multiple meanings and messages can be at play in a given context with regard to a particular symbol. Other persons within the same social networks who view and react to one person's symbolic expression will often see in it one or more of the metaphoric messages intended by the designer. They may also, however, read from it other metaphoric meanings not intentionally communicated by the author (Bruner 1993: 332; Fabian 1985: 145–47). The symbolic expression can thus be created and used in a way that has a separate polyvalent impact—the array of metaphoric meanings read into the representation by viewers of the symbol—that overlaps to some degree with the polysemous design of the author (Tilley 1999: 28–33; Turner 1967: 20–31).

However, these dynamics do not leave archaeologists at a loss to say anything useful in attempting to analyze the creation and use of particular symbolic expressions in different cultural settings and time periods. When particular forms of symbolic representation appear and reappear with some degree of consistency over time and in related cultural circumstances, that persistent pattern and its changes over time provide a subject for analysis (Rosaldo, Lavie, and Narayan 1993: 5–6). While the spoken words of past social interactions may be lost to us, the archaeological record often shows persistent patterns of material forms of symbolic expressions that can be interpreted in the context of one or more past cultural traditions and associated meaning systems (Tilley 1999: 31; Turner 1973: 1101). Thus, analysts can detect patterns of representations and attempt to describe and interpret the cultural traditions that inspired past actors in their creation and use of particular symbolic motifs and the associated metaphors incorporated in those compositions. Persuasive interpretations and explanations can be formulated when supported by multiple lines of evidence addressing the attributes and context of the material culture in question.

The archaeologist's interpretative reconstruction of the primary array of metaphors and meanings expressed in particular symbols over time will not fully capture the array of metaphors intended by specific creators of those symbolic communications. Nor will it perfectly capture the array of metaphors and meanings other readers within a past cultural tradition would have taken away from the symbol. Yet, an archaeologist's interpretative construction, if assembled with rigor and constrained by a closeness of fit to the available evidence, will overlap at least in part with the primary and repeated metaphors intended by past authors and read by past viewers of the material culture bearing those symbols (Firth 1973: 208; Hegmon 1992: 527; Tilley 1999: 260–66).

A Core Symbol of the BaKongo Culture

The spectrum of emblematic versus instrumental, abbreviated expressions of a core symbol can be illustrated with the BaKongo cosmogram. The Ba-Kongo people consisted of a cluster of groups who spoke the KiKongo language, shared a cultural system called the BaKongo, and inhabited the area referred to historically as Kongo (MacGaffey 2000c: 35–36). That geographic area consisted of territories now located in the nations of the Democratic Republic of the Congo, Gabon, the Republic of the Congo, and Angola, in a region that historians often refer to as west central Africa (Janzen 1977: 112; MacGaffey 2000c: 35; see fig. 1.2). This discussion will introduce a key facet of this culture, and the historical contexts in which it operated will be explored in greater detail in the next chapter.

A core symbol of the BaKongo culture was an ideographic religious symbol, or cosmogram, called *dikenga dia Kongo* or *tendwa kia nza-n' Kongo* in the KiKongo language (Fu-Kiau 2001: 22–23; Janzen and MacGaffey 1974: 34; Thompson and Cornet 1981: 43; see fig. 3.1), which I will refer to as the dikenga. Ethnohistorical sources and material culture evidence demonstrate that the dikenga existed as a longstanding symbolic tradition within the Ba-Kongo culture before European contact in 1482, and that its use continued in west central Africa through the early twentieth century (Janzen 1977: 81; MacGaffey 2000b: 8–11; Thompson and Cornet 1981: 27–30, 44–45; Thornton 1998: 251). In its fullest embellishment, this symbol served as an emblematic representation of the BaKongo people, and summarized a broad array of ideas and metaphoric messages that comprised their sense of identity within the cosmos (see, for example, Gundaker 1998: 8–10; MacGaffey 1986: 136, 169–71; Thompson 1997: 29–30).

Figure 3.1 is a rendering of the full dikenga. The composition's multiple components summarize and represent a remarkable array of key ideas and metaphoric meanings. The dikenga consists of intersecting vertical and horizontal axes, set within a circle or ellipse, with smaller circles or disks at the four ends of those crossed lines (Jacobson-Widding 1991: 182–83; MacGaffey 1986: 43–46; Thompson 1997: 29–30). The small disks represent the "four moments" of the sun and cosmos, with the top symbolizing north, the sun at noon, a masculine element, the land of the living, the apex of a person's earthly life and power in that life, and the upper realm of the Godhead. The bottom disk represents south, the sun at midnight, a female element, the

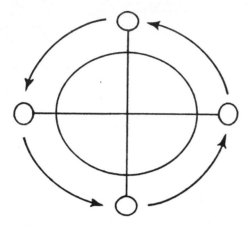

Figure 3.1. Dikenga dia Kongo, a core symbol of the BaKongo culture. (Image by the author)

land of the dead and the spirits, and the apex of a person's spiritual power. The right-hand disk represents east, the sun at dawn, the power of potentiality and transition, and the nascence of the spirit, soul, and earthly life in a cosmic cycle. The left-hand disk represents west, the sun at dusk, the power and transition of death, and the movement from the living to the spirit world. Movement in this depicted symbolic cycle is conceptualized as proceeding counterclockwise (Gomez 1998: 148–49; Janzen and MacGaffey 1974: 34; Thompson 1983: 108–9).

The surrounding circle or ellipse conveys the cyclical nature of earthly life and the natural world, the spiritual journey of the soul, and the reincarnative evolution of spirits. The crossed lines communicate an array of meanings concerning both the oppositional ordering of the cosmos and the invocation of spiritual powers into the land of the living. The vertical "power line" connects the Godhead above with the lower realm of lesser spirits, ancestor spirits, and the dead. It also communicates the invocation of spiritual power from below into the land of the living above. The horizontal line is the "line of Kalunga," which is the boundary line between the supreme God and the lesser spirits, and also the boundary between the land of the living and the realm of the spirits and the dead (Thompson and Cornet 1981: 28, 44; Thornton 1983: 9). Both living persons and the souls of the dead are conceptualized as cycling through incarnations, the living becoming the dead, the dead forming souls and ancestors, and ancestors evolving into more powerful spirits. These cycles are depicted by the wheeling element of the surrounding circle and the progression of the four moments of the cosmos (Balandier 1968: 155; Thompson 1997: 29–30).

The opposing realms of upper and lower unfold in additional metaphoric oppositions expressed in this emblematic version of the dikenga. The upper land of the living is inhabited by people with dark complexions, opposed and mirrored by the lower realm of the land of the dead and spirits, inhabited by souls of a white color. The east and west points are powerful points of transition—of birth, demise, and rebirth—and are associated with red as the color of birth and death. The upper land of the living is conceptualized as a mountain range, mirrored at the Kalunga boundary by a comparable mountain range in the land of the dead. The Kalunga line is a boundary for which the surface of water is a metaphoric image, and the mirroring flash of water and other reflective surfaces invokes this immediate interrelation of the land of the living and that of the spirits. The crossed lines represent the BaKongo belief that spirits pervasively imbue the land of the living, and can be summoned to cross the boundary and come to the aid of an individual, family, or community to provide aid in subsistence and protection against disease, misfortune, and harmful spirits (Janzen and MacGaffey 1974: 34; Thompson and Cornet 1981: 27–30).

A more abbreviated and instrumental form of the dikenga, consisting solely of the crossed axes, omits the surrounding cycle of lives and souls and the four moments of the cosmos with their multiple, metaphoric oppositions (Jacobson-Widding 1991: 183; MacGaffey 1988b: 516; Thompson and Cornet 1981: 43–44). The crossed lines provide a more focused and selective invocation of the intersection of the spirit world and the land of the living for immediate social action. Among the BaKongo people, this was the "simplest form" of dikenga rendering, and was used when individuals took oaths of truthfulness or undertook private rituals to seek spiritual aid (MacGaffey 1986: 118).

These crossed lines were typically drawn upon the ground, and a person would stand at the intersection of the lines when swearing an oath. Similarly, a ritual specialist would draw the lines upon the ground to demarcate a private, ritual space in which a spirit would be summoned to aid an individual supplicant. The crossed lines could also be drawn or etched onto objects in combination with vocalized prayers to create protective objects and amulets. Thus, this abbreviated version of the emblematic form of the dikenga typically served more private and instrumental purposes (Jacobson-Widding 1991: 201; MacGaffey 1991: 4; Thompson and Cornet 1981: 43–44).

Marking Social Group Contours

A primary use for emblematic symbols is the communication of social group identities and membership. As an expression of central beliefs of religious character, the creation and use of objects to invoke spiritual powers could be expressive of a practitioner's social group identity (A. Cohen 1976: 102). This will not always be the case, because particular religions often crosscut many social group identities (Yinger 1994: 264). However, if that religious belief system is one shared within a population that has the bounded characteristics of a social group, then such religious practices may be part of the key criteria of membership in a group identity as well (Emberling 1997: 318–20; Wolf 1972: 150). Thus, artifacts of such past religious beliefs may provide one line of interpretative evidence indicating past group identities. A concentrated study of the expressive elements in those artifacts could yield evidence of consistent patterns from which possible group identities of the creator or users of the artifact can be inferred (Fennell 2000: 304–5).

In contrast, instrumental expressions of core symbols may often develop into *assertive* stylistic expressions (for example, Wiessner 1983, 1984, 1985, 1990). Social actors will typically employ assertive and instrumental symbolic expressions in settings where there is intragroup competition or they are pursuing individual interests, such as self-protection (DeBoer and Moore 1982: 152–53; Hegmon 1992: 523–24; Wiessner 1990: 109). The belief systems exercised through personalized and instrumental religious expressions provide social actors with a means of self-initiative and methods for explaining and responding to misfortune, disease, malign events, and the conduct of adversaries who seek to subjugate them (Leone and Fry 1999: 384; Mbiti 1990: 196; McKee 1995: 41; Orser and Funari 2001: 63; Raboteau 1980: 286; Wilkie 1997: 83–84).

Archaeologists have often viewed some artifacts of religious significance as potential *cultural markers* or *ethnic markers* (Paynter 2000b: 184–85). Those phrases can be read in different ways. In one approach, it is the analyst who does the "marking," by first theorizing that past cultural actors shared a particular belief system with which members shaped their material culture in a largely unconscious, passive manner. The analyst can then view a pattern in material culture expressions as the consistent manifestation of a shared meaning system and mark that pattern for use in identifying members of that cultural group. In another approach, an ethnic marker is viewed as representing a past social actor's conscious efforts to create material culture expressions that signal group identity and membership to others. Consistent patterns can exist within such material culture, because each member purposefully and consciously expressed elements of the group's shared meaning system in those objects. Of these two approaches, the latter is typically more appropriate when considering the purposeful creation in material culture of symbolism expressing core religious beliefs and spiritual invocations (Fennell 2000: 284; Sackett 1985: 154, 157; Shanks and Tilley 1992: 143–44; Wiessner 1990: 107).

What does it mean to refer to a social group as an identifiable entity, such as the "BaKongo culture"? Particular culture groups should not be viewed as essentialized or static in character, but rather as dynamic, socially constructed networks of relationships and related group identities. Anthropologists have often referred to such social groups as ethnicities and to the process of their creation as ethnogenesis (see, for example, Banks 1996; A. P. Cohen 2000; De Vos 1975; Eriksen 1993; Friedman 1989, 1994; Roosens 1989). I refer to groups that possess a shared meaning system and social cohesion with the interchangeable terms of *social group, ethnic group, culture group,* and *social network.* Insights into cultural dynamics can be gained by analyzing the degrees of solidity, permeability, or disappearance of particular social group identities and their associated boundaries in different settings and over time. Thus, when we find evidence of different social groups interacting, analysis can focus on the degree to which members of each group utilize material expressions to signal their collective identity, and on the ways in which that identity persists or dissipates over time (see, for example, Barth 1998a: 16; 2000: 27–35; Franklin and Fesler 1999: 2–4; Hegmon 1992: 527–28; Sider 1986: 94).

These theories of social group interaction were not created in the abstract, but rather developed as methods for making sense of the social complexity observed firsthand by anthropologists. For example, Fredrik Barth's study of ethnic group identities in the Afghanistan region demonstrated that ethnic affiliations are socially constructed and not based on simple blood relations. Rather than define themselves by a large aggregation of beliefs and practices, members selected "only certain cultural traits" and made those the "unambiguous criteria for ascription" to the group (Barth 1998b: 119). When individuals ceased living a lifestyle that permitted them to satisfy those key attributes of a particular group, and where there was "an alternative identity within reach," the result was "a flow of personnel from one identity to another" (133). The features of a particular social group identity and its beliefs and practices might not change internally in some settings and time periods, because many persons simply chose a different identity to which they would subscribe (Barth 1998b: 133–34; 2000: 28–35). However, where tensions existed within a group and no alternative networks were accessible, or where diverging from the key cultural criteria was not very costly to the group's coherence, then the "basic contents or characteristics of the identity" would often be modified over time by members of the group (Barth 1998b: 134).

Consistent with this analysis, Edward Spicer (1971) outlined the observable characteristics of a variety of ethnic groups as "persistent cultural systems." Using historical examples, he found that each group experienced and outlived repeated efforts by state organizations to assimilate them through economic, political, and religious means. Such a cultural group typically developed "well-defined symbols of identity differentiating it from other peoples," including other ethnic groups and the state organization that it had opposed (797). The "formation and maintenance" of each cultural system was "intimately bound up" with such "conditions of opposition" to other groups (797). Thus, ethnic group identity may often be created and reinforced in opposition to outwardly imposed pressures (Friedman 1989: 254–56; Kelly and Kelly 1980: 134–35; Pollard 1994: 79–80).

Another fundamental theoretical question arises in anthropological investigations of such group dynamics: what is the general relationship between an individual, a social group of which he or she is a member, and the shared meaning system to which the members of the group subscribe? For example, should an analyst's interpretative framework be based on an assumption that individual actors were pervasively conditioned by the cultural traditions to which they subscribed and were enculturated? Can a cultural system be viewed as somehow existing separate from the individuals who subscribe to it, and does that cultural system continuously shape the conduct of those individuals? In the alternative, should an analyst assume that individuals played an active role as social agents in determining their own expressive conduct and in constructing the shared meaning systems in which they operated? Similarly, should a cultural system be viewed as existing only as it is conceptualized and acted out by individuals, and therefore as susceptible to modification and change by those actors?

These questions have played a central role in debates within the social sciences for some time. "It is no exaggeration to state that the problem of how to conceptualize the relationship between individual or group agency and wider social processes has been a primary problem of both the philosopher and the social theorist since the Enlightenment and beyond" (Shanks and Tilley 1992: 123; see also Dobres and Robb 2000: 4; Rorty 1979: 3–9). It is beyond the scope of this discussion to address the full array of debates and competing arguments that have focused upon these basic issues of social structures and agency, and the many subsidiary questions that flow from those concepts. Instead, I outline here the basic analytic assumptions I employ in this study and the general theoretical framework within which I address the relationship of individual "agents' perceptions of ethnicity and associated modes of interaction, and the cultural contexts and social relations in which they are embedded" (S. Jones 1997: 87).

The characteristics of a constant, moment-to-moment interaction of structure and agency have been addressed by theories such as Pierre Bourdieu's (1977) concept of habitus and Anthony Giddens' (1979) concepts of structuration and practical consciousness. Stated simply, these theories posit that the structure of a group's shared meaning system and accumulated rules and traditions for behavior provides both motivations for and constraints on the ways in which individual members of the group think and behave at any given moment. That structure, however, exists only as it is carried out moment-to-moment in the interactions of the individuals who subscribe to that culture group. Those persons can, in turn, modify the structure over time through their individual choices and innovations in performing those cultural beliefs and rules of conduct (for example, Bruner 1993: 321–23; Giddens 1979: 64–73; Sapir 1949: 515). The chapters of this book explore how these processes unfolded over time among the diasporas of the BaKongo, Yoruba, Fon, and Palatine German peoples, among others.

Bourdieu's theory of a habitus provides a very useful framework for evaluating the interdependence of the individual and social group, and of structure and agency. The habitus is a social structure consisting of a shared system of beliefs and practices learned by each member of a social group from an early age onward. This structure provides each group member with a set of durable dispositions toward certain ways of perceiving the world and conducting oneself (Bourdieu 1977: 78–93; see also Giddens 1979: 64–66; S. Jones 1997: 88). The habitus thus accounts for routinized modes of conduct and sets of learned dispositions that are applied by social actors in varied contexts. As such, the habitus will shape individuals' beliefs, perceptions, and practices in an often unconscious and routinized manner (Bourdieu 1977: 77; see also Giddens 1979: 69–73; S. Jones 1997: 88–89).

In the context of socially constructed ethnic groups, the habitus plays a similar function. The "sensations of ethnic affinity are founded on common life experiences that generate similar habitual dispositions" so that a "commonality of experience and of the preconscious habitus it generates" in turn "gives members of an ethnic cohort their sense of being both familiar and familial to each other" (Bentley 1987: 32–33). In this way, a "shared habitus engenders feelings of identification" that are "consciously appropriated" by members of the group and "given form through existing symbolic resources" employed by those group members (Bentley 1991: 173; see also 1987: 39). Individual agency operates in an interactive relationship with such dispositions. As the habitus is carried out and expressed by the conduct of group members who subscribe to that worldview from moment to moment, those individuals can generate incremental changes in the collected dispositions of the habitus over time. Such changes can also be influenced by pressures created by external alterations in the broader social and environmental contexts in which that group operates (Bourdieu 1977: 78; see also Dietler and Herbich 1998: 247; Giddens 1979: 64–73; Hegmon 1998: 273; S. Jones 1997: 89–90).

Expressions of Group Identity and Individual Purpose

Archaeologists confront another related and basic question: how does material culture relate to this interdependence of individual agency and social group structures? Are the objects of a culture created in an almost passive manner, as the mere by-products of cultural behavior? Or do objects play a role in conscious, meaning-imbued conduct, and in perpetuating the cultural belief systems that shaped their creation and use? In addressing these questions, Bourdieu's practice theory and concept of habitus have again proven useful (Wilkie 2000: 11; see also Shackel 2000: 233). In the interdependent dynamics summarized by the concept of habitus, "artifacts are recognized as situated within cultural negotiations and infused with meaning" (Wilkie 2000: 11). Both routinized and purposeful conduct should be expected of the individual members of any social group, so that "while material culture can be used in automatic, unconscious ways during the course of everyday life, it is also used in active, expressive ways, that are conscious on the part of actors" (Wilkie 2000: 13; see also Dobres and Robb 2000: 6–7).

Some studies of material culture have viewed objects as the products of the passive application of mental templates or behavioral processes. Other analysts have applied theoretical frameworks in which material culture is viewed as an active part of cultural practices, created with conscious activity and purpose (Dietler and Herbich 1998: 239; Hodder 2000: 22; Paynter 2000a: 11). Such analysts have also found that objects of material culture often play a key role in communicating the belief systems through which they were designed, selected for acquisition, or used (Csikszentmihalyi and Rochberg-Halton 1981: 17–18; Paynter 2000a: 16; Yentsch and Beaudry 2001: 224–26). Material culture thus functions in varying contexts as a primary medium for creating, confirming, or modifying cultural beliefs and practices, as well as serving as a vehicle for expressing those beliefs in a routinized way (for example, Wilkie 2000: 10–11).

This view of material culture as an active component of social conduct applies as well to the stylistic patterns in material culture. The shared meaning system and collection of rules for action in each social group influence the types and forms of material culture that members of the group prefer to create and utilize. This type of cultural preference has been analyzed frequently as a choice of style. As Michelle Hegmon (1998: 265, emphasis in original) states, "style is not just a passive by-product of cultural norms or mental templates. Style *does* something."

Style can be defined as an aspect of form and appearance of material items that is in addition to "that required by utilitarian function," so that style represents "a choice, conscious or capable of being raised to the level of consciousness, between equally viable functional alternatives" (David, Sterner, and Gavua 1988: 365). This stylistic aspect of the form and appearance of particular objects of material culture can communicate information about the cultural preferences, beliefs, and self-perceptions of the persons who created or used the objects shaped by that style (for example, Beaudry, Cook, and Mrozowski 1991: 165–67, 174; Douglas and Isherwood 1979: 65; Hegmon 1998: 265; D. Miller 1987: 190). As a communicative medium, style conveys information through symbolic modes of expression. Bringing these concepts of style together with insights on core symbols, we can anticipate that stylistic expressions will include a continuum from relatively emblematic messages to the more individually assertive and instrumental.

H. Martin Wobst analyzed the likely characteristics of emblematic stylistic expressions in an influential article published thirty years ago. He asserted that stylistic expressions that served to identify a group affiliation would most likely be targeted at outside groups at a social distance from the emitters of the material expression. The stylistic shaping of the material expression would thus serve to communicate an intragroup affiliation in an intergroup context (Wobst 1977: 323–25). He argued that it was unlikely a person wishing to communicate a group identity would expend time and labor creating a stylistically shaped material object to communicate such a message to a fellow member of his or her own group. Such an intragroup message would be unnecessary, "would be known already or generally could be more easily transmitted in other communication modes" (324). In contrast, he contended that the use of material culture would be efficient and effective for communicating such messages of identity to outside groups with whom one interacted less frequently, but who would still be able to "decode" or "read" the message signaled in the objects (Wobst 1977: 324; see also Hegmon 1992: 520–22). Material expressions that serve in this capacity should typically possess a uniformity and clarity in their design and in the messages conveyed (Wobst 1977: 323–34; see also Wiessner 1983: 257).

Wobst thus proposed that a social actor would undertake the stylistic shaping of material culture to communicate social group identity only when it was efficient to do so. Social actors would be expected to weigh the costs of time, materials, and labor expended in making the object versus the benefits of the material expression's communicative impact (Wobst 1977: 325). He based this proposition on the argument that it would be a "dysfunctional waste of energy and matter" for a social actor to invest time and labor in creating a stylistically shaped object to communicate with persons with whom that individual interacts on a regular basis (325). This would be the case, for example, if that actor could easily communicate the same information verbally, which has a lower cost (325).

The general theoretical propositions of the communicative functions of style articulated by Wobst have been tremendously useful to archaeological analysis. However, his propositions concerning efficiency are problematic for a number of reasons. First, his approach imposes western assumptions of self-interested rational actors and related cost-benefit preferences onto all social actors in varying past cultures. In the absence of persuasive empirical evidence, such assumptions remain ethnocentric and untenable (Dietler and Herbich 1998: 241). Second, it could be entirely efficient, even from Wobst's cost-benefit viewpoint, for a social actor to use an object of material culture to communicate within a social group of persons with whom she or he interacts on a daily basis. Although more time, material, and labor are invested in creating such an object, the object is an efficient and repetitive communicator once it is in place and on display, relieving the creator from repeated verbal utterances of the same message. Contrary to Wobst's assumptions, talk is not always "cheap," and such verbal utterances are ephemeral and require a speaker's repeated emission over time. In contrast, an object emits a stylistic message repeatedly and constantly as it is displayed to an audience that understands the language of the style.

Wobst (1977: 324) similarly proposed that social actors would use stylistically shaped material culture to communicate group identities primarily in settings where the material object would be highly visible to a targeted audience of outsiders who could understand the message. Yet, the use of stylistically shaped material culture in intragroup settings could make tremendous sense as well, even within a cost-benefit perspective. Objects used and displayed in a setting with relatively low visibility to outsiders may achieve high visibility and efficiency of communication to a different audience of insiders (see, for example, DeBoer and Moore 1982; Sterner 1989). More recently, Wobst has recognized the persuasiveness of these alternative views (Sterner 1989: 451; Wobst 2000), which have been supported by extensive evidence compiled in archaeological and ethnographic research (for example, Bowser 2000; David, Sterner, and Gavua 1988; DeBoer and Moore 1982; Hegmon 1998; Sterner 1989).

There are yet more complications to consider when trying to understand such rich cultural domains. What happens when multiple social groups interact? The continuum of core symbol expressions, extending from emblematic examples to private and instrumental uses, becomes particularly relevant in social settings where multiple cultures are at play. A spectrum of core symbol expressions typically exists within each culture's religious beliefs. In many social settings, however, a dominant religion emerges. This is the religious belief system of those persons who are in controlling positions in the society (Scribner 1987: 44; K. Thomas 1971; Yoder 1965).

For example, in the colonial and antebellum periods in North America, many European-Americans who exercised control over a wide array of social settings propounded Christianity as the proper form of religious belief and observance that should be practiced by all members of society (Yoder 1965). Others in this period believed that enslaved African Americans should not be converted to Christianity, for fear that conversion would necessitate emancipation. This did not, however, lead to a view of African religions as approved alternatives, but was rather accompanied by an indifference to the spiritual lives of enslaved African Americans by many persons who sought to subjugate them (Berlin 1998: 60–61; Gomez 1998: 288; Raboteau 1980: 66, 98–99, 103–7, 148–49; Wills 1997: 14).

Dominant religions often have the effect of driving other religious belief systems "underground" (Morgan 1998: 612; Shorter 1972: 148; Yoder 1990: 95). These nondominant religions are often referred to as "folk religions" by historians, folklorists, and anthropologists (for example, K. Thomas 1971; Yoder 1965). The public exercise of group rituals of such folk religions typically becomes impracticable, due to the social pressures imposed by members of the dominant religion. If group rituals of a folk religion are undertaken, they typically are convened in secret, away from the watchful eyes of disapproving members of the dominant religion. However, the primary way the folk religion is continued is through private, instrumental invocations of the core symbols of that belief system (for example, Scribner 1987: 44).

Thus, when persons who practiced a dominant religion in one region are removed from that context and placed into a new area where they are not in control, they often have to abandon the public display of group exercises of their religion. They are able to continue the exercise of their beliefs only through individualized, instrumental expressions in private settings. In time, they may adopt the dominant religion that holds sway in that new setting and attend its public ceremonies, all the while practicing the beliefs of their previous religion in private surroundings (Gundaker 1998: 75–76; K. Thomas 1971: 221–32; Yoder 1965: 36–39).

Archaeologists, folklorists, and historians have often studied past social settings in which there was evidence of a continuing exercise of private, instrumental expressions of a religion in the space of households, and yet there was no evidence of the public display of group exercises of that belief system. When addressing such subjects, analysts often employ a variety of terms to describe such individualized practices, including phrases such as folk superstition, conjuration, cunning, magic, divination, witchcraft, hoodoo, and voodoo (for example, Deetz and Deetz 2000; Fennell 2000; Ferguson 1999; Leone and Fry 1999; Powdermaker 1939; Wilkie 1995, 1997). While such distinguishing terms are useful indications that only individualized invocations are under study, it is important to emphasize that these private uses were just one part of a past array of beliefs and practices within a full and comprehensive religion. The past suppression of public and group exercise of one religion by the impact of another, dominant religion does not mean that individualized invocations of the nondominant religion represent the mere "debris" of that belief system (Turner 1973: 1105). Those private, symbolic deployments instead typically serve as vital continuations of what was once a comprehensive worldview (Butler 1990: 159).

In this study, I examine the degree to which particular forms of material culture can be interpreted as the product of specific ethnic group affiliations and related traditions of stylistic and symbolic expression. An analysis of various African and European diasporas illustrates how the processes of group identity, individual agency, and emblematic and instrumental expressions operated interdependently in particular contexts. In the next chapter, we look in more detail at the history of the BaKongo people. Doing so lays the groundwork for formulating predictions of how their beliefs and expressions could have continued to develop in the New World even in the face of the European slavery system's brutality and oppression.

4

A Model for Diaspora Analysis

Can one credibly interpret crossed lines scratched into bowl bases, marbles, spoons, and coins, or crossed lines demarcated by the position of buried caches of objects at African American sites in North America as the solemn expressions of a particular African culture, such as the BaKongo? Such a proposition would be greatly strengthened if there existed specific evidence that persons enculturated in BaKongo beliefs and practices had lived at each of those sites. This observation raises the initial issue of whether individuals abducted into slavery and subjected to the horrors of the Middle Passage across the Atlantic could have retained any of their cultural beliefs and practices.

Some historians have contended that the traumatic experiences of enslavement effectively destroyed Africans' memories and knowledge of the cultural traditions that existed in the homelands from which they were abducted (for example, Frazier 1966a, 1966b; Whitten 1962). In addition, some scholars of African cultures have argued that many of those belief systems lacked a concept of individuality similar to that found among western societies, so that an "individual" could not "exist alone except corporately" (Mbiti 1990: 106; Mogobe 1988: 10; compare R. Handler 1994: 31–34). However, such a contingency should become less relevant when examining the impact of enslavement, which removed individuals from the previous social networks in which such specific corporate norms would have operated.

Other studies have demonstrated that enslaved Africans succeeded in retaining detailed memories of their original cultures, and that they passed these beliefs and traditions on to later generations throughout the Americas (for example, Herskovits 1941; Perdue, Barden, and Phillips 1976). Similarly, other analysts find extensive historical evidence of concepts of individualism among a variety of African cultures, which should have facilitated a person's ability to adapt to new group settings (for example, Comaroff and Comaroff 2001: 276–77; MacGaffey 1970a: 261–62; Morris 1994: 139–40, 145–46). Although enslaved Africans were unable to transport their social structures to America, individuals could bring their learning and cultural knowledge with them. Torn from their previous social relationships and thrown into new settings in American plantations and big houses, individuals abducted from African societies needed to apply their cultural knowledge creatively in forging new relationships (for example, J. Miller 2002: 42, 60). In addition to the average members of each cultural group abducted into slavery, healers, diviners, priests, priestesses, and political leaders were frequently abducted as well, and brought with them even more specialized beliefs and practices (Mintz and Price 1976: 10; Raboteau 1980: 50; Sobel 1987: 6).

Mintz and Price (1976: 6–7, 21) argued persuasively that enslaved African Americans most likely forged new social relationships with one another by focusing on their common cultural and cosmological assumptions, creating innovative forms of expression in their new settings. Subjugated persons would have focused less on trying to retain the "formal elements" of their different African cultural traditions, such as specific kinship or political modes of organization (6–7). One avenue for these creative efforts would have involved individuals' greater use of instrumental symbols to invoke spiritual aid and protection for themselves and their new cohort. Captive Africans in the Americas likely placed much less emphasis on utilizing emblematic symbols expressive of their past group identities.

To explore these processes, consider an array of artifacts uncovered at sites occupied by persons of African American heritage in the late seventeenth through nineteenth centuries in North America. A number of these artifacts bear attributes similar to those of the Demory site skull figure. For example, at a variety of plantation sites in South Carolina and Virginia dating from the late seventeenth century to the early nineteenth century, archaeologists recovered pieces of colonoware pottery associated with use by African Americans. A number of these pieces of pots and bowls had crosses scratched into their round bases (Ferguson 1992: 110–16; 1999: 121–27; Orser 1994: 38–39). Most of these incised pottery remains were recovered from river bottoms near the locations of past rice plantations in South Carolina (Ferguson 1992: 146; 1999: 121–22). At the Locust Grove plantation in Kentucky, archaeologists uncovered a white clay marble and a silver teaspoon with X marks incised into them, and glass prisms from a chandelier in the artifacts of a domestic site occupied by African Americans in the period of the 1790s through 1860 (Young 1996, 1997).

Archaeologists excavating the basement level of the Charles Carroll house in Annapolis, Maryland, occupied between 1721 and 1821, uncovered objects deposited in caches under the floorboards of adjacent workrooms. These objects included quartz crystals, a smooth black stone, a glass bead, pottery pieces decorated with cross and asterisk marks, and pierced discs and coins (Adams 1994: 1–2; Galke 2000: 23–25; L. Jones 2000: 2; Leone and Fry 1999: 372–73; Logan 1995: 154–55; Russell 1997: 64–65). Similar finds were uncovered from African American occupations at the nearby Brice, Slayton, and Adams-Kilty houses, dating in the middle to late nineteenth century (Leone 2005: 199–224; Neuwirth and Cochran 2000; Rivera 2005; Ruppel et al. 2003: 326–27).

The Levi Jordan plantation site in Brazoria, Texas, yielded particularly intriguing artifacts (K. L. Brown 1994, 2001; K. N. Brown and K. L. Brown 1998; K. L. Brown and Cooper 1990). This site was occupied from 1848 through 1888, when it was rapidly abandoned due to eviction proceedings. African Americans lived in quarters at the plantation, worked as enslaved labor until emancipation, and later lived and worked at the site as tenant farmers. They were forced off the land in approximately 1888 by the plantation owner's heirs in a manner that resulted in sudden abandonment of their dwellings (K. L. Brown 1994: 96–98, 102–3; 2001: 101). Artifacts uncovered at several of those house sites presented distinct assemblages indicating that a number of the residences had been occupied by persons who possessed well-defined social and economic roles. For example, archaeologists identified one house site as the residence of a seamstress, and others as past dwellings of a carver, a carpenter, a political leader, and a curer (also referred to as a healer, magician, or conjurer) (K. L. Brown 1994: 101, 106–7; K. L. Brown and Cooper 1990: 15).

The "curer's cabin" at the Jordan plantation site contained four caches of objects in the floor space of one room. These caches were not located at the corners of the room, but rather along the perimeter at each of the cardinal directions. The caches contained, among other things, round iron kettle bases and white chalk; a concentrated deposit of iron wedges or knife-blade fragments; a series of silver coins; two iron kettles with heavy chain fragments, white ash, and clay; and burned iron nails, shells, and ash (K. L. Brown 1994: 108–10; K. N. Brown and K. L. Brown 1998: 2). Another African American dwelling nearby, which the archaeologists referred to as the "political leader's cabin," contained a concealed brick embossed with crossed lines surrounded by an ellipse (K. L. Brown 1994: 112, 115).

Archaeologists investigating these sites in South Carolina, Kentucky, Maryland, and Texas have each interpreted these artifacts as representing objects of religious significance derived from the beliefs of the BaKongo culture. Based on material similarities and contextual evidence, the artifacts are viewed as expressing symbolic compositions consistent with the BaKongo dikenga or with related objects of spiritual invocation called *minkisi* in the KiKongo language (K. L. Brown 1994; K. L. Brown and Cooper 1990; Ferguson 1992, 1999; Franklin 1997; Galke 2000; Leone and Fry 1999; Neuwirth and Cochran 2000; Patten 1992; Samford 1996; Young 1996, 1997). These interpretations have been viewed skeptically by some commentators, who caution that archaeologists should be careful and explicit in the logical steps taken in arriving at such inferences of particular cultural affiliations (see, for example, Deetz 1995, 1996; Fennell 2000; Howson 1990; B. Thomas 1995).

For example, it is often unclear whether these interpretations are based on an approach that invokes a direct and specific historical link between the occupation site and persons known to have come from the BaKongo culture (compare Steward 1942). Some analysts, such as Leland Ferguson (1992, 1999), have attempted to show that persons abducted into slavery from the Kongo area were brought to the general region in which the archaeological finds were located. If more direct and specific types of evidence exist, however, they have not been identified in the archaeologists' studies. Similarly, it remains unclear whether these interpretations are based on an approach that employs some form of ethnographic analogy (see Ascher 1961; K. L. Brown 2004; Stahl 1993; B. Thomas 1995; Trigger 1995; Wylie 1985). If such a method has been applied, it is often unclear in published reports as to what specific approaches were utilized.

Other sources of information that archaeologists in North America could potentially consider are the findings of archaeological investigations at historic-period sites in Africa (for example, Singleton 2001: 179; 2006: 259–60). For example, one can imagine how useful it would be to compare the artifacts of BaKongo or Yoruba religious beliefs uncovered at eighteenth-century village sites in Africa with the artifacts uncovered at African American sites that date to later in that century. A number of archaeological projects have been completed that focus on sites in west and west central Africa dating to the time period of the transatlantic slave trade (for example, DeCorse 2001; Reid and Lane 2004). However, those archaeology projects at various locations in Africa have not yet addressed the particular questions raised when examining the remarkable artifacts under scrutiny at North American sites. I hope that as historical archaeology expands in African locations, such comparative data will become increasingly available in the future.

Interpreting Cultural Expressions through Ethnohistorical Analogy

For each of the North American sites described previously, corroborative and contextual evidence supported the proposition that the artifacts in question were located in the living quarters of enslaved or free African Americans (see, for example, K. L. Brown and Cooper 1990: 18; Wilkie 1997: 102). There is, however, no direct documentary or archaeological evidence at any of those sites to demonstrate that one or more of the past inhabitants abducted from the Kongo area or were in some way closely associated with a member of the BaKongo culture. Such specific evidence would be required if one were to apply a "direct historical approach" and interpret these artifacts as particular expressions of core symbols of the BaKongo culture (compare Steward 1942).

Other potential sources of direct evidence typically fall short of such proof as well. For example, the records of individual slave shipments arriving in North American ports are often unhelpful. Those records usually fail to identify individuals or the locations within west or west central Africa from which each person was abducted (DeCorse 1999: 135; Lovejoy 1989: 378). Identifying the ports on the African coast from which slave ships departed also fails to provide specific evidence for particular persons. Slave ships embarking from African ports often carried persons abducted from many varied locations in the interior of the country and transported long distances to those ports (DeCorse 1999: 136–37; Posnansky 1999: 25; Walsh 2001: 141). Recent work by historians has greatly increased available data on the relative percentages of persons abducted from different African cultures for the transatlantic slave trade. Yet, we still typically lack data that can link specific individuals at sites in the Americas with the particular locations in Africa from which they were abducted.

In the absence of direct evidence linking occupants of these sites with individuals known to have been enculturated in the BaKongo belief system, an analyst should instead formulate an explicit interpretative framework based on an ethnohistorical analogy. One can then compare and contrast in a more systematic manner the ethnohistorical information concerning a specific African cultural system with the material culture evidence found at the relevant sites in North America. Such an approach using an ethnohistorical analogy requires one to compile a detailed account of the beliefs and practices of an identifiable culture in one place and time, referred to as the "source" of the analogy. One then compares and contrasts the attributes of that source with the material culture uncovered in another time and place (Ascher 1961; Stahl 1993; Wylie 1985).

A first step in constructing an ethnohistorical analogy is to demonstrate that the cultural system selected to provide the source information is relevant to the subject of material culture to which it will be applied (Stahl 1993: 248–50; B. Thomas 1995: 153; Trigger 1995: 450–52; Wylie 1985: 101). To illustrate this, let us address this question to the subject of the BaKongo culture. The BaKongo religion was practiced by a large percentage of the population in the Kongo and Angola areas of west central Africa throughout the period of slavery. People abducted into slavery and brought to the North American colonies came from a variety of regions in Africa, however, not just Kongo and Angola. Nonetheless, one can readily demonstrate the general relevance of the BaKongo culture as a potential source of cultural beliefs and practices for occupants of slave quarters in North American sites.

Continuing studies of the transatlantic slave trade, building off the work of Curtin (1969), Richardson (1989), and others, have estimated that approximately 26 percent of captive Africans brought to North America came from west central Africa, 24 percent from the Bight of Biafra, 15 percent from Sierra Leone, 14 percent from Senegambia, 13 percent from the Gold Coast, and 4 percent from the Bight of Benin (Gomez 1998: 29; see fig. 1.2). Other studies estimate that more than one-third of Africans abducted into slavery and taken to North America came from the region of west central Africa (Eltis 2001: 44, table II; Morgan 1998: 62–68; Thompson and Cornet 1981: 32).

The operations of the slave trade could have presented further obstacles to the ability of individuals to retain and practice their BaKongo beliefs over time. For example, it is possible that persons abducted from the Kongo area could have lost their original cultural beliefs and practices before arriving in North America if they were first forced to adapt to the settings of plantations in the Caribbean for a number of years. Recent studies show, however, that the vast majority of Africans abducted into slavery and brought to British North America were transported there directly from locations in Africa, rather than from other locations in the Caribbean or South America (Eltis 2001: 36–37). For example, Lorena Walsh (2001: 144–45) calculated that 93 percent of persons abducted into slavery and brought to the Chesapeake region were brought there directly from Africa "or were transshipped from the West Indies after only a brief period of recuperation from their transatlantic ordeal." Examining newly expanded databases of slave shipment records, she found that "[a]lmost all of the 18,000 slaves estimated to have been imported into Maryland in the eighteenth century came, as in Virginia, directly from Africa" (148).

A significant percentage of those captives brought to Maryland came from west central Africa, ranging from 13 to 48 percent in the period of 1731–1773 (167, table I). In the period of 1710–1769, approximately 3,860 enslaved laborers were imported into Virginia from the Angola region within west central Africa, out of a total of approximately 52,504 captives imported into that colony from all African locations in that period (Holloway 1990: 11; see fig. 1.2). Other census calculations show that enslaved persons imported from the Angola region of west central Africa into South Carolina comprised approximately 59 percent of all slaves imported into that colony in the period of 1733–1744, 14 percent in 1749–1787, and 52 percent in 1804–1807 (Holloway 1990: 7).

Thus, significant numbers of persons were abducted from the Kongo and Angola regions and taken directly to the areas where the North American archaeological sites in question were located. This fact is not sufficient to provide a direct historical link for each site. It does demonstrate, however, the relevance of using the attributes of the BaKongo beliefs and practices in formulating an ethnohistorical analogy for interpreting the potential meaning and significance of the material culture uncovered at such African American sites in North America.

After compiling a detailed description of this source for our analogy, we need to apply it to the artifacts and context of the North American sites to determine the degree to which the attributes of the source provide a closeness of fit for interpreting the meaning and significance of those objects. In addition, the context in which the artifacts are found at each site is of critical importance when formulating inferences of their meaning, use, and significance in those settings (K. L. Brown and Cooper 1990: 16–19; Posnansky 1972: 34; Stine, Cabak, and Groover 1996: 64–65).

The particular character of the interpretation proposed here raises another relevance criterion for the source of the analogy. My research question proposes that persons learned in BaKongo cultural beliefs and practices were abducted into slavery in the sixteenth through nineteenth centuries and brought to sites in North America, where they continued their practices and taught these traditions to others with whom they interacted. The ethnohistorical evidence should therefore provide details of a BaKongo culture that existed in west central Africa in time periods predating the related artifacts uncovered in the North American sites. In contrast, prehistoric archaeologists often employ current-day ethnographic analogies that postdate the subject of the artifacts under analysis. This methodology is acceptable for their purposes, because their interpretations are typically limited to the question of the general functions once served by certain types of artifacts or artifact assemblages (see, for example, Binford 1967; Costin 1996: 117–18). However, the type of historic-period analysis proposed here involves much more specific questions of cultural belief systems, applied to much richer contextual evidence, to assess the potential meaning and significance of particular artifacts (B. Thomas 1995: 151–54).

The level of specificity involved in this type of analysis makes a requirement of chronological relevance appropriate. I am not proposing the use of an ethnographic analogy to yield only a general interpretation that these artifacts at North American sites were simply of a general spiritual or ideological character, rather than purely utilitarian in nature. Nor do I seek to assess an interpretation that such artifacts simply exhibit some form of homogenous, "pan-African" spiritual character (Lovejoy 1997: 10; B. Thomas 1995: 153). The ethnohistorical analogy proposed here is designed for the purpose of credibly assessing an interpretation that these artifacts show the attributes of spiritual expressions consistent with a specific culture group—in this case, the BaKongo. The use of such a specific analogy also provides a means to assess the extent to which there may have been changes and innovations in those expressive motifs over time and in the new settings in which African Americans lived.

This requirement of chronological relevance raises methodological challenges. Extensive ethnographic data concerning many African cultures were compiled in the late nineteenth and early twentieth centuries. One should not, however, rely solely on ethnographic data of a particular African society compiled in the late nineteenth or early twentieth century to construct an analogy for application to artifacts in North America that date from earlier time periods (J. Handler and Lange 1978: 210; Howson 1990: 78–81; Jamieson 1995: 43; Palmer 1995: 224; B. Thomas 1995: 152–53). To do so, one would have to assume that the characteristics of the African society under analysis had remained static for centuries preceding the time of ethnographic description (Posnansky 1999: 22; Singleton 1999: 8). Although some facets of a culture may have remained consistent for a number of decades or centuries, this fact should not be assumed, but instead should be established by ethnohistorical and material culture evidence from the earlier time periods relevant to the study.

Finally, when employing ethnohistorical analogies, analysts should refrain from "mapping" a "wide range of social traits" from the source side of the analogy onto the subject of interpretation based only on limited similarities in some forms of belief systems and associated material expressions (Stahl 1993: 252–53; see also Schmidt 1995: 125; B. Thomas 1995: 154). For example, one may find evidence of symbolic objects in North American sites that are consistent with the attributes of an instrumental and abbreviated expression of the BaKongo dikenga in private settings. However, one should not, based on that finding alone, assume that occupants of those sites in North America also displayed symbolic renderings consistent with an emblematic expression of the dikenga to assert group identity in public settings. Similarly, one should not assume that an individual who performed a role as a ritual specialist and healer within the slave quarters of a North American plantation would have possessed all the social status and attributes of a comparable specialist within the BaKongo culture in west central Africa (B. Thomas 1995: 154).

Formulating an explicit and detailed ethnohistorical analogy, which compares primary facets of the BaKongo culture in west central Africa with the characteristics of the African American artifacts under consideration here, yields two main benefits. First, a more systematic study provides a greater body of evidence with which to judge the accuracy of these interpretations of artifacts. Second, a thorough consideration of the BaKongo religion as practiced historically in the Kongo region reveals dynamics of the emblematic and instrumental symbolism utilized within that belief system. A comparative use of an ethnohistorical analogy points out not only elements of correspondence, but instances of divergence between facets of the source and of the material culture under analysis (Stahl 1993: 252–53; Wylie 1985: 107). Such elements of correspondence and divergence can be seen in the repertoire of material expressions used within the BaKongo culture in Africa, those expressed in African American domestic sites in North America, and those expressed in newly embellished forms in settings in the Caribbean and South America. This focus, in turn, permits a richer analysis of the social significance of the artifacts uncovered at those sites.

BaKongo Culture in West Central Africa

Consider, now, the body of evidence comprising the source for this ethnohistorical analogy. Extensive and detailed information about the BaKongo people, their culture, and their religion is available from accounts dating back at least to the time of Portuguese colonists' arrival in Kongo in 1482 (see, for example, Janzen 1977: 77; MacGaffey 1986: 21–24; 2000b: 7–8; Vansina 1966: 6–7). Unlike other African cultures farther to the north, the BaKongo people were not significantly affected by the spread of Islam (Alexander 2001; Gomez 1998). In contrast, European officials and Christian missionaries generated many ethnohistorical accounts of the BaKongo culture from the late fifteenth century onward, often with the assistance of members of the BaKongo people. Thus, some of the primary sources of earlier ethnohistorical information consist of accounts written by Europeans, rather than oral histories or written accounts recorded directly by BaKongo authors (see Vansina 1962: 126–28).

In addition, Swedish missionary Karl Laman (1953, 1957, 1962, 1968) compiled remarkably detailed ethnographic accounts of the BaKongo culture and religion in the period of 1891 through 1919 (Laman 1953: vii). Some commentators have questioned the usefulness of the extensive data provided in Laman's accounts, in view of his role as a missionary in that late time period (for example, B. Thomas 1995: 153–54). However, a close examination and critical reading of Laman's methods and results establishes the value of his work. The consistency of his findings with those of earlier observers also supports the relevance and usefulness of his data.

From 1891 onward, Laman began collecting ethnographic information on the BaKongo religion as it then existed in practice and in oral history (Jacobson-Widding 1991: 214–15; MacGaffey 1991: 2). He formulated detailed questionnaires and recruited a number of his student evangelists, who were members of the BaKongo people, to use those guidelines in interviewing the elders and ritual specialists in their communities. Laman structured this collection process in a way that indicated he was interested in compiling and preserving an accurate record of this culture. Sixty-eight primary informants provided extensive information, filling over 430 notebooks and more than 10,000 manuscript pages (Jacobson-Widding 1991: 214–15; Janzen 1972: 319–21; MacGaffey 1991: 2). Analysts who have studied his compilations in detail have viewed the ethnographic information as credible and relatively unbiased (for example, Jacobson-Widding 1979, 1991; Janzen and MacGaffey 1974; MacGaffey 2000b; Thompson and Cornet 1981). In addition, evidence from other, earlier ethnohistorical sources provides corroborating data and extends the time period of key facets of the BaKongo culture back to the sixteenth century (for example, Thompson 1993: 48–54; Thompson and Cornet 1981: 27–30, 44–45).

The numerous accounts of Christian missionaries and European officials in the sixteenth and seventeenth centuries must also be read critically to extract useful ethnohistorical information while avoiding reliance on biased characterizations (Thornton 2002: 73; Vansina 1966: 8–9; compare J. Handler 2000). For example, early missionaries often described indigenous beliefs and practices in disparaging terms. An array of BaKongo religious beliefs and practices, including the use of material culture to invoke spiritual aid, would often be described as the "barbaric" worship of "fetishes." Similarly, missionaries occasionally reported that the indigenous religious practices were mired in declension and incoherence, a view supportive of the missionaries' aspirations of replacing those beliefs with their own. In contrast, when emphasizing the challenges they faced, missionaries often noted the vitality and resistant character of the local beliefs and practices (Thornton 1977: 512–14). An analyst should read the accounts of such missionaries and colonial representatives to extract the basic factual descriptions of the BaKongo religious materials, practices, and beliefs, while setting aside the past authors' qualitative characterizations and assessments (for example, Thornton 2002: 73; Vansina 1962: 128).

Utilizing such critical readings, analysts have extracted and compiled a remarkable body of detailed, credible information concerning the economic, political, and religious traditions of the BaKongo people (Balandier 1968: 22). Anthropologists and historians working with these ethnohistorical accounts and later ethnographic observations find a remarkable continuity in the principal facets of the BaKongo religion from the sixteenth century through the late nineteenth century (Balandier 1968; Ballard 2005; Hilton 1985; Jacobson-Widding 1979, 1991; Janzen and MacGaffey 1974; MacGaffey 1986, 2000b; Thompson 1993; Thornton 1983, 1998). Their observations are based not on mere assumptions of constancy or the "conservative" character of cultures, but rather on the critical reading of numerous ethnohistorical accounts that span that time period (compare DeCorse 1999: 134). This continuity resulted largely from the particular historical dynamics of political strategies of BaKongo ruling factions over time and the related effects of indirect European colonial rule and Christian missionary strategies (MacGaffey 1986: 179).

The indigenous Kingdom of Kongo held control of much of the west central region in Africa from at least the fourteenth century onward. That kingdom included territories that are now located in portions of the Democratic Republic of the Congo, Gabon, the Republic of the Congo, and Angola (see fig. 1.2; MacGaffey 1986: 21–24; Thompson and Cornet 1981: 27). The kingdom was likely founded sometime between 1275 and 1350, according to the record of successive kingships up to the time of Portuguese contact in 1482 (Balandier 1968: 35; Balandier and Maquet 1974: 206). Before that time, the BaKongo people were organized in clans, groups of clans called *kandas*, and chiefdom structures, which continued to underlie the later kingdom organization (Thornton 1983: 19). The royal families who attained dominant political power within the kingdom by the late 1400s were typically members of a limited number of kandas (Thornton 1983: 35). Both chiefs and kings endeavored to control interregional trade in a variety of goods, including copper and ivory (Balandier 1968: 137–38; MacGaffey 2000c: 39). At the time of European contact, the kingdom encompassed approximately 116,000 square miles of territory and likely included a population of two to three million people (Balandier 1968: 29; Balandier and Maquet 1974: 206).

The BaKongo royalty were among the first to adopt Christianity, but they did so primarily for the pragmatic purpose of bolstering their political power (Broadhead 1979: 632–33; Sweet 2003: 110–14). For this and other reasons, the BaKongo people adopted Christianity in a relatively superficial manner that did not alter their traditional religious beliefs (Balandier 1968: 47; Broadhead 1979: 632–33). The royal families often came to view Christianity warily, in part because of the Christian missionaries' condemnation of polygamy, a practice that was integral to the royal families' social and political alliances and their accumulation of power (Balandier 1968: 47, 180–81).

The kingdom began to fragment not long after the first European contact, and it later expanded and contracted with successive acquisitions and losses of territory (Balandier 1968: 29, 33; Broadhead 1979). The royal families of Kongo both adopted and renounced Christianity throughout the late fifteenth through seventeenth centuries to suit their shifting political purposes (Janzen 1977: 78). Regional political struggles and internecine wars led to the increasing abduction into slavery of members and leaders of the losing factions during the sixteenth and seventeenth centuries (Balandier 1968: 62, 68–69). By 1665, European colonial rule, implemented by Portugal and later by Belgium and France (see fig. 1.3), replaced the kingship structure with a system of chiefdoms, while retaining a general approach of indirect rule (MacGaffey 1986: 179).

After the defeat of the Kongo Kingdom, civil wars ensued among competing chiefdom factions of the BaKongo people and with other neighboring polities in the 1665–1718 period (Balandier and Maquet 1974: 207; Thornton 1998: 120). One of the impacts of such wars was an increase in the abduction of persons into slavery, including groups living in areas farther inland from the coast (Eltis 2001: 34–35; Nwokeji 2001: 61; Thornton 1998: 120). The transatlantic slave trade finally came to a close in the west central region of Africa in 1863 (MacGaffey 2000b: 18).

Extensive documentary, material culture, and oral history evidence indicates that the core elements of BaKongo culture survived the period of the slave trade (Janzen 1977: 81; MacGaffey 2000b: 8–11; Thornton 1998: 251). The BaKongo people were able to retain and speak the KiKongo language through the eighteenth and nineteenth centuries. They were also able to practice many of the central facets of the BaKongo religion, particularly in relatively private settings. Although members of the BaKongo culture adopted Christianity, they did so in a very selective manner, translating most of the Christian concepts and icons into the BaKongo worldview (Berlin 1996: 259–60; 1998: 73; Thornton 1983: 63).

Primary elements of the BaKongo religion included a concept of a supreme Godhead, called Nzambi Mpungu in KiKongo, who was the creator of all things (Laman 1962: 53; Raboteau 1980: 9). However, Nzambi was viewed as a remote creator, uninvolved in the daily affairs of the living (for example, Vansina 1966: 30). Nzambi created a variety of spirits, ancestor spirits, souls, the land of the dead, the land of the living, and the natural world as part of the cosmic structure and cycling of all things. The living may make supplication to these spirits to aid them in subsisting and to protect them from disease, misfortune, and the attacks of adversaries (Janzen and MacGaffey 1974: 34–35; Raboteau 1980: 9).

The BaKongo dikenga expressed the cosmic structure of these cycles, various entities, and complementary realms. The crossed lines of the dikenga were viewed as "Nzambi's writing" and were not to be drawn by any person without solemnity (Laman 1962: 56). Ethnohistorical sources and material culture evidence demonstrate that the dikenga was already in existence as a longstanding symbolic tradition within the BaKongo religion before European contact in 1482 (Janzen and MacGaffey 1974: 34; Thompson 1993: 48–54; Thompson and Cornet 1981: 27–30). In its fullest embellishment, including crossed lines, surrounding ellipse, and four moments of the cosmos, this ideogram likely served as an emblematic symbol for the group identity of all members of the culture (MacGaffey 1986: 136, 169–71). In its abbreviated form, consisting of crossed lines, the dikenga was incorporated pervasively into instrumental rituals, which were performed extensively in public and private settings for community and individual supplications to the spirits (Laman 1962: 21; MacGaffey 1991: 4; Thompson and Cornet 1981: 37).

The BaKongo believed that *basimbi* (also spelled *bisimbi* for the plural and *simbi* in the singular) were the intermediary spirits whom the living could summon and to whom they could make supplications for aid and protection (MacGaffey 1991: 6; Thompson 1983: 107). Basimbi were powerful forms of spirits. Some were created directly by Nzambi and others originated as the souls of living persons, which evolved through multiple cycles of death and rebirth as living person, then soul, then ancestor, then simbi (Laman 1962: 33, 68). "As the basimbi (from simba, to hold, keep, preserve) safeguard the country, man could not exist anywhere without them" (33). Simbi spirits were strongly associated with bodies of water, although there were also basimbi associated with the land as the creators of mountains (33, 41–42). This BaKongo concept of intermediary spirits was notably distinct from the Yoruba and Fon concepts in west Africa (see fig. 1.2) of a pantheon of sub-deities, each with specific personalities (Raboteau 1980: 9–12).

The BaKongo believed that the land of the dead mirrored the land of the living, and that the personalities and attributes of the dead paralleled those of persons who had once lived (Laman 1962: 14–20; Thornton 1983: 9). "The journey to the land of the dead takes the form of the ascent of a high mountain. When the traveler has reached the top he is dead, and can no longer see his village" (Laman 1962: 15–16). In turn, the souls of the dead could evolve, through several reincarnative cycles, into more powerful simbi spirits (Laman 1962: 17; Thompson 1983: 108–9).

One can thus see the repeated metaphors that are captured in the elements of the dikenga. For example, the horizontal Kalunga line in the dikenga was conceptualized as dividing two mountain ranges, opposed at their bases and separated by the mirroring surface of a body of water (Janzen and MacGaffey 1974: 34; Thornton 1983: 9). Ethnohistorical sources dating from the sixteenth and seventeenth centuries show that the Kalunga line and the surface of water were both viewed metaphorically as a great boundary, the realm through which the living gain access to the spirit world and the newly deceased pass into the other world (Thornton 1983: 9). BaKongo people believed that the powers of the spirit world shaped the events of the living and natural worlds, and that all evil, good, power, and authority were derived from the other world (Thornton 1983: 9). The intermediary spirits were thus pervasively present, and could be summoned to make themselves manifest and focused within the land of the living to provide aid to particular persons or communities.

Members of the BaKongo people made supplications to and requested the aid of particular basimbi, ancestor spirits, or souls of the dead by creating physical containers into which a manifestation of one of those spirits could be summoned and focused (Laman 1962: 34, 44–45, 67; MacGaffey 1991: 1–6; 2000b: 82–83). These physical objects were called *minkisi* in KiKongo (*nkisi* in the singular). Minkisi were typically created by ritual specialists called *banganga* (*nganga* in the singular). The supreme Godhead, Nzambi, cannot be incorporated into minkisi in the way basimbi or ancestor spirits can be captured within them (Jacobson-Widding 1979: 135; Janzen 1977: 70; Laman 1962: 56). Nzambi was viewed as having created the universe, people, spirits, transformative death, and the power of minkisi. The Godhead was thus viewed as being removed from mortal concerns, and supplications were made instead to the ancestor spirits or the other intermediary spirits created by Nzambi (Laman 1962: 57, 67–68; Raboteau 1980: 9; Van Wing 1941: 85).

The compositions of various types of minkisi were replete with metonymic and metaphoric meanings that were summarized in the components of the dikenga (MacGaffey 1991: 4–6; Thompson and Cornet 1981: 37). A metonymic message is composed using an object or substance that has a literal and tangible relationship with the subject that it is now employed to represent. For example, dirt from an ancestor's grave could be used to represent the spirit of that deceased individual. A metaphoric reference uses an object, word, or substance to stand for a subject without having such a literal relationship to it. For instance, one might use the color white to represent an invocation of the spirit world.

The minkisi were typically created and used in association with a ritual space demarcated by crossed lines drawn upon the ground, and the crossed-line motif was often incorporated into the decorative design of an individual nkisi object itself (Laman 1962: 149, 152, 156; 1968: 37; MacGaffey 2000b: 107–8; Van Wing 1941: 86). Banganga created the minkisi and performed both private and public ritual functions that incorporated them. These rituals included both divination to determine the causes of misfortune or illness, and enactment of supplications to obtain protection, cures, or retribution (Thornton 1983: 59–62).

A nkisi object usually consisted of a container, which could be a wooden sculpture, ceramic bowl or pot, gourd, animal horn, raffia fiber or cloth bag, woven leaves, or other enclosing vessel (MacGaffey 1991: 5). The nkisi was animated by the powers represented metaphorically and metonymically by the *bilongo* substances placed within it and upon it. These bilongo expressed the invocation of the spirit world into the land of the living and the relevant attributes of the summoned spirit (Janzen and MacGaffey 1974: 35–36; Laman 1962: 68; MacGaffey 1988a: 190–91). A nkisi was thus viewed as the container for a manifestation of an invoked spirit, and the object itself was not worshipped as an idol (Jacobson-Widding 1979: 132; Janzen 1977: 71; Van Wing 1941: 86). The BaKongo people believed that a nkisi could lose the spiritual manifestation contained within it if the bilongo were removed, if the nganga who created it failed to follow the proper restrictions that attended the nkisi, or if the nganga died (MacGaffey 2000c: 38).

Members of the BaKongo believed that many minkisi were created after a simbi or other spirit overtook and possessed a nganga or other initiate with a powerful ecstasy. After that, the nganga or initiate would dedicate himself or herself to that simbi and create a nkisi to summon and contain a manifestation of it. The nkisi would thereafter have a life of its own, containing an element of that spirit in the land of the living, and it would be used for repeated supplications over time (Laman 1962: 69; MacGaffey 2000a: 232). As part of the proper ritual use of a nkisi, the nganga would typically follow specific rules of behavior, such as abstaining from sexual intercourse or the consumption of different types of food when preparing to make a supplication (Jacobson-Widding 1979: 68; Janzen and MacGaffey 1974: 26; MacGaffey 1991: 33–34; 2000a: 232). Some accounts report a belief that only male banganga could summon certain types of spirits into minkisi, whereas both male and female banganga could invoke other types of spirits (Balandier 1968: 221; Thornton 1983: 16–17).

A great variety of minkisi were created over time, some designed to contain more powerful spirits capable of lethal actions, and others designed to contain more benign spirits for the purposes of specific tasks of healing or for protecting an individual or household (Janzen and MacGaffey 1974: 37; MacGaffey 1991: 5–6, 33–34; Van Wing 1941: 86–87). This variety was reflected in the wide array of objects and substances used as containers and bilongo (MacGaffey 1991: 5, 63–67, 85). White clay or white ash provided metaphors of the purity of God, the spirits, and the dead. Reflective surfaces of seashells, quartz crystals, and mica or mirror fragments were metaphoric for the water boundary between the living and the world of spirits, and thus communicated the invocation of spiritual forces into the world of the living. Seashells, nutshells, and some types of roots also provided metaphors for wombs and containers of lives, souls, and spirits. Bird skulls or feathers supplied metaphors for spirits through the connotation of flight and the realm of the sky. Animal claws and teeth provided metaphors of the power and forcefulness of particular spirits. Fragments of clinging vines and roots were used as symbols of a summoned spirit's ability to locate malevolent spiritual forces and to bind and subdue them (MacGaffey 1986: 132, 137–48; 1993: 32–42; Van Wing 1941: 86).

Other items used as bilongo invoked metaphors through the punning association of the item's name with a word for a desired attribute of a summoned spirit or a word descriptive of the affliction that the spirit would be able to cure (Jacobson-Widding 1979: 140; Janzen and MacGaffey 1974: 6; MacGaffey 1991: 5). For example, the bilongo might include a nut named *nkiduku* to invoke *kidukwa*, the KiKongo word for protection (MacGaffey 2000c: 44). The nganga who created a nkisi likely recited these names of the bilongo in a solemn, ritualized manner while composing the object (Jacobson-Widding 1979: 140; MacGaffey 2000c: 38).

White clay presented multiple metaphoric meanings for the BaKongo. The land of the dead was called *nsi a bafwa* in KiKongo, and was viewed as being a realm that mirrored the land of the living. The land of the dead was viewed variously as being located underground, in forests, in cemeteries, across rivers or the ocean, or under water (MacGaffey 2000b: 27–28). However, the land of the dead was also called *Mpemba*, which was the same word used for white kaolin clay. White represented the color of the dead, the pure, the innocent, the enlightened, and the Godhead (Jacobson-Widding 1991: 181; MacGaffey 2000b: 27, 82). In contrast, the color red was symbolic of transformation and movement between the worlds. For this reason, corpses and ritual initiates were often adorned with red coloring in key ceremonies (Jacobson-Widding 1991: 183; MacGaffey 2000b: 27).

White kaolin clay was found in streambeds, providing both a metonymic and metaphoric association with water, the spirit world, and the dead. A nganga could communicate with the dead in divination ceremonies that typically included preparation and adornment of the area around his or her eyes with pigment made from white chalk or clay, conveying a capacity for spiritual vision (Laman 1962: 18; MacGaffey 1988a: 197). Kaolin was also a very frequent component of minkisi designs, included both as a bilongo substance and as an adornment to the outside of the nkisi (MacGaffey 2000b: 82; Van Wing 1941: 86). Other materials representing the flash of the water boundary and power of the spirit world were used as well, such as seashells, mica, or mirror fragments to enclose the bilongo medicines of the nkisi and to adorn the containing object (MacGaffey 2000b: 82–83).

The banganga ritual specialists were often viewed as possessing and exercising a sacred form of power that could be contrasted with the political power of the ruling class. However, they were not viewed as a caste of priests. Any member of the BaKongo people could become a nganga on experiencing a simbi's calling and dedicating herself or himself to the proper use of minkisi (Jacobson-Widding 1979: 68; Laman 1957: 132). The banganga were feared for their powers, but they were also viewed with respect and appreciation for their abilities to cure and bring blessings on communities and individuals seeking aid (Laman 1957: 132; Van Wing 1941: 86–91). The greater the number and variety of minkisi that an individual nganga created, possessed, and worked with, the greater the array of specific divination, healing, and protective measures the nganga would be able to provide to those who sought his or her aid. Those banganga whose efforts were believed to be successful would in turn obtain higher status and earnings (Janzen and MacGaffey 1974: 37; Laman 1957: 132).

Some seventeenth-century accounts report that banganga were recruited at times to bestow blessings and invocations for success in battles (Balandier 1968: 121). At other times, chiefs and members of the royalty sought to co-opt the ritual specialists' roles and their perceived powers into their political arena in order to promote their authority and legitimacy as governing officials (Broadhead 1979: 632–33; Laman 1957: 138; MacGaffey 2000a: 232). The symbolism of the BaKongo dikenga was incorporated in design motifs of royal and chiefly regalia, as well as in special forms of woven cloth that could be traded and possessed only by persons of high status (Bassani 1983; 2000: 277–84; Gibson and McGurk 1977). Different types of minkisi were often used in coronation ceremonies for chiefs and paramount chiefs, and a nganga would often play a role in the ceremony (Laman 1957: 144–45, 150–51). Similarly, in the seventeenth and eighteenth centuries, chiefs were often viewed as possessing a nganga's ability to control the spiritual powers of minkisi (MacGaffey 2000b: 12–13).

Minkisi could be used for more private purposes, as well as for more public displays and applications (Laman 1953: 83; MacGaffey 1986: 136, 169–71; Thompson 1993: 48–54). When a nkisi was employed for the use and protection of a village, "nkisi-houses" were often built with "low walls, so that anyone could see the nkisi and call upon him" for aid (Laman 1953: 83). Some nkisi-houses were carefully concealed, so that they could not be desecrated by outsiders and would be accessible only to members of the community (83). A nganga might take up residence within such a nkisi-house at times, necessitating an expansion of the structure. Banganga also frequently kept many of their minkisi in their own dwellings and conducted related rituals in their homes or transported the minkisi to the houses of persons who sought their services (Laman 1953: 83; MacGaffey 2000b: 82; Van Wing 1941: 88–89).

Banganga might be requested to assist in childbirth by providing medicines to invoke spiritual aid for a healthy birth (Laman 1957: 3; Van Wing 1941: 86–87). They were often also requested to place protective blessings on newborns and homes. Many minkisi were designed for the purpose of aiding childbirth and protecting or curing children from disease or misfortune (Janzen and MacGaffey 1974: 37; Laman 1957: 4–23). Others were designed for use in bestowing blessings after childbirth and in key social rituals, such as ceremonies in which a child was given his or her proper name (Laman 1957: 5–23). Banganga used a wide variety of minkisi to cure or protect against disease, illness, and misfortune, often employing designs with simpler forms of containers and bilongo (see, for example, MacGaffey 1991). They also employed other healing techniques in combination with the minkisi, such as creating herbal medicines to be taken internally, and using bleeding techniques and curative baths for their patients (Laman 1957: 59–78; Van Wing 1941: 86–91).

Some forms of minkisi were created and used in prominent, public rituals (Janzen and MacGaffey 1974: 37). For example, the powerful nkisi Nkondi was often used for public ceremonies of oath taking and for consecrating political and social agreements. "For agreements between villages concerning marriage, hunting, help and support in case of war, etc., the chiefs from both sides convene. They confirm the agreement on oath and with invocations of nkisi Nkondi, confirming the latter by driving iron wedges and the like into him" (Laman 1957: 113). The same procedure was employed when laws or treaties were enacted to apply to the territories of multiple chiefdoms (Laman 1957: 117, 159–60; MacGaffey 2000b: 109–10). In efforts to protect an entire village from disease or misfortune, two banganga might convene at a crossroads leading into the village, draw a cross upon the ground, pour water onto the crossed lines, and undertake other ritual measures to safeguard the community (Laman 1962: 156). Similarly, households or villages could be protected by burying selected minkisi in their vicinity and avenues of approach (Janzen and MacGaffey 1974: 45).

When one considers the characteristics of various BaKongo spiritual traditions, Nkondi was notable for the use of iron wedges and knife blades as part of the ritual materials. Whereas fragments of iron were frequently reported as possible forms of bilongo, representing strength and resilience, such a focused use of iron appeared primarily in the accounts concerning Nkondi. This differed from other African religions, such as that of the Yoruba, which placed far greater emphasis on the use of iron materials in religious objects dedicated to principal sub-deities, such as Ogun, a god associated with war and iron (Barnes 1989).

Earlier ethnohistorical accounts report that ironworking was an honored craft among the BaKongo people, who believed that it often involved the application of mystical powers for the transformation of materials (Balandier 1968: 224–25; Denbow 1999: 414–16). Various methods of metallurgy were likely introduced into the region from east Africa during the fourteenth century. Yet, ironworking was not controlled exclusively by upper classes or guilds within the BaKongo, and was instead a craft that anyone who was capable could undertake (Balandier 1968: 107–8).

Forms of the nkisi Nkondi were created and used by banganga for more private purposes as well. These compositions were often viewed as hunter minkisi, which contained manifestations of a powerful simbi spirit that could track down, bind, and vanquish malevolent spirits and other forces that were assailing the persons who made supplication to Nkondi for aid (MacGaffey 1988a: 199). The container was usually designed as an anthropomorphic or zoomorphic figure in a pose conveying power and lethal capabilities. These containers ranged in size from a few inches to a few feet in height, with large forms often employed in public rituals (MacGaffey 1993: 33, 75–76). The bilongo of such a nkisi frequently included fragments of binding vines, animal teeth, and claws as metaphors for its lethal powers. Other metaphoric bilongo, such as fragments of reflective crystals and white clay were often included, along with decorations of crossed lines on the exterior of the wooden body of the nkisi. The bilongo were usually placed inside a cavity created in the body of the sculpture and enclosed with a reflective piece of seashell, mica, or mirror (MacGaffey 1993: 32–42, 75–79).

Members of the BaKongo culture would typically seek the aid of nkisi

Nkondi if they believed malevolent spirits were assailing them. To do so, they requested the help of a nganga known to possess such a nkisi. Such a personal supplication was undertaken in a private ritual attended by the person seeking help and the nganga who possessed and interacted with the nkisi. The nganga would often draw crossed lines upon the ground, oriented in the cardinal directions, to demarcate the ritual space in which this supplication would be made (Jacobson-Widding 1991: 201). The intersection of these lines represented the desired intersection and communication between the spirit world and the land of the living (Thompson 1990: 153). The nganga and supplicant would first swear their righteous and truthful purposes by taking oaths while standing upon the crossed lines and addressing the Nkondi (Thompson and Cornet 1981: 44).

If the supplicant was ill, the nganga would have him or her lie on the crossed lines with feet pointing west, perhaps drawing a circle to surround the person and crossed lines (Jacobson-Widding 1991: 201; MacGaffey 1986: 118). The nganga would then symbolically drive the illness out of the person and into obliteration in the direction of the west (Laman 1962: 144, 149; MacGaffey 1986: 118). In the course of the ritual the nganga typically would place the nkisi at the intersection of the crossed lines as well (Thompson 1990: 153; Thompson and Cornet 1981: 151). The nganga and supplicant would then recite prayers to request specific aid from Nkondi and to incite it to action. In addition, they would drive a small iron wedge or iron nail into the body of the wooden Nkondi to record this act of supplication and oath taking, and to further animate the nkisi to exercise its powers (Gell 1998: 59–61; Laman 1957: 113, 117, 159–60; MacGaffey 2000b: 98–99, 106–7; Thompson and Cornet 1981: 38).

European colonization and Christian missionary activities from the late fifteenth through the late nineteenth centuries failed to destroy this rich belief system expressed in the BaKongo dikenga and minkisi (Balandier 1968: 50–51; Thornton 1983: 67–68). Catholic missionaries were most active in the region from the time of initial European contact onward, with the assistance of Portuguese colonial interests. Protestant missionaries sponsored by the British and Dutch also became active in the region in the eighteenth and nineteenth centuries (MacGaffey 2000c: 38). The BaKongo people converted to Christianity and adopted its beliefs only in a highly selective manner throughout this period. This process of selective adoption was aided by the fact that European missionaries often used KiKongo terms for key Christian concepts, thus translating Christian beliefs into BaKongo counterparts (Thornton 1977: 512–13; 1983: 63).

Priests were viewed as performing the same roles as banganga, and the crucifix, statues of saints, Eucharist, and church buildings were viewed the same way as minkisi and related ritual buildings (Hilton 1985: 94; Thornton 1977: 512–13; 1983: 63). There were occasional purges ordered by the Ba-Kongo royalty and paramount chiefs during the colonial period, including the burning of minkisi and imprisonment of particular banganga. This was selective condemnation, however, and these events were typically followed by the promotion of other banganga and the creation of other minkisi by competing political factions within the BaKongo (Balandier 1968: 47–48, 254–55; Thornton 1983: 65).

The BaKongo easily understood and reinterpreted the Catholic concepts of saints, seraphim, and the Holy Spirit as entities translatable into the BaKongo belief in basimbi and other intermediate spirits (Thornton 1998: 259). In contrast, the BaKongo largely rejected Catholic concepts of heaven and hell, which were highly inconsistent with their traditional cosmology (Hilton 1985: 94). By the mid-seventeenth century, the BaKongo people had come to view the crucifix as the principal nkisi of the Christian banganga (the priests), and they erected wooden crosses throughout the region (Balandier 1968: 102, 242, 254; Hilton 1985: 102). According to seventeenth-century missionary records, the country was "'full of crosses of wood'" and the people "'saluted them devotedly and knelt before them,'" treating them as a new and powerful form of nkisi (Hilton 1985: 102; see also Balandier and Maquet 1974: 208–9). Thus, the symbol and object of the Christian cross was not adopted as a cosmological symbol that displaced the BaKongo dikenga, but rather as a new form of nkisi container.

In fact, Catholic priests often substituted wooden versions of the Christian cross in place of minkisi that had been positioned in fields or other communal spaces to provide protection (Thornton 1977: 513). Missionaries similarly placed crosses upon BaKongo meeting houses that had been designed for use by initiation cults and for training banganga. These meeting house ceremonies included BaKongo rituals in which the initiates were viewed as dying from their former status and being transformed into a new form and status as banganga (Thornton 1977: 513–14). Missionary priests also found that baptism was a primary Christian sacrament of interest to the BaKongo people, with their religious beliefs in the transformative character of the water boundary. Priests therefore used baptisms as a favored way to attract potential converts (Thornton 1977: 514). The blending of the dikenga with the Christian cross and other sacraments thus occurred in many ways that served to reinforce the BaKongo cosmology, rather than displace it.

Predicting Facets of Symbolic Expression in New Settings

This extensive body of evidence concerning the BaKongo culture in west central Africa provides the elements for constructing an ethnohistorical analogy. A predictive model incorporating that source of analogy can be employed in analyzing and interpreting the potential meaning, significance, and use of artifacts of spirituality created by members of a BaKongo diaspora. The principal elements of material culture delineated and characterized in this analogy consist of the dikenga and related forms of minkisi. More specifically, the dikenga was manifested in different forms depending upon the specific context and use to which it was placed. When used for public rituals to express group identity and solidarity, the dikenga was often utilized in its fully embellished and emblematic form of expression, with crossed lines, surrounding cyclical ellipse or circle, and four moments of the cosmos. When used in community or private rituals for the purpose of invoking spiritual aid to protect or heal a village, household, or individual, the dikenga would often be expressed in an abbreviated form of crossed lines and associated with forms of minkisi positioned along the axes or intersection of that cross.

Within the BaKongo culture, the more emblematic uses of the dikenga were usually associated with public rituals conducted by political and religious specialists. However, it is unlikely that persons abducted into slavery could replicate the political and religious organizational structures of the BaKongo culture in New World plantations (see Mintz and Price 1976: 6–7, 21). In such circumstances of subjugation, members of the BaKongo diaspora would likely exercise their expressions of cosmology and self-identity in private and covert settings (Orser 1994: 39, 42; Raboteau 1980: 215). The BaKongo people had practiced a broad array of such private rituals within west central Africa, typically by demarcating the appropriate spaces with the crossed lines of the dikenga and using nkisi objects in association with that space. Although minkisi were at times maintained within public nkisi-houses, they were also frequently utilized within the dwellings of the banganga or their clients, or positioned to protect individual households and villages.

Banganga held positions of elevated status within the BaKongo culture. They played vital roles in a broad array of political rituals, public religious rituals, and invocations of spiritual aid for individuals seeking healing, self-protection, or retribution. While many banganga were no doubt abducted into slavery, it is less likely that they were able to enjoy comparable social status within plantation settings in the New World (Mintz and Price 1976:

10; Raboteau 1980: 50; Sobel 1987: 6). In time, they could adjust to their new circumstances and begin performing the services of a healer, diviner, and specialist in invocations of spiritual aid within their immediate communities (Genovese 1976: 221; Orser 1994: 37). In turn, they could teach their evolving sets of beliefs and practices to other members of their communities, with some facets of the BaKongo traditions continuing, some changing, and others falling away.

The degree to which such beliefs and practices were exercised, both in frequency and intensity, was dependent in part on the degree to which plantation owners and overseers worked to preclude enslaved persons from engaging in such conduct (Levine 1977: 60; Raboteau 1980: 53, 66). The rate of change in those beliefs and practices also depended upon the degree to which particular slave communities consisted of a significant number of persons enculturated in the BaKongo culture, or instead consisted of persons enculturated in a diversity of African cultures. In many New World settings, Africans and African Americans enculturated in the traditions of diverse cultures interacted within local slave communities. The religions of the Yoruba, Fon, Bambara, and BaKongo, to mention just a few, are notable in their richness and diversity of beliefs, practices, and modes of ritual and symbolic expression (for example, Gomez 1998; Morgan 1998: 610–11; see fig. 1.2).

The broad array of nkisi designs created by the BaKongo people presents particular challenges to the effort of predicting discernible patterns in related material culture in New World settings. Due to the compositional emphasis on metaphoric meanings, both the containers and contents of minkisi are often made of naturally occurring and fairly prosaic materials. Containers made of wood or natural fibers will typically decompose in the soils of the archaeological record. Bilongo consisting of pieces of vines or other organic materials will similarly perish. Bilongo that invoke the reflective flash of the water boundary, such as quartz crystals, shells, or polished stones, are naturally occurring objects that will usually endure within the archaeological record. However, such objects might have been collected and deposited in New World house sites without any relationship to BaKongo religious beliefs and practices. White clay and white chalk have similar characteristics. Such objects as crystals, shells, and polished stones also could have been collected and deposited by persons who subscribed to European-American religious beliefs and practices entirely separate from and independent of the BaKongo (Fennell 2000: 286–87; Perry and Paynter 1999: 303). Similarly, other African religions treated objects of white color or grave dirt as religiously symbolic as well (Mbiti 1970: 155; Raboteau 1980: 34; Thompson 1983: 134–38).

The particular context in which artifacts are found is critically important to the strength of an interpretation that those objects were created pursuant to beliefs and practices derived from the BaKongo cosmology. Such an interpretation will be stronger if a variety of bilongo-like objects are located in a concentrated collection, rather than being dispersed throughout the space of a dwelling. This analysis will be even more robust if there exist multiple concentrations of bilongo-like objects, located in a spatial pattern that indicates the demarcation of the crossed lines of a dikenga along the cardinal directions within a private space. However, these elements of contextual evidence alone should not suffice. Archaeologists should look for multiple lines of supporting evidence to establish that the site was inhabited by persons likely to have been enculturated in BaKongo beliefs. Analysts should also assess the degree to which the site may have been inhabited or used by persons likely to have been enculturated in other European-American or African American belief systems that could have generated similar artifacts (Fennell 2000: 286–87).

Archaeologists should proceed with similar care when interpreting crossed lines inscribed upon artifacts as representing expressions of the dikenga. A significant number of such artifacts have been found at historic-period sites in the United States (see fig. 1.1). These are often small, everyday items with crossed lines scratched into them, such as ceramic bowls and pots, white marbles, pewter or silver spoons, and coins (for example, Davidson 2004; Ferguson 1992, 1999; Franklin 1997; Young 1996, 1997). Some of these objects include white material, such as the bright color of pewter and silver metals when scratched, or objects made of kaolin (Young 1996, 1997). This bolsters the interpretation of these objects as expressions of BaKongo beliefs, because it presents two known metaphoric features that were often used in combination by the BaKongo in west central Africa.

However, the mere presence of crossed lines on small amulet-like objects could as easily be interpreted as the product of other European-American or African American beliefs. Anglo-American and German-American religious traditions included the use of a cross mark or saltire as an invocation sign on objects designed to create protective charms or curses (Davidson 2004: 28–31; Fennell 2000: 299–302; E. Smith, Stewart, and Kyger 1964: 156). Other African religions also utilized the symbol of crossed lines and the crossing of paths as an invocation of the spirit world (Gundaker 1998: 65; Stuckey 1987: 92). The interpretation of crossed lines on particular artifacts or in the spatial configuration of features upon the ground as a primarily BaKongo expression will be stronger if evidence exists of other, accompanying metaphoric references that are also consistent with BaKongo beliefs and practices. The surrounding circular motif manifested in the shape of an inscribed marble, coin, or bowl base provides reinforcing evidence of related metaphors. Additional supporting evidence should be sought, however, because the symbol of a circle as representative of cosmic cycles was not unique to the BaKongo.

Using this body of data from an ethnohistorical analogy and predictive model, we can now examine archaeology sites in New World settings in a more rigorous and systematic manner. The next chapter analyzes archaeological sites, material culture, and ethnohistorical evidence in North America, Cuba, Haiti, and Brazil, to explore expressions of BaKongo cultural heritage, and transformations in those beliefs and practices over time and in different locations. Intersecting belief systems of the Yoruba and Fon cultures are also considered.

5

African Diasporas and Symbolism in the New World

In his extensive study of "slave religions" in the Americas, Albert Raboteau (1980: 86) stated that "in the United States the gods of Africa died." He contended that various forms of "African theology and African ritual did not endure" in the slave communities of North America "to the extent that they did in Cuba, Haiti, and Brazil" (86). More recently, Laura Galke (2000), one of the archaeologists who worked on the Carroll House site in Annapolis, Maryland, declared that Raboteau was mistaken. Surely, she argued, the numerous findings of nkisi-like objects at slave sites in the United States show that the BaKongo cosmology was alive and well in America in the seventeenth through the nineteenth centuries. In essence, they are both correct.

Private Rituals in North America

Documentary, oral history, and archaeological evidence related to sites in North America (fig. 1.1) show no evidence that the BaKongo religion was observed in public displays of group-oriented rituals using emblematic forms of the core symbol of the BaKongo. Instead, only private and covert forms of ritual were undertaken, each employing instrumental and abbreviated forms of the dikenga to obtain protection and well-being for the individuals involved. The institution of slavery and the dominant religion of Christianity had pushed the BaKongo beliefs off the stage of publicly displayed group rituals. Adherents to the BaKongo religion were, however, able to continue practicing forms of the private, instrumental rituals that the BaKongo people had observed regularly in west central Africa.

PROTECTIVE INVOCATIONS IN ANNAPOLIS

The artifacts uncovered at the Carroll House in Annapolis provide a persuasive example of such a continuation of private nkisi rituals in North America. Documentary evidence showed that Charles Carroll of Carrollton maintained this house as one of his family's principal residences from the mid-1700s through 1821. He employed up to nineteen enslaved African

Americans at this location in the early 1780s and a lesser number in the early 1800s (Galke 2000: 22–23; L. Jones 2000: 2). Many enslaved Africans imported into the Maryland and Chesapeake areas in these periods came from the region of west central Africa (Walsh 2001: 148). Thus, it is probable that Carroll obtained persons enslaved from the Kongo area, although direct evidence is lacking.

Concentrated collections of a variety of objects were located under the floorboards of adjacent rooms in the basement level of the Carroll House. Supporting evidence indicated that these rooms were likely used as the living and work space of enslaved African Americans who worked as house servants (Galke 2000: 22–23; L. Jones 2000: 2; Leone 2005: 200–5). The objects could be interpreted as reflecting multiple metaphors of significance within the BaKongo tradition. Quartz crystals, polished stones, and glass fragments invoked the flash of the water boundary. Disks of white bone invoked the color of the spirit world and the dead, and the circular form of the cosmic cycle. A fragment of a pearlware bowl, with an asterisk mark as a decoration, could have been viewed both as a symbolic container of other bilongo-like objects and as providing an invocation of the crossed lines of the dikenga (Galke 2000: 23–24; L. Jones 2000: 2; Leone 2005: 200–3; Logan 1995: 154–55). If so, a decorative motif applied to a pearlware bowl by a pottery manufacturer in England was later reinterpreted as a "found" rendering of the dikenga by an African American in Maryland.

CROSS MARKS ON POTTERY

Crossed lines appear as well on the round bases of colonoware pottery uncovered at African American sites in the Carolinas and Virginia (Ferguson 1992: 111–16; 1999: 121–23; Orser 1994: 38–39; see fig. 1.1). This form of earthenware pottery was produced as a result of a blending of African American and Native American ceramic forms and production techniques (Ferguson 1992, 1999; Mouer et al. 1999). Many of these incised pottery fragments were located underwater in rivers of South Carolina (Ferguson 1999: 121–23). These locations are in areas occupied in the past by enslaved Africans and African Americans who worked on nearby plantations. A large percentage of the enslaved persons who arrived in South Carolina came from west central Africa (Holloway 1990: 7; see fig. 1.2).

Four attributes of these colonoware artifacts thus correlate with the potential composition of a nkisi-like object produced pursuant to inspirations from BaKongo beliefs. Ceramic pots and bowls were used as containers for some forms of minkisi by the BaKongo people. The crossed lines scratched within the circumference of a surrounding, circular bowl base could invoke elements of the dikenga. The use of such objects at sites along the edges of bodies of water also could have been consistent with private rituals invoking the boundary with the spirit world or invocations of simbi spirits associated with bodies of water (Ferguson 1999: 124–26; see also Denbow 1999: 420; MacGaffey 2004).

Documentary accounts from the nineteenth century in South Carolina provide supporting evidence of African Americans who subscribed to such BaKongo spiritual beliefs (R. Brown 2004). Edmund Ruffin was a Virginia plantation owner who traveled in the South Carolina coastal areas in 1843 to survey for calcinated rock deposits. He was interested in exploring methods for agricultural reform that used such deposits as potential ingredients for "liming" and "marling" fertilizers (Ruffin 1992: xi–xiii). Ruffin kept a diary of his survey activities in the coastal area of South Carolina—the same region where incised colonoware pottery would later be recovered and studied by archaeologists. He recorded that enslaved African Americans at the Woodboo plantation described their belief in "cymbee" spirits that inhabited springs, pools, and other bodies of water (166). Another nineteenth-century author recorded similar beliefs in simbi spirits among African Americans at the nearby Pooshee plantation (Thompson 1998: 61).

Ferguson (1998: 4–6) believes one can infer that the small colonoware jars and bowls were likely used in the preparation of medicines in ritual undertakings, and that the vessels were later cast into the water. However, the use of cross and circle motifs, and the association of water with religious rituals were beliefs and practices common to a number of Native American, African American, and European-American religions (Ferguson 1999: 118, 124, 127; Stuckey 1987: 34–35, 92). Ferguson (1999: 127) suggests that the multivocal character of these symbols facilitated cultural interactions and the sharing of ideas among African Americans and Native Americans who worked and lived together under the burdens of enslavement.

MULTIVALENT FIGURES OF AN ENCLOSING HAND

Another set of artifacts uncovered at archaeology sites in North America likely illustrates the dynamic intersection of European-American and African American belief systems. Several sites of the living and work areas of enslaved African Americans in the nineteenth century have contained the remains of small hand figures, typically manufactured of brass or another copper alloy. Anne Yentsch (1994: 32–33) and her colleagues recovered a hook-and-eye fastener in the shape of a closed hand from the fill of a crawl space at the site of the Charles Calvert house in Annapolis, Maryland. The Calvert house was owned by a wealthy Anglo-American family for several

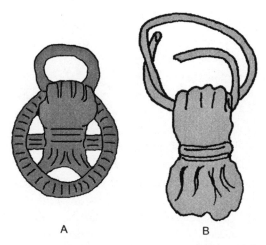

A   B

Figure 5.1. Types of small hand figures uncovered at archaeology sites, including the Calvert house in Annapolis, the Poplar Forest plantation in Virginia, and the Hermitage plantation in Tennessee: *a.* stamped brass fastener or ornament, usually 0.40 to 0.50 inches long across both circles combined; *b.* likely a watch charm, approximately 0.75 inches long from the base of the wrist to the top of the hand, made of molded metal holding a loop of wire, uncovered at the Hermitage site (see Heath et al. 2004; McKee 1995; Russell 1997; Yentsch 1994). (Images by the author)

decades starting in 1719, and was occupied by members of that family and by African Americans working as enslaved servants. The hand figure, only one-half inch in size, likely functioned as the hook assembly to an ornate clothing fastener. Yentsch (33) observed that an individual of African American heritage could have perceived such an object as providing symbolic protection against witchcraft. However, the archaeological context did not provide evidence that the object was deposited in an area utilized primarily by the African American servants, rather than by the Anglo-American occupants of the house (32).

Several other hand figures have been uncovered at sites specifically associated with the occupation and work areas of African Americans in the nineteenth century. These objects share similar characteristics to the one found in Annapolis: a hand closed in the form of a fist is set within a surrounding circle and a crossbar bisects the circle perpendicular to the wrist at the base of the hand. The closed hand typically "holds" a smaller ring that extends out from the larger circle (see fig. 5.1a). This design was often created out of a single stamped figure, one-half inch or less in diameter, of brass or copper alloy. Hand figures of this type have been uncovered from the sites of living quarters once occupied by African American laborers at Andrew

Jackson's Hermitage plantation in Tennessee (McKee 1995; Russell 1997; see fig. 1.1) and Thomas Jefferson's Poplar Forest plantation in Virginia (Heath et al. 2004). Another hand figure uncovered at the Hermitage plantation is different. This version was made of molded metal, with a slightly larger, closed hand that is not set within a circle and instead holds a loop of wire (McKee 1995; Russell 1997; see fig. 5.1b).

These small artifacts raise a number of interesting questions: Were these items simply utilitarian objects, or were they used in some other way? What was the purpose of each of these items as a manufactured object—were they ornate clothing fasteners, jewelry, or something else? If these were "popular culture" items of manufactured jewelry or clothing fasteners, what inspired the manufacturers to use a design that included such an ornate hand figure? How were these items used and perceived by the African American individuals who possessed them?

The examples of the item with a hand set inside a circle were most likely a form of manufactured ornament referred to as a stamping. These products were sewn onto clothing and accessories as adornments or used as part of hook-and-eye fasteners (Bury 1991: 355–59). The other example from the Hermitage, which was a slightly larger, molded hand figure that held a loop of wire, was most likely a manufactured watch charm or jewelry charm. A smaller metal or glass ornament would have originally hung from the loop of wire as part of this charm (Fales 1995: 165, 368; Israel 1968: 419; see fig 5.2). Hand figures have been incorporated in manufactured jewelry designs for centuries. Prominent examples, dating from the early and middle nineteenth century, include hand-shaped necklace clasps and jewelry charms in the design of a hand that held a loop of wire from which smaller charms were suspended (for example, Fales 1995: 165, 182, 368; Hinks 1975: 36; see fig. 5.3).

If these items uncovered at archaeology sites were such manufactured objects of popular culture, what would have inspired the manufacturers of jewelry and clothing fasteners to use such a design? Jewelry manufacturers often used symbolic motifs derived from religious beliefs or from the emblems of benevolent societies and guilds when creating design motifs for mass-produced and commercialized charms and ornaments (Fales 1995; Hansmann and Kriss-Rettenbeck 1966; Israel 1968: 419–22). Three symbolic motifs from European folk religions and Catholicism rise as primary candidates for the past design inspirations of the enclosing hand figures: the *mano fica*, the Manus Dei, and the protective symbolism of the wounds of Christ.

A mano fica charm, also called a *figa* or *higa*, is in the shape of a hand closed into a fist, with the thumb thrust between the first two fingers in a

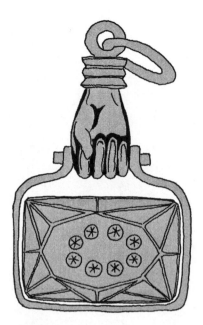 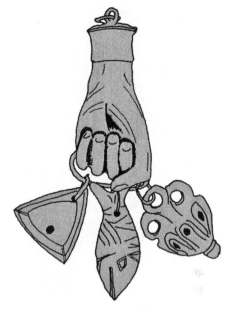

Figure 5.2. Example of a commercially produced watch charm incorporating a molded metal hand figure holding a loop of wire (see Israel 1968). (Image by the author)

Figure 5.3. Example of a European jewelry charm incorporating a figure of a hand holding a loop of wire from which other charms are suspended (see Hansmann and Kriss-Rettenbeck 1966). (Image by the author)

gesture of fertility and vitality (Deagan 2002: 89–99). The fertility symbolism of this charm is evident in its name as well as the gesture. The Italian word *fica* means vulva, which in turn is derived from the Latin word *ficus*, for the fruit of the fig tree (Moss and Cappannari 1976: 8).

Figas have served as popular amulets throughout the Mediterranean region for centuries, and were often used as protection against the perceived dangers of "evil eye" curses (Elworthy 1900: 176–77; Tait 1986: 211–13). Beliefs in a form of evil eye curse have been widespread across cultures for millennia. This belief consists of the fear that some individuals can cast curses through malevolent intent and motivations of envy, communicated by a fixed gaze cast upon a targeted person, crops, livestock, or other property (Maloney 1976: v–vii; J. Roberts 1976: 221–26). Protections against such remote expressions of malevolence typically involve regular wearing of protective amulets such as figas.

The figa symbol likely was adopted as one form of protective charm against the evil eye due to its association with fertility and vitality. Parents often placed figas on children to protect them during the vulnerable period of youth (Deagan 2002: 89; Elworthy 1895: 255–58). Figas were brought to the New World with Spanish colonization of the Americas. Examples have been uncovered at archaeology sites throughout the Spanish colonial sphere, at locations in South Carolina, Florida, the Caribbean, and South America, dating from the sixteenth through eighteenth centuries (Deagan 2002: 89, 95–99; see fig. 1.1).

Were figa charms the historic referent that jewelry manufacturers had in mind when they designed the hand figures that were uncovered at the Hermitage and Poplar Forest plantations? It seems unlikely. Jewelers certainly knew how to make a figa charm, and they produced many of them over centuries, with the distinctive gesture of the thumb inserted between the fingers (Elworthy 1900: 176–77; Tait 1986: 211–13). That configuration is not included in the closed hand figures of interest here (fig. 5.1).

The symbolism of the wounds of Christ and the Manus Dei present more likely sources for the design inspiration of such manufactured charms depicting a closed hand within a circle (Stafford 1942: 32–34; Webber 1971: 140–44). A symbolic motif focused upon by Catholic denominations and related folk religion invocations, the five wounds of Christ consisted of the piercing of the Messiah's hands, feet, and heart in the course of crucifixion (Deagan 2002: 83–84; Strauss 1975: 62–63; Webber 1971: 140–44; Yoder 1990: 81, 100). These manifestations of the passion of Christ's sacrifice were used in extensive devotional art to symbolize the creation of grace as a flowing source of spiritual power and benevolence created by the crucifixion. The hand is often depicted with the fingers closing over the wound of a spike hole (see, for example, Yoder 1990: 81, 100).

Amulet symbols of an *open* hand have been used to convey messages of sacredness, power, and benediction in a number of cultures for millennia (Elworthy 1900: 169–74; Webber 1971: 49–54). For example, the "Hand of Fatima" is the name within Islam for a symbol consisting of an open, extended hand, communicating benevolence, abundance, and good fortune. This symbol, and similar ones that predated Islam, were incorporated into personal charms used to ward off malevolent forces such as the evil eye (for example, Hansmann and Kriss-Rettenbeck 1966: 197; Hildburgh 1906: 459).

Within Christian symbolism, the Manus Dei, or "Hand of God," has been rendered as an open, extended hand overlaying a "tri-radiant nimbus" (Stafford 1942: 33; Webber 1971: 49–54). The three rays, representing the Holy Trinity, bisect one half of the circular nimbus, which is itself a symbol of sanctity and divinity (Stafford 1942: 33; Webber 1971: 50). The open hand typically fills the other half of the nimbus and partially overlays the three rays. Another Christian symbol included the cupped, enclosing hand of God, holding the souls of the righteous and overlaying a similar nimbus bisected by radiant lines (Stafford 1942: 32–34; Webber 1971: 49–54). The latter symbol relates to gospel passages observing that the "'souls of the righteous are in the hand of God'" (Webber 1971: 50). By the time of the twelfth century, a similar symbol of Christ's sacrifice and benevolence, consisting of an extended hand of beneficence framed by a tri-radiant nimbus, was engraved as an emblem over the main door of the Cathedral of Ferrara in Italy (Elworthy 1900: 195).

Symbolism related to Christ as the Messiah more directly employed depictions of an enclosing hand. For example, small metal figures of a closed hand were incorporated into strings of paternoster beads. *Pater Noster* stands for Our Father and the Lord's Prayer, and these bead strings were the predecessor of rosary beads within Catholic denominations (Deagan 2002: 65; Lightbrown 1992: 528–29; Winston 1993: 621). These bead strings were held in the hand; worn about the neck, arm, or wrist; or attached to clothing with a brooch. An individual would use them while repeating prayers as an act of devotion and penance (Deagan 2002: 65–66; Winston 1993: 621–22). Prayers typically consisted of the Ave Maria or the Lord's Prayer, and one repeated those prayers while meditating on the life events of the Messiah (Winston 1993: 620–22, 631–32). An example of paternoster beads created sometime in the late fifteenth or early sixteenth century was composed of small wood beads with several small metal figures, including a closed hand, three nails, a hammer, a crown of thorns, a cloak, and the head of Christ bearing a crown of thorns (Lightbrown 1992: 528–29).

No doubt based on the religious symbolism of the wounds of Christ, many folk religion charms were created throughout southern and central Europe, at least from the fifteenth century onward, consisting of a closed hand holding a loop of wire from which smaller charm objects were suspended. The smaller charm objects attached to these compositions varied greatly, but often included other symbols of Christianity (such as a fish, a cross, a triangle shape for the Trinity, or a censer), symbols of fertility (such as phallic figures), and images of human anatomy or livestock for which cures and protection were sought (for example, Hansmann and Kriss-Rettenbeck 1966: 162–67, 199, 211; see fig. 5.3).

When archaeologists brushed the dust away from the small hand ornaments uncovered in the soils of Tennessee and Virginia, they uncovered items that were likely the product of generations of symbolic references extending far back into European history. Emblematic symbols within Christian religious denominations were incorporated into the instrumental folk religion charms of Europeans over the course of centuries. With the rise of mass-produced goods, manufacturers in the nineteenth century incorporated popular images from folk religion charms into small items stamped out by machine or configured as watch charms. Customers in North America may have purchased such mass-produced items from local merchants because they found the ornamentation attractive without assigning to them any of the past symbolism that could have attended them.

Yet, at the Tennessee and Virginia plantation sites, these small hand ornaments appear to have been owned and utilized by individuals of African American heritage. What meanings might those individuals have associated with these small hand ornaments? Enslaved laborers could have obtained these items through barter and trade with others in the plantation community, or by purchasing them from local merchants (Heath 1999: 50–58; B. Thomas 2001: 20–23).

Archaeologists have speculated that an African American owner of one of these objects may have obtained and used it as a protective charm because it looked similar to a figa charm (for example, McKee 1995: 40; Singleton 1991: 162). Figa charms were in fairly widespread use in the Americas by the middle of the nineteenth century (Singleton 1991: 162–63). African Americans in Virginia or Tennessee could have learned of this cultural tradition if they had spent time in more southerly plantation regions or had interacted with others who subscribed to such beliefs (Russell 1997: 67). However, the hand charms found in Tennessee and Virginia lacked the figa's distinctive gesture of thumb thrust between the fingers (fig. 5.1). This notable difference of configuration makes this interpretation unpersuasive.

Archaeologists have also suggested that the African American owners of these small hand figures may have viewed them as representative of the Hand of Fatima (McKee 1995: 40; Russell 1997: 67). Many West Africans of Islamic heritage were abducted into the transatlantic slave trade, and may have communicated knowledge of Islamic charms to others with whom they associated in the slave quarters of North America (Chireau 2003: 46; Fett 2002: 42). However, the fist-shaped artifacts from Tennessee and Virginia were quite distinct in appearance from charms that depicted the open and extended Hand of Fatima.

Another possibility is that these uncovered artifacts had been viewed as symbolic for a form of conjuration composition that was itself called a hand in African American folk religion traditions of the nineteenth century (McKee 1995: 40; Singleton 1991: 163). Under these cultural traditions, one created a material composition as part of a protective invocation to ward off malevolent spiritual forces. In interviews, formerly enslaved persons frequently recounted that such material compositions were referred to by a number of terms, including *hand, gris-gris, mojo,* and *jack* (Chireau 2003: 47; Russell 1997: 66–67). The small hand ornament may have been viewed as a symbolic substitute for another material composition that would have been called a hand. Such punning idioms were a prominent feature of nineteenth-century African American folk religion practices. When creating a material composition to invoke spiritual forces, African American practitioners often chose compositional elements based on similarities in the names or shapes of those ingredients with characteristics of the maladies to be averted or cured (for example, D. Brown 1990: 22).

If such a punning substitution of symbols was involved in the use of these hand ornaments, the process could have been even more involved than has yet been suggested. Such punning idioms were also a significant feature of BaKongo cultural practices in which ritual specialists created material compositions as part of their supplications for healing and protection (Jacobson-Widding 1979: 140; Janzen and MacGaffey 1974: 6; MacGaffey 1991: 5; 2000c: 44). In addition, the phonetic root of *hand* resonates with relevant terms of the BaKongo culture. In the KiKongo language, the "word magician, *nganga,* comes from *vanga,* to make, and could be translated 'operator'" (MacGaffey 1970b: 28). Similarly, words for "activation" and "to operate" can be rendered as *vanda* and *handa* in KiKongo (Janzen and MacGaffey 1974: 6, 46). Another phonetic similarity lies in the KiKongo word *kànda,* which means "palm of the hand" (Denbow 1999: 418; MacGaffey 1986: 126). Thus, the use of the word *hand* for a ritual composition could have involved a punning derivation from phonetically similar KiKongo terms to communicate an act of dexterous creation. Indeed, another term for conjuration objects in North America was *wanga,* which was derived in this way from the KiKongo language (Hall 1992: 302; C. M. Long 2001: 4, 39). In contrast, words like *gris-gris* have roots in the Mande language of west Africa (see fig. 1.2) and the past influence of Islamic cultures in that region (Chireau 2003: 46; Hall 1992: 163).

One might suggest at this juncture that persons of BaKongo heritage may have perceived Christian imagery in the small figure of an enclosing hand, because many of the BaKongo people were introduced to Catholicism by Portuguese missionaries while in the Kongo. However, there is little evidence to indicate that missionaries utilized such symbolic images of the hand in the course of their activities. Missionaries instead primarily utilized the symbols of the crucifix and the water of baptism (for example, Thornton 1977: 513–14).

It is possible that African American individuals had acquired and used these small hand ornaments as ritual symbols because they perceived the significance of the figure of a creative hand within the heritage of BaKongo cosmology. If that were the case, they may also have subscribed to other beliefs related to the BaKongo culture, including the relationships between the realms of the spirits and the living, and key BaKongo symbols that summarize those relationships. These small hand ornaments would be of compelling interest to a person who subscribed to BaKongo cosmology. The hand figure—which would represent the creative capabilities of the nganga—is centered within an encircling cycle of the cosmos and rests upon a horizontal crossbar (see fig. 5.1a) that could be read as the Kalunga boundary line separating the living and spirit worlds. Moreover, the hand reaches up from that boundary and grasps the top point of the surrounding circle, which is a position on the cosmic cycle that is symbolic of powerful acts of the living (Robert F. Thompson, pers. comm.).

Thus, these small ornaments likely embody intersecting lines of history that reach from the symbols of Christ's passion spreading across the Mediterranean to the expressions of self-determination through individualized ritual invocations by enslaved African Americans in the New World.

SYMBOLIC EXPRESSION AT THE DEMORY HOUSE SITE

Can one interpret the context and attributes of the skull figure uncovered at the Demory house site in Virginia, with its inscription of initials and crossed lines, as an expression derived from the BaKongo belief system? Historical studies of the North American slave trade demonstrate that many persons of BaKongo heritage were brought into the Virginia region as enslaved laborers (for example, Holloway 1990: 11; Walsh 2001: 144–48). Census lists, tax records, and Peter Demory's 1843 estate inventory show that the family owned enslaved African Americans throughout much of the antebellum period. One or more of those individuals could have been knowledgeable about beliefs and practices that were derived, at least in part, from the BaKongo culture.

The person who created this object could have intended the use of a skull figure to invoke death or fear of death in the targeted person. The crossed lines, or X mark, on the figure could have been used as an abbreviated, instrumental form of the BaKongo dikenga, intended to invoke spiritual forces to activate the curse. The crossed lines are inscribed on the figure within the circular form of the skull, perhaps providing additional elements of a dikenga invocation. The clay object appears to have been placed at a point roughly central in distance between the north and south doorways of the house's main workroom (fig. 2.2). Yet, there was no evidence of other deposits within the floor that would create axes within the room along the cardinal directions. Nor were there accompanying objects expressing the symbolism of white color for the land of the dead and spirits. I also found no associated items with notably reflective surfaces to invoke the flash of the water boundary between the land of the living and the spirit world. The skull figure itself is made of a red-yellow clay, which might have been viewed as representing the red color symbolic of the power of death and transformation.

This composition could have been buried under the floorboards pursuant to beliefs that it would work its magic on the target as that person walked over the hidden figure. The simple burying of such a distinctive conjure item also could have the significance of invoking death. The initials MD or HD also match the names of members of the Demory family, including Peter's wife, Mary, their son Mahlon, daughter Margaretha, or grandson Harry. These initials could have been intended to identify the individual targeted by the invocation. However, the initials RS cannot be explained as identifying a targeted person. Detailed census lists, tax rolls, land deeds, voting ledgers, and local church records reveal no one with those initials living in the area during the relevant time periods (Fennell 2003a: 165–83).

If an alternative interpretation can account for all attributes of this object and its context, including the significance of the initials RS, then that explanation will have greater persuasive value. Such an alternative account focuses on the meaningfulness of this object within the folk religion beliefs of German-Americans in the upper Potomac and northern Shenandoah region in this time period. Those beliefs and practices have a separate and independent history from the beliefs systems spread through African diasporas. This alternative explanation, detailed in chapter 6, proves more persuasive than an interpretation of the skull figure as an expression of beliefs derived from the BaKongo culture.

TENTATIVE STEPS OF ETHNOGENESIS IN TEXAS

A remarkable blending of multivocal, instrumental symbolism of diverse African cultures appears at the Levi Jordan plantation site in Brazoria, Texas (see fig. 1.1). No direct evidence established that persons enculturated in the BaKongo religion lived at that site (K. L. Brown 1994: 96–98; B. Thomas 1995: 153). However, available data on the history of the Atlantic slave trade shows that members of the BaKongo culture were likely imported into the region, either directly or through points in the Caribbean such as Cuba (K. L. Brown 1994: 97; K. L. Brown and Cooper 1990: 12; see fig 1.1). The artifacts uncovered in four caches in the so-called curer's cabin present a number of poignant attributes (fig. 5.4). The four caches contain concentrated collec-

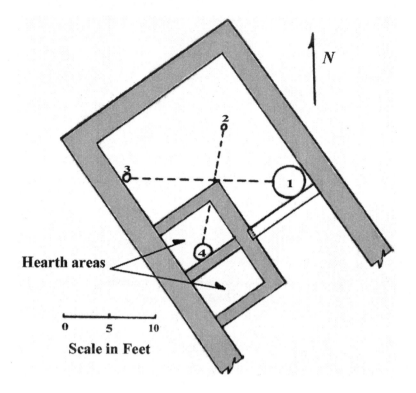

Figure 5.4. Floor plan of the curer's cabin at the Levi Jordan plantation site and location of caches (see K. L. Brown 1994). (Image by the author)

tions of objects deposited at the four cardinal directions along the perimeter of the room. This is notable, since the room itself was not oriented along the cardinal directions (K. L. Brown 1994: 108–14; fig. 5.4). An alignment of axes with the cardinal directions was incorporated as one of multiple metaphoric associations of the dikenga. Thus, these deposits could have been intended to demarcate the crossed lines of a dikenga within the space of this cabin. The objects also could have been components of minkisi placed along the axes and intersection of this dikenga when ritual invocations were undertaken.

One deposit consisted of a concentration of small iron wedges, which could be described as contrived fragments of a knife blade (in area 1 in fig. 5.4). The archaeologists working on this site propose that these are the remains of a form of nkisi Nkondi—a hunter nkisi into which one would drive an iron wedge to record the taking of an oath and a request for aid (K. L. Brown 1994: 111–12; K. N. Brown and K. L. Brown 1998: 2–3). If such a nkisi had been created in this space, the body would most likely have been made of wood, a material that frequently disintegrates in the soils of the archaeological record. A cavity within the wooden figure would have held a cache of bilongo objects, some of which may have been inorganic and some others organic and perishable over time. Close to the iron wedges the archaeologists found water-worn pebbles, fragments of mirrors, several seashells, and a part of a small white porcelain doll (K. L. Brown 1994: 108–9, 113; K. N. Brown and K. L. Brown 1998: 2–3).

The archaeologists refer to this structure as a curer's cabin in part because of the variety of nkisi-like deposits within it. This variety suggested that an experienced curer or healer had lived there and performed his or her services for others in private rituals undertaken in the space of the cabin. This view supports the likelihood that a nkisi of the Nkondi style may have been created and used there, because such a nkisi was viewed by members of the BaKongo culture as very powerful and as manageable only in the hands of an experienced ritual specialist. Such hunter minkisi, if misused, were believed to inflict harm on those persons who mishandled them (Janzen and MacGaffey 1974: 37).

Adjacent to the concentration of iron wedges were two round bases of cast iron kettles with a piece of white chalk, fragments of medicine bottles and a glass thermometer, and two bullet casings sealed into a tube form (area 1 of fig. 5.4). These could be interpreted as objects consistent with other minkisi deposits and items used in divination, with the iron kettles used as trays on which crossed lines would be drawn with white chalk when commencing a divination ritual. The thermometer once held mercury, a silver liquid often associated with magical properties and spiritual forces (for example, Bell 1980: 85). Objects uncovered in the other deposits in the curer's cabin included several silver coins, dated 1853 and 1858, that were stacked along a line running north-south at the northern point of the room's floor (K. L. Brown 1994: 108–9, 113; 2001: 102; area 2 of fig. 5.4). On the south side of the room, a cavity covered by bricks inside the hearth contained a concentrated deposit of burned shells, burned iron nails and spikes, and white ash (K. L. Brown 1994: 113–14; K. N. Brown and K. L. Brown 1998: 3–4; area 4 of fig. 5.4). The series of coins, fragments of glass, burned shell, iron nails, and ash could invoke the flash of the spirit world, land of the dead and ancestors, and cycles of the cosmos, while their placement would demarcate the axes of a cosmogram (K. L. Brown 1994: 108–15; K. N. Brown and K. L. Brown 1998: 2–4).

The west end of this configuration presented artifacts that did not directly fit the predictable attributes of BaKongo-inspired religious items (area 3 of fig. 5.4). At this location, the archaeologists uncovered two iron kettles deposited upright, with one inside the other and ash placed in between their bases. The upper kettle contained soil, small bone fragments, seashells, and metal objects. Fragments of a third, smaller kettle rested on top of the two larger kettles, and a heavy iron chain was wrapped around the circumference of the largest kettle. Other objects were located in the space immediately surrounding these kettles, including seashells, metal buttons, bone fragments, a bolt, several spikes, a bayonet, a hinge, and a piece of an iron plow. It was not clear whether all of these objects were placed in this area purposefully (K. L. Brown 1994: 113–14; 2001: 102; K. N. Brown and K. L. Brown 1998: 2–3).

This configuration of nested iron kettles wrapped in a heavy chain does not correlate directly with the known forms of minkisi design utilized by members of the BaKongo culture. While BaKongo beliefs included the use of iron materials as a form of bilongo object, such a concentrated use of iron containers was seldom employed within the Kongo. It is a design far more consistent with the *amula* compositions of the Yoruba culture, which were typically dedicated to an *orisha* named Ogun (also spelled Oggún) (K. N. Brown and K. L. Brown 1998: 3). Archaeologists analyzing the Jordan site made this interpretation by examining forms of amula known in New World settings, such as examples from Cuba (K. N. Brown and K. L. Brown 1998: 3; B. Thomas 1995: 153; Thompson 1983: 54–56). This interpretation is also supported by historical information concerning the Yoruba religion as practiced in earlier periods in west Africa (see fig. 1.2).

The Yoruba culture possessed a large pantheon of sub-deities, called orisha, to which believers could make supplication and prayers for protection or intervention in the affairs of the living (Cuthrell-Curry 2000: 460–61; Drewal, Pemberton, and Abiodun 1989: 15–18). Although this region was impacted by the arrival of Christian and Islamic influences, the Yoruba religion was not significantly displaced by those developments (S. Barrett 1991: 14–18; Salamone 1991: 55–62). Members of the Yoruba culture in west Africa prayed to individual orisha in the privacy of their homes, in public shrines within their villages, and at regular, large-scale ceremonies (Mbiti 1970: 240, 268; Thorpe 1991: 92, 99).

Ogun was a principal orisha, associated with the powers of iron and war, and supplicants made offerings of iron to Ogun at shrines within their homes when seeking this sub-deity's aid and protection (Barnes 1989: 2, 5–6; Thorpe 1991: 94). Ironworking technologies had spread throughout sub-Saharan Africa in the period of 500 BC through AD 300, and beliefs related to Ogun as an orisha predated the colonial period in west Africa (Barnes 1989:

4–5; Barnes and Ben-Amos 1989: 42; Goucher 1999: 144–47). Ogun was associated with the powers of transformation and related symbolic motifs that included the color red (Barnes 1989: 2, 17; Barnes and Ben-Amos 1989: 53–58). Altars to the orisha were often oriented toward specific cardinal directions (Drewal 1989: 62). An amula was an object composed primarily of elements of iron and used to make supplication to Ogun and focus the protective powers of that orisha into the space where it was placed (for example, Thompson 1983: 54–56).

The artifacts of the curer's cabin at the Jordan plantation thus appear to present evidence of the interaction of distinct traditions and practices derived from separate African cultures. It is in such a setting that the powerful utility of instrumental and abbreviated symbolism becomes apparent. The fully embellished and emblematic dikenga of the BaKongo would have little direct import as a summarizing symbol to someone who was instead educated in the Yoruba religion and culture. Yet, a configuration of four altars at each of the cardinal points within a private space would be consistent with the Yoruba practice of individual, ritual supplications to the orisha (Mbiti 1970: 240; Thompson 1997: 30–31). Thus, the spatial layout of the four ritual caches in the curer's cabin would make sense to a member of the Yoruba culture as well, but due to the application of different religious metaphors read off the same symbolic configuration.

This example of the negotiation and blending of different African belief systems could have taken place within the social network at the Jordan plantation itself, as one instance of a complex process that played out among individuals in many New World settings. However, the ritual composition of nested iron cauldrons in the west portion of the curer's cabin could also have represented a different instance of intercultural negotiation that took place elsewhere in the Americas, in the form of the Afro-Cuban belief system called Palo Monte Mayombe. If the population of the Jordan plantation included an individual who had lived in Cuba and had subscribed to the Palo belief system, the westernmost composition in the curer's cabin could represent a ritual composition called a *prenda* to Zarabanda (K. L. Brown 1994: 110). The histories of the development of Santería and Palo as distinct belief systems in Cuba provide further examples of the complex processes of such intercultural negotiations.

Yoruba and BaKongo Dynamics in Cuba

The experiences of African descendants in colonial Cuba were shaped by processes notably distinct from those seen in Haiti, Brazil, or North America (see fig. 1.1). Spanish colonial administrators in Cuba initiated a strategy in the sixteenth century to create mutual aid societies, called *cabildos* or *co-fradías*, which served to cluster Afro-Cubans into different ethnic categories (Brandon 1993: 70–71; Klein 1986: 183–85). This was a strategy of "divide and rule" designed to foster social differences across groups within the enslaved population so that they would not find a unifying focus through which to rebel against the colonial government (Klein 1986: 185). This strategy in turn contributed to the cohesive continuation and development of different African cultural systems on Cuban soil. In contrast to the extensive blending of diverse African cultures that would be seen in Haiti and Brazil, Cuban cabildos contributed to rich continuations of Yoruba culture in the development of Santería and to largely separate developments of BaKongo beliefs in Palo Monte Mayombe.

Spanish colonial investment in Cuba started in 1511, and the first enslaved Africans were imported onto the island in 1517 (MacGaffey and Barnett 1962: 2–3). Colonial and plantation activity on Cuba remained limited through the late eighteenth century (Duany 1985: 103; MacGaffey and Barnett 1962: 4). With the beginning of a slave rebellion in Haiti in 1792, colonial investors began focusing on Cuba as a new center for sugar plantations (Duany 1985: 103). By 1823, Spain's colonial possessions in the New World consisted primarily of Cuba and Puerto Rico (MacGaffey and Barnett 1962: 7–8). By the 1830s, the intensive investments in sugar, coffee, and tobacco production in Cuba made it one of the highest profit-producing colonies in the world (Duany 1985: 103).

Importation of enslaved Africans to Cuba was permitted under the law through 1820, and smuggling of slaves continued in the region through 1862 (MacGaffey and Barnett 1962: 6–7; J. Miller 1976: 109–11). Slavery was not abolished until 1886, and Cuba remained a colony of Spain until gaining independence in 1898 (MacGaffey and Barnett 1962: 10–12). The population of Africans on the island increased dramatically starting in the late eighteenth century (Brandon 1993: 53). "Between a million and a million 200,000 slaves were introduced to Cuba from 1517 to 1880, but only about 600,000 of these came before 1761" (Duany 1985: 104). Enslaved Africans brought to Cuba had been abducted from a number of cultures, including the Ashanti, Ewe, Fon, BaKongo, and Yoruba (Howard 1998: 44–46, 60; see fig. 1.2).

A number of distinct Afro-Cuban subcultures developed throughout the colony's history as a result of the government's promotion of the cabildo system of mutual aid societies that functioned as social and religious centers. While the first cabildo in Cuba was recorded in 1598, the Spanish colonial government promoted this system primarily in the period from 1691 through the early 1880s, and particularly in the regions around major urban settlements such as Havana, Matanzas, and Santiago de Cuba (Brandon 1993: 71; Duany 1985: 107). A similar dynamic of populations clustering according to ethnic affiliations developed in more remote, rural locations in Cuba, where fortified *palenques* were established by escaped African slaves, who were referred to as *cimarrones* (La Rosa Corzo 2003; Matibag 1996: 22). For example, some palenque settlements were largely populated by persons of either BaKongo or Yoruba heritage (Ballard 2005: 98–99). By the time of emancipation in 1886, the cabildo system was disfavored within the Cuban legal regime and was largely replaced by Afro-Cuban religious organizations called *reglas* (Ayorinde 2000: 73; Brandon 1993: 72, 82).

Yoruba-speaking persons and their descendants formed a Cuban ethnic affiliation called the Lucumí. A cohesive political and governmental unit called the "Yoruba" did not exist in such a form in west Africa, and was instead represented by a number of related social groups who shared common cultural and language traditions. Such related groups from west Africa coalesced into new ethnic affiliations as part of the dynamics of New World settings (Childs and Falola 2004: 5; Lovejoy 2003: 33). "Just as the Apulians, Sicilians, and Calabians all became Italians in the United States, Oyos, Egbas, Ijebus, and Ijeshas all became Lucumis in Cuba" (Brandon 1993: 55). Within cabildos operated by Lucumís, the religion of Santería developed as an expression of Yoruba cosmology and the selective incorporation of symbolic motifs from Spanish Catholicism (Brandon 1993: 73–74; González-Wippler 1989: 3–5).

Santería, "way of the saints," identifies a number of Catholic intercessory saints as representing certain orisha (González-Wippler 1989: 10). In Yoruba cosmology, a supreme deity, Olodumare, created the universe, sub-deities, spirits, and humankind, but remained remote from human propitiation and prayer (Brandon 1993: 12–17). Humans could instead make supplications to the orisha for aid and intercession, and to obtain the vitality of a spiritual energy called *ashé* (González-Wippler 1989: 5). Principal orisha within Santería include Elegguá, who opens paths to the other orisha; Oggún, god of iron and war; and Shango, god of thunder (Ayorinde 2004: 212–15).

In a process that likely began as a subversive exercise of worshipping according to the Yoruba religion while appeasing officials of the colonial government and church, the orisha of Santería were identified with symbolic motifs of certain saints. "As the Yoruba had become the Lucumi in Cuba, so the Yoruba religious vision had become santería, an attempt to honor the gods of Africa in the land of the Catholic saints" (Murphy 1993: 32). Shaped in part by colonial strategies that divided the populace along ethnic lines,

Santería grew within the Lucumí cabildos as a cultural belief system that represented an enduring expression of Yoruba cosmology. Santería developed with notably limited incorporation of influences from other African religious systems, such as the BaKongo or Mandinga (Ayorinde 2004: 209; see fig. 1.2).

In contrast, the religious system developed in the Cuban cabildos affiliated with BaKongo ethnic heritage involved much greater interactions and blending of BaKongo and Yoruba symbolism and beliefs (Howard 1998: 44, 60–61). This Afro-Cuban belief system was called Palo Monte Mayombe, Palo Monte, Regla de Palo, or Reglas Congas. It included facets directly related to the BaKongo cosmology, combined with intercessory spirits that corresponded to powerful orisha within Santería (Cabrera 1979: 128; Matibag 1996: 153–55; Wedel 2004: 29).

For example, Oggún of Santería was worshipped as Zarabanda within Palo Monte Mayombe and was associated with war, iron, and powers of transformation (Cabrera 1979: 128; González-Wippler 1989: 249). Altars to Oggún or Zarabanda were therefore constructed in a similar manner. An altar to Zarabanda was composed of a prenda, consisting of an iron cauldron wrapped in chains and filled with other iron objects such as tools and weapons (Matibag 1996: 163; Olmos and Paravisini-Gebert 2003: 41, 83–84).

Elements of Catholic beliefs were incorporated into both Santería and Palo Monte Mayombe due to the imposition of the Spanish colonial regime and the cabildo system. The greater flexibility of Palo Monte Mayombe than Santería to incorporate elements of other African religious systems may have resulted from its more "pragmatic" orientation toward individualized problem solving (Wedel 2004: 55). In contrast, Santería involved a more cohesive expression of largely Yoruba beliefs, with much less incorporation of facets of BaKongo cosmology. This likely occurred because the Lucumí cabildos in which Santería flourished were characterized by a "higher degree of internal organization" than were the Kongolese cabildos (Duany 1985: 107).

The ritual compositions dedicated to Zarabanda within Palo Monte Mayombe are remarkably similar to the nested iron cauldrons and related objects uncovered by archaeologists in the curer's cabin at the Jordan plantation site in Texas. The other ritual deposits within that curer's cabin also exhibit strong associations to BaKongo beliefs and practices. Focusing on such intercultural dynamics increases our appreciation of the cultural flexibility of past actors and their innovativeness in creating new social networks and shared symbolic expressions under difficult circumstances (see C. H. Long 1997: 27; Mintz and Price 1976: 23–24; Sacks 1979: 144). In individual uses, we see evidence of the symbolism being selected in the form of simpler, instrumental compositions.

Consider the possible choices of an African American individual who was educated in the traditions of the BaKongo religion, lived in slave quarters, and interacted with persons more familiar with other African religious traditions. By reducing the extensive array of design components from the fully embellished BaKongo dikenga (cross, circle, and four disks) down to a simpler form of cross symbol, this person would have an increased ability to communicate in a religiously meaningful way during interactions with those other African Americans (see Firth 1973: 211–40; Sacks 1979: 6–7). Over time, their interactions could solidify into new social networks for which they could develop emblematic symbols to express their new group identity. Those emblematic symbols could be composed of the components of their previously varied instrumental symbolism. Cultural developments in Haiti and Brazil, to which this discussion now turns, provide exemplary illustrations of these diachronic dynamics.

Innovation of New Emblems in Haiti and Brazil

The blending of different instrumental symbols of African religions into new emblematic symbols occurred more fully in those regions where the European colonial institutions were less rigid and surveillance and control frequently lax. Plantations and slave communities within western Saint Domingue (later called Haiti) and Brazil provided such opportunities (Mulira 1990: 35; see fig. 1.1). In each region, the abbreviated forms of core symbols from multiple African religions were combined to create new, ideographic symbols that served as "virtual national expressions" of group identity (Thompson 1990: 155). Such a blending of varying religious beliefs and practices in the formation and consolidation of new social networks can thus be viewed as examples of ethnogenesis (Roosens 1989: 9–20; Yinger 1994: 263). I propose that this process is best conceptualized using a theoretical construct of ethnogenic bricolage. I compare and contrast this concept with theories of creolization in the concluding chapter of this study.

In both Haiti and Brazil a number of factors contributed to this rich blending of African traditions. The population of enslaved Africans and African Americans was far greater than the number of European plantation operators and their associates. Control and surveillance were less strict than in other slave-owning areas, and plantation operators tended to seclude themselves from the daily affairs of the workforce. Social interaction and communications between enslaved persons were undertaken with greater ease and regularity. Religious and political leaders were able to assert themselves within local slave communities, organizing the residents socially while employing beliefs, practices, and expressive motifs derived directly from African traditions (see, for example, L. Barrett 1977: 193).

Europeans first brought enslaved Africans to Saint Domingue in the sixteenth century. The majority of those persons were abducted from the areas of the Gulf of Benin, Kongo, and Angola, with most coming from the region in which the BaKongo people resided (see fig. 1.2). The religion of Vodun developed as a blending of African belief systems in Saint Domingue from the early 1700s onward, a period in which increasing numbers of captive Africans were imported from varied locations. Elements of the Catholicism of the French colonialists were incorporated as well. With strong instigation from the ritual specialists of Vodun, the enslaved population rebelled over the span of a decade and won their independence in 1804, creating the nation of Haiti (Eltis 2001: 46; Genovese 1976: 174–75; Trouillot 1995: 37–43; Vanhee 2004).

The word *Vodun* (or *Vodou*) was derived from the Ewe language and referred to lesser deities within the religious beliefs of the Fon people of the Dahomey region in west Africa (Klein 1986: 181; see fig. 1.2). However, Vodun represents a rich blending of numerous African religions, including the Fon, Yoruba, and BaKongo. As Leonard Barrett (1977: 199) stated, Vodun represented "a divine confederation honed on African pragmatism" and an example of the "flexibility" that enabled African traditions to survive and evolve in Saint Domingue. Vodun beliefs include a broad array of sub-deities, called *loas* (or *lwas*), each with variant names from the principal contributing religions.

The loas called Legbe, Guede, and Dambella are typically treated as the most prominent in Vodun rituals. Legbe represents the guardian of gates and boundaries between worlds, and is a direct variant of the Yoruba orisha named Eshu and Elegba. Supplication is typically made to Legbe at the start of any ceremony to request permission to seek spiritual intercession into the land of the living. Thereafter, other spirits or loas might be requested to provide specific forms of aid (Barrett 1977: 199–200; Metraux 1972: 28–29; Rigaud 1985: 9, 92).

Each of the principal Vodun loas is represented by an ideographic symbol, typically drawn upon the grounds of ritual spaces displayed to the public. These are called *vèvè* ground blazons (or the *vever*) and are typically two to three square feet in size (Barrett 1977: 200; K. M. Brown 1976: x–xi; Metraux 1972: 163). *Vèvè* was originally a word from the Fongbe language of the southern Dahomey region, and was used in that area of west Africa to refer to ceremonial circles drawn on the ground to demarcate a protective space (K. M. Brown 1976: ix; Thompson 1997: 23). Like the crossed lines of the BaKongo dikenga, the Vodun vèvè denote the center of the ritual space on which supplications can be made for spiritual assistance. Each rendering of a blazon is believed to summon the associated loa to become manifest in that space, and other ritual objects are typically placed at the center of intersecting lines within the blazon's pattern (K. M. Brown 1976: xi, 46; Laguerre 1980: 30, 166; Metraux 1972: 165; Rigaud 1985: 92). Ethnohistorical sources record the appearance of early forms of ground blazons in a slave community in Saint Domingue in the late eighteenth century (Thompson 1997: 26–27).

Haitian vèvè are typically rendered on the floors of Vodun temples, at the exterior entrance to those temples, at the base of trees deemed sacred to particular loas, and in cemeteries (K. M. Brown 1976: 46; Rigaud 1985: 79–80). Some may be rendered as adornments on the walls of temples (Gundaker 1998: 165). These detailed drawings are rendered with a variety of media, including kaolin; wheat flour; cornmeal; wood ashes; powdered leaves, bark, roots, or charcoal; red brick powder; rice powder; or gunpowder (Gundaker 1998: 165; Rigaud 1985: 92).

Figure 5.5 shows an example of a Vodun blazon associated with the loa called Simbi. Simbi is a loa of many variant forms, and is derived in part from the BaKongo concept of simbi spirits (de Heusch 1989: 293–96; Gundaker 1998: 165; Rigaud 1985: 93). In this vèvè the crossed lines of the BaKongo dikenga have been combined with numerous symbolic motifs along the axes which represent blended concepts from the Yoruba and Dahomean cosmologies (K. M. Brown 1976: 412). As Grey Gundaker (1998: 165) observed, such "designs sum up the attributes of the lwa . . . and are composites spreading out from central crossmarks—the crossmark itself being the intersection of worlds mediated by the lwa Legba, the master of thresholds, uncertainty and writing." These ideographic renderings, combining an array of instrumental core symbols into new emblems, were not used solely in private rituals, but were instead deployed as part of public expressions of group identity (Gundaker 1998: 165; Thompson 1990: 155).

A similar but separate process unfolded among the enslaved Africans and Native Americans in plantations of Brazil (see fig. 1.1). Portuguese colonial efforts promoted the establishment and operation of large-scale plantations in this region, focused primarily on sugar production, from the early sixteenth century onward. The first captive Africans imported into Brazil were abducted primarily from the areas of Senegal and Sierra Leone (see fig. 1.2).

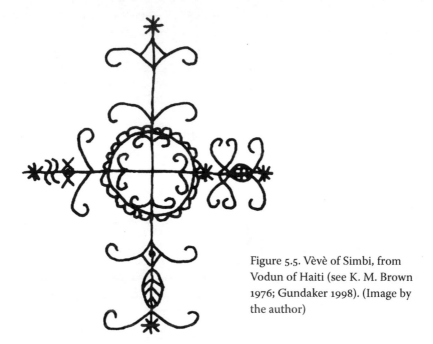

Figure 5.5. Vèvè of Simbi, from Vodun of Haiti (see K. M. Brown 1976; Gundaker 1998). (Image by the author)

However, from the late sixteenth century onward, the Portuguese obtained most enslaved people for import into Brazil from the area of Angola and Kongo (Eltis 2000: 189; Orser 1996: 42, 51–52; Sturm 1977: 218).

Plantation owners in this region of Brazil typically ran large-scale operations with less consistent control and surveillance of their workforce than occurred at locations in North America. As a result, enslaved persons had greater opportunities to engage in social interactions within their communities over time. Moreover, many rebelled and won their freedom from the plantations, creating "maroon" communities of escaped slaves (Orser and Funari 2001: 66). Nonetheless, slavery persisted in Brazil until the late nineteenth century, and nearly two million newly enslaved persons were imported into the region between 1811 and 1870 (Wolf 1982: 316, 373).

Historic-period documents record cultural practices among enslaved Africans in Brazil that can be related to particular African societies from which individuals were abducted. For example, a colonial report from 1721 described divination practices and beliefs that strongly corresponded with BaKongo rituals. An enslaved man named Domingos was described as an "Angolan" and was known as a talented diviner in the area of a city in Bahia. He began his divination ritual "by drawing a cross in the dirt with his finger" (Sweet 2004: 144). Domingos then conducted divination inquiries

along those drawn axes with a nkisi-like composition contained in a cala-
bash (144–45).

Over time, communities within Brazil developed a new set of beliefs and
practices, later to be called Macumba, through a blending of different African religions, Catholicism, and Native American religions. The concepts of
BaKongo minkisi, Dahomean Vodun, Yoruba orisha, and the intercessory
saints of Catholicism were creatively integrated using the complementary
elements of those religions (Genovese 1976: 179–80; Thompson 1983: 113;
1990: 156). Similarly, the indigenous Tupí-Guaraní people of Brazil, called
Tupinambá by the Europeans, possessed religious beliefs concerning ancestor spirits that blended readily with ancestor beliefs of the BaKongo and the
Yoruba concepts of orisha (Genovese 1976: 180; Orser 1996: 48–49; Sturm
1977: 219).

This articulation of religious concepts included a careful combination of
abbreviated symbols from the contributing cultures. Ground blazons, called
pontos riscados (for "marked points" of invocation), developed in this Brazilian tradition as well. These pontos were typically rendered in chalk or
sand on the floors of shrines and other public ritual spaces (Bastide 1978:
298; Thompson 1983: 113–15; 1990: 155–56). Each intercessory spirit, often
characterized with the combined names and attributes of a saint, ancestor,
orisha, or simbi, possessed a ponto which would summon a manifestation of
that spirit to render aid. These pontos were rendered both in transient forms
during particular rituals and as permanent expressions in publicly visible
locations (Thompson 1983: 115–16).

For example, the crossed lines of the BaKongo dikenga were combined
with the concept of Eshu Elegba as the mediator of the crossroads between
the spirit world and the land of the living. Elegba was viewed as being un-
predictable and inclined to punish those who trifled with the spirit world. In
turn, Elegba's attributes were merged selectively with symbols for the Satan
figure of Catholicism, with Elegba challenging and testing the righteousness
of individuals, but not representing an opponent to the Godhead (Thompson 1983: 114; 1990: 156). Figure 5.6 shows an example of a ponto for Elegba
within the Macumba tradition, which blends the intersecting lines of the
dikenga with the pitchfork motifs of Elegba, and a spinning pinwheel motif suggestive of the dynamism and unpredictability of that guardian of the
crossroads (Thompson 1983: 114; 1990: 156).

This blending of elements from different African religions with facets of
European and Native American beliefs developed in Haiti and Brazil with "a
depth and visibility virtually unknown in the United States" (Genovese 1976:
179). Such intercultural blending of multiple African belief systems was also

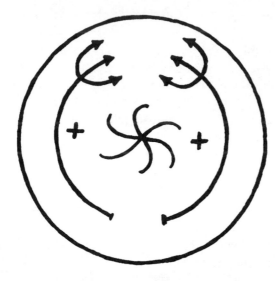

Figure 5.6. Ponto of Eshu Elegba, from Macumba of Brazil (see Thompson and Cornet 1981). (Image by the author)

largely absent from the development of Santería in Cuba, but was evident in facets of Palo Monte Mayombe, with its selective incorporation of orisha and related symbolism (Olmos and Paravisini-Gebert 2003: 82–83). Palo Monte Mayombe also developed complex "firma" blazons that were similar in character to vèvè and pontos riscados (for example, Ballard 2005: 131; Matibag 1996: 161). These religious systems developed in Cuba, Haiti, and Brazil, and the associated material expressions of key symbols were deployed as part of larger-scale processes of social organization and the consolidation of new group identities. Central elements of a variety of African religions were combined and developed for continuing observance, not just in the private rituals of households and covert meetings, but in public displays that signaled an evolving group cohesion to anyone within view. I define this process as ethnogenic bricolage, and I explore the facets of this dynamic further in chapter 7.

Afro-Christian Dynamics in North America

In the African American communities of North America, we do not see evidence of this process of ethnogenic bricolage based on diverse African religions. Instead, the vast majority of religious artifacts recovered at African American sites in the United States dating to the eighteenth and nineteenth centuries reflects only private, instrumental symbolism. Why?

Two primary factors inhibited the development of new, emblematic symbolism from the components of instrumental symbols of multiple African religions in the United States. First, in the early generations of enslaved laborers in North America, from the seventeenth through the early eighteenth century, high levels of surveillance and control of slaves' lives largely precluded their ability to develop and deploy such new, emblematic symbols. Plantation owners and overseers in the North American colonies typically implemented a much greater level of control over the daily lives of their labor force than did many plantation operators at locations in the Caribbean and South America (Genovese 1976: 179, 211; Raboteau 1980: 53). Second, from the early eighteenth century onward, many enslaved persons in North America adopted evangelical Christianity as a new set of beliefs and practices. Through subscription to such denominations, African Americans were able to shape local church congregations, promote group solidarity, and employ associated symbolic expressions in open, public displays (Blassingame 1972; Harding 1997).

Some analysts emphasize a third factor as well: the United States formally outlawed the importation of enslaved persons after 1808 (see, for example, Genovese 1976: 211). As Raboteau (1980: 92) stated, in "North America, a relatively small number of Africans found themselves enslaved amid a rapidly increasing native-born population whose memories of the African past grew fainter with each passing generation." However, this factor is of questionable significance. Scofflaws no doubt continued a considerable amount of illegal importing of enslaved persons into the United States throughout the decades leading up to the Civil War. Moreover, the question remains of the degree to which individuals enculturated in particular African traditions succeeded in passing those beliefs and practices on to others within their community in America, regardless of where those other persons were born.

The early generations of Africans and African Americans could practice rituals derived from their African religions only when outside the scope of surveillance. The twentieth-century narratives of formerly enslaved persons report that such meetings, when held, were usually convened in hollows, hush arbors, and other secret locations in the vicinity of the plantations (C. H. Long 1997: 26; Perdue, Barden, and Phillips 1976: 53, 94, 124; Raboteau 1980: 215; Rawick 1978: 23). These limitations greatly inhibited the formation of new styles of group ritual and group expression that could have been developed out of a blending of different African religious traditions. Such a blending of African traditions occurred instead in those parts of the Caribbean and South America where European colonial institutions were less fixed and surveillance less strict (Barrett 1977: 193; Mulira 1990: 35).

In that same period, up through the early eighteenth century, plantation owners in North America preferred that their enslaved laborers exercise no religious observances. Plantation owners, overseers, and their associates frequently disapproved of the exercise of African religious beliefs, fearing that such conduct would lead to instances of group solidarity and resistance among the slaves. They similarly disfavored the conversion of enslaved persons to Christianity. Many slave owners were apprehensive that conversion would lead to arguments that Christianized African Americans should not be subjected to bondage. Some believed that they would lose significant amounts of labor time if their slaves began attending services regularly. Plantation owners primarily feared, however, that enslaved laborers would become increasingly restive after conversion, due to Christianity's concepts of religious equality and self-determination (Berlin 1998: 60–61; Genovese 1976: 211; Levine 1977: 60; Raboteau 1980: 66, 98–99, 103).

By the early eighteenth century, two trends made it easier for African Americans to adopt Christianity as a dominant religion for public observance. An increasing number of colonies passed laws declaring that conversion to Christianity would have no effect on a person's status as an enslaved laborer. This development alleviated many of the concerns of plantation owners. In addition, successive waves of evangelical movements within the Christian faith spread across the colonies, promoting conversion of as many persons as possible (Berlin 1998: 138; Gomez 1998: 21; Levine 1977: 60–61; Raboteau 1980: 98–99).

Many African Americans were attracted to this religious movement, which emphasized the value of every soul, no matter one's station in life, and the comparable struggle of every individual against sin and corruption. The evangelists also frequently expressed religious grounds for condemning material opulence, pretension, and unequal wealth. An emphasis on the sacrifices and pains of the Savior during mortal life, and comparable salvation after death, presented sympathetic and familiar themes. Old Testament promises of God's liberation of the chosen and downtrodden provided comparably attractive beliefs (Berlin 1998: 138–39; Levine 1977: 60–61).

The evangelical movements were particularly strong in the Virginia Tidewater area and in Maryland (see fig. 1.1), moving northward from there from the 1740s onward. Such evangelical "awakenings" occurred in waves of revivals in one decade after another in that time period (Berlin 1998: 138, 272; Levine 1977: 61; Raboteau 1980: 66). This process accelerated in northern states in the late 1790s as new evangelical churches were formed with the aid of local African American leaders. Elsewhere during the eighteenth century, in areas such as the low country of the Carolinas, many African Americans resisted evangelists' proselytizing and instead endeavored to retain various forms of their African religious heritage (Berlin 1998: 172, 252; Genovese 1976: 211; Raboteau 1980: 149).

The core symbols of Christianity contained motifs that resonated with the symbolism of a number of African religions. Sterling Stuckey (1987: 34–35, 92) argues persuasively that persons learned in the BaKongo religion would have viewed the Christian cross, as it was used in group worship in the colonial and antebellum periods in the United States, as a symbol consistent with the dikenga. Moreover, as those persons converted to Christianity and participated in its group rituals of worship, they shaped their liturgical practices to reflect the ring shouts and call-and-answer techniques of traditional BaKongo ceremonies (Gomez 1998: 4; Raboteau 1980: 64; Stuckey 1987: 93–95). "By operating under cover of Christianity, vital aspects of Africanity, which some considered eccentric in movement, sound, and symbolism, could more easily be practiced openly" (Stuckey 1987: 35).

Crossed lines would have been read in varying ways by members of different African religions, such as the Fon, Yoruba, Asante, or BaKongo. That symbol was still meaningful in a spiritual sense to members of each of those religions, however, even if interpreted differently in its details (Raboteau 1980: 34, 85; Stuckey 1987: 92; Thompson 1997: 21–27). Through these interactions and constraining social influences, many African Americans continued to practice African religious beliefs in private, instrumental contexts, while shaping evangelical Christianity into a new form for public observance and promotion of their group interests and solidarity (Genovese 1976: 211).

In the next chapter, we focus again on the Demory house site in Virginia and its symbol-laden material culture. Just as a number of African belief systems were targets of subordination in the New World, numerous belief systems in European cultures confronted the dominant deployments of Christianity. A diaspora of commoners from the war-torn countryside of the districts of Germany provides another illustration of instrumental symbolism carried to the New World in the eighteenth and nineteenth centuries.

6

European Diasporas and the Persistence of Magic

The preceding chapters examined the ways in which facets of a number of African cultures were carried to New World locations and were variously continued in practice, changed over time, and blended with elements of other cultural traditions. While the attributes of the skull figure uncovered at the Demory house site in Virginia ostensibly fit with an instrumental and abbreviated form of the BaKongo dikenga, an in-depth analysis shows this is likely not the case. Other sources of rich cultural traditions operated in the northern Shenandoah and Upper Potomac River valley regions (see fig. 1.1) surrounding the Demory site during the eighteenth and nineteenth centuries. These included the varied beliefs and social practices brought into the area by German immigrants. This chapter further explores this history of German-American cultural traditions, related deployments of instrumental symbolism, and facets of ethnogenesis among such immigrant communities.

From the Palatinate to Virginia

German immigrants and their descendants comprised a significant proportion of the settlers in the northern Shenandoah and Upper Potomac River valley regions during this time period. I use the term *German* here as a simplifying label for a complex reality. For example, the immigrants who departed from particular regions of Germany in the eighteenth and nineteenth centuries certainly did not represent all of Germany nor promote a German nationalist identity or ideology in the countries or colonies to which they moved (Kessel 1990: 89; Yoder 1985: 42–43). Nor did they possess some inherent characteristics that one would refer to as being German. They did, however, share with one another a common language as well as similar experiences in their past ways of making a living and conducting themselves in the rural regions of Germany. They similarly shared common experiences and motivations that led to their immigration.

On the basis of such shared language, knowledge, and experiences, many of these immigrants and their descendants formed new social networks in the regions to which they emigrated. Similar shared experiences brought Scots-Irish (also called Scotch-Irish) immigrants together in new social networks in America. As Patrick Griffin (2001: 4) observed in his study of immigration in this time period,

> In the New World, especially in the Middle Colonies, identities . . . became more coherent over the course of the eighteenth century. Within a region of great diversity, migrants from Europe created ethnic, religious, or, as some would argue, ethnoreligious identities to carve out meaningful cultural space in a plural world. Each group of migrants to the New World overcame the religious and regional divisions of their place of origin to invent markers of membership that bound the group together. Only in America, therefore, did men and women who left Scotland become Scots, or migrants from German-speaking regions of Europe discover a semblance of German unity. This process of invention called on these migrants to resurrect Old World ways, often religious traditions and practices, and infuse them with new meanings.

Many of the German immigrants who eventually moved into the upper Potomac and northern Shenandoah area came from the broad region of the Palatine districts of southwestern Germany (Fogel 1915: 1–2; see fig. 1.3). The Palatine states, located along the Rhine Valley and the area of modern-day Switzerland, suffered extensive disruptions and instability during numerous wars of the seventeenth and eighteenth centuries (Mörz 2002: 333; Otterness 2004: 9, 12). Repeated instances of warfare among French, German, Spanish, and Austrian interests inflicted tremendous damage on the region. The area's instability was exacerbated by periods of poor harvests and the increasing burdens of taxes and debts imposed upon resident families who subsisted primarily by farming. These adverse conditions prompted many families to emigrate to England, other parts of Europe, and eventually to the British American colonies (Fogleman 1996: 5–6, 80; Kulikoff 2000: 190, 197; Moltmann 1985: 15; Otterness 2004: 12, 22). Emigrations motivated by such hostile conditions are often referred to as a form of diaspora.

Thus, many German immigrants from the Palatinate sought the basic benefits of stability and the opportunity to make a living in a less volatile social and natural environment. Between 1702 and 1727, approximately 40,000 to 50,000 German immigrants arrived in Pennsylvania, attracted by exactly these opportunities and the colony's promise of greater political and religious tolerance (Williams 1938: 46). Approximately 60,000 more Germans emigrated to the American colonies over the next couple of decades. Additional waves arrived in decreasing numbers through the late 1700s and early 1800s (Kulikoff 2000: 190). Members of this large-scale movement came from diverse locations within southwestern Germany and from a variety of political, religious, and cultural backgrounds. They also encountered some variation in their spoken dialects of the German language. Among their numbers were many individuals proficient in crafts and professions, families experienced primarily in agrarian production, and persons of a variety of religious affiliations, including Catholic, Protestant, and Judaic denominations (Fogleman 1996: 21–22, 80; Kulikoff 2000: 197; Otterness 2004: 4, 9; Wust 1969: 104–5, 206–7).

These German immigrants tended to move as family groups, rather than individually, a trend that contributed to their propensity to maintain close-knit social units. Those who lacked money to pay ship fares for transatlantic travel typically funded their passage by working as indentured servants upon arriving in America. In time, they pooled resources so that they could move on and settle on backcountry farmsteads (Kulikoff 2000: 201; R. Mitchell 1977: 104; Moltmann 1985: 16; Nolt 2000: 65–66; Wust 1969: 105–6). German immigrants employed traditions of community-based social networks in establishing and running their new households in Pennsylvania, Maryland, Virginia, and other American colonies. They did so without necessarily employing a self-identity of being German in the early stages of those settlements. However, their cohesive, enclave-based social networks were increasingly defined by neighboring outsiders as being expressions of German, Palatine, or Dutch traditions and ethnicity. (In this context, *Dutch* is an Anglo-American corruption of the word *Deutsch*.) This emphasis would later be adopted as a shorthand form of social identity by the members of those enclave communities (Fogleman 1996: 71, 74–81; Kercheval 1850: 50–51; Nolt 2000: 65–66).

Those interested in promoting the settlement of particular colonies, such as the Penn family, recruited immigration of families from Germany through several means. Such efforts included advertising with pamphlets that emphasized the availability of inexpensive farmlands in frontier areas and the religious and political freedom that immigrants would enjoy (Otterness 2004: 26). Officials in Virginia similarly encouraged European immigrants to settle on the northern and western reaches of the colony "in an effort to form buffer groups between the inimical French and Indians to the north and the seated parts" of Virginia's eastern Tidewater region (Williams 1938: 46; see also Kulikoff 2000: 158; Wust 1969: 17–19). These efforts to recruit immigrants through pamphlets distributed overseas proved successful with many of the Palatine residents, among whom literacy was high. "One-half to four-fifths of adult male German immigrants to Pennsylvania from 1730 to 1775 were literate, able to read about American freedom and eastern serfdom" (Kulikoff 2000: 190).

The efforts of Pennsylvania officials to attract German immigrants were so successful that families of German heritage comprised approximately three-fifths of the total population of Pennsylvania by 1747 (Weatherly 1986: 8). By 1760, "a clearly defined 'Pennsylvania German' landscape existed . . . within which virtually all German-speakers of the colony lived, regardless of whether they were recent arrivals or descendants of immigrants from three-quarters of a century earlier" (Fogleman 1996: 81). Pennsylvania's success in attracting so many newcomers throughout this period had spillover effects for neighboring colonies. By the 1730s, the availability of affordable farm-lands had begun to decrease in Pennsylvania, prompting many immigrant families to move south into western Maryland and northern Virginia (Rice 1995: 351, 354).

Maryland authorities had attempted to attract German immigrants to settle in western Maryland, rather than continue south into the Shenandoah Valley and Loudoun areas (Wust 1969: 38; see fig. 1.1). Lord Baltimore issued a proclamation in 1732 assuring prospective settlers "'that they shall be as well Served in their Liberty & property in Maryland as any of his Majesty's Subjects in any part of the British Plantations in America'" (quoted in Wust 1969: 38). For example, families that settled in western Maryland within three years of this 1732 proclamation were offered up to two hundred acres of land with no purchase price and no rents due for three years. These efforts by Maryland interests succeeded to a certain extent, but many German immigrants moved on and settled in Virginia (Kessel 1990: 89–90; Wust 1969: 38).

Officials of the Virginia colony had undertaken similar efforts to promote immigration into the frontier areas on the northern and western parts of that colony. Virginia law had earlier required all residents to participate in local Anglican or Episcopal churches, and the membership lists of those congregations were used for a variety of governmental purposes. However, these requirements were relaxed following the English Toleration Act of 1689 and a similar law passed in Virginia in 1699, which opened the way for settlement by immigrants who were members of other religious sects (Keller 1990: 81; Poland 1976: 40–41).

In addition, the governor of Virginia succeeded in obtaining a treaty with the Iroquois Confederation in 1722 in which that Native American group agreed to withdraw north of the Potomac River and west of the Blue Ridge Mountains (Poland 1976: 4; Williams 1938: 31). The Iroquois Confederation was further coerced into relinquishing all land claims in Virginia in the 1744 Treaty of Lancaster. Settlement began increasing in northern Virginia and the Shenandoah Valley after the 1722 treaty, and German-speaking families began forming lasting settlements in the Shenandoah Valley in the 1730s. Some of these families had arrived directly from Germany, whereas others had first settled in Pennsylvania, Maryland, or New Jersey and a second generation then moved to the Shenandoah Valley (Poland 1976: 4; Roeber 1993: 141–42; Williams 1938: 31).

In western Maryland, the Shenandoah Valley, and north Loudoun County, German families settled in separate farmsteads, rather than concentrated villages, a change from their settlement patterns in southwest Germany. Yet, they tended to settle these farms near one another, and they maintained local social networks in which they provided one another with labor, equipment, products, and loans of currency. These families quickly adapted to new economic circumstances by taking advantage of the market for exporting their surplus crops and livestock. They were able to sell their agricultural products into commercial channels serving growing market centers on the east coast, including Philadelphia, Baltimore, and Alexandria (Kercheval 1850: 50–51; Kessel 1990: 88, 101, 103; R. Mitchell 1990: 13; Williams 1938: 49–50.

German-American families in this region also tended to pass on family wealth through a system of "partible inheritance," similar to that employed in southwest Germany, to provide as much to all their children as they could (Kessel 1990: 101–2; Otterness 2004: 21). Under this approach, the male head of the household typically bequeathed a portion of the family wealth to each child, while arranging for the family farm to pass largely intact to one son for continued operation (Kessel 1990: 101–2). As discussed later, Peter Demory took this approach in dividing his estate among his wife and several children.

Distinct enclaves of German immigrant families resided in the Shenandoah Valley and neighboring Piedmont by the 1750s, and the valley was home to approximately 23,000 German settlers by 1790 (Fogleman 1996: 82–83; Kercheval 1850: 50–51; R. Mitchell 1977: 106). German social networks proved resilient in the Shenandoah Valley area, and "remained a significant cultural force" throughout that region until at least the early 1800s (R. Mitchell 1977: 107; see also Kercheval 1850: 51; Wust 1969: 95). These German-Americans in Virginia were members of a variety of religious denominations, including Lutheran, Reformed, Mennonite, Dunker, and Moravian sects. The German language was used in both church and public services among these residents until about 1830, when it began to be replaced by English (Kercheval 1850: 50; R. Mitchell 1977: 105–7).

Although a variety of religious denominations were represented in the waves of German immigrants settling in Virginia in this period, the majority of families were associated with Lutheran or Reformed (also called Calvinist) congregations. These residents tended to utilize churches and related primary schools as social centers in their settlements (R. Mitchell 1990: 12). For these congregations, "religion and ethnicity became important, mutually supporting aspects of immigrant culture in their new communities" and played a key role in distinguishing them from surrounding populations (Fogleman 1996: 88–89). Local congregations of these two denominations also cooperated with one another, often sharing local meeting houses and schoolhouses (Nolt 2000: 69). Both denominations were challenged by the evangelical movements of the Great Awakening in the period of 1740–1790, and those external pressures likely served to further emphasize the commonalities of the two congregations to their members (Longenecker 2002: 73–74; May 1976: 51–52; Nolt 2000: 70).

The residents of the "German Settlement" of Loudoun County, Virginia (see fig. 1.1), were also primarily members of Lutheran or Reformed congregations. This settlement name was applied primarily by Anglo-Americans to designate the area inhabited by approximately sixty-five German-American families who had moved from Pennsylvania into northern Loudoun County in the early 1730s (Goodhart 1999: 121; Head 1908: 111–12; Weatherly 1986: 8; Wust 1969: 37–38). Such a concentrated influx brought individuals skilled in a variety of crafts, including "carpenters, millers, clock makers, silver smiths, kettle makers, tinners, cabinet makers, hatters, tailors, boat makers, chair makers, distillers and preachers" (Goodhart 1999: 121; see also Weatherly 1986: 8). The area of this settlement of neighboring farms was approximately 125 square miles in size, bounded by Catoctin Mountain on the east and Loudoun Valley and Short Hill Mountain on the west, and extending south approximately ten miles from its north edge on the Potomac River (Goodhart 1999: 120; Poland 1976: 6; Wust 1969: 266).

These Loudoun residents raised livestock and surplus crops for sale, in an area of particularly fertile farmlands, and sold their products into market channels served by competing port cities along the east coast. Within a few decades of growth, other business operations developed within the community, including eight distilleries, several flour and grist mills, and two woolen and cotton mills (Goodhart 1999: 121–22; Weatherly 1986: 22; Williams 1938: 49–50). The social cohesiveness of this German settlement in

Loudoun County was reinforced by a relative degree of geographic isolation from the other settlers in the county (Stevenson 1996: 17–18; Weatherly 1986: 9). A neighboring concentration of Quaker families developed on the southern edge of the German settlement, and this Quaker community also maintained its own self-sufficient character. These Quaker families came from earlier settlements in New Jersey, Pennsylvania, and western Maryland, and some had immigrated directly from England and Wales. This Quaker settlement formed an additional buffer separating the German settlement from the areas in southern and eastern Loudoun County where primarily Anglo-American families had settled (Poland 1976: 6; Stevenson 1996: 17–18, 323; Williams 1938: 32, 50).

The family farmers of both the German and Quaker communities in north Loudoun County shared several characteristics, including lifestyles of frugality and industriousness. They tended to be more successful farmers than others in the county, including the larger-scale Anglo-American farm operators (Williams 1938: 50). Members of the German and Quaker communities practiced crop rotations and used manure to fertilize their fields in a way that boosted the productivity of their farms above that of others in the region during the late 1700s. However, these two communities did not interact politically or socially to an appreciable degree during this period. When the hostilities of the Revolutionary War erupted in the 1770s, many members of the German community fought for one side or the other, whereas members of the Quaker community tried to avoid involvement in such violent conflict (Weatherly 1986: 13, 17; Williams 1938: 135–36, 159).

These two communities generally shared a common view of slavery. Members of the Quaker community strongly promoted emancipation. Residents of the German settlement largely agreed, and very few German-American families owned slaves in this area of Loudoun County (Goodhart 1999: 125; Williams 1938: 59; Wust 1969: 124). The Demorys appear to have been one of the few families of German heritage in the Loudoun Valley who owned enslaved persons. The German residents of the Shenandoah Valley also largely chose to avoid the use of enslaved laborers during this period. German-American farmers throughout the Upper Potomac, Loudoun, and Shenandoah Valley regions tended to focus their production efforts away from crops such as tobacco and hemp, which required constant labor and attention throughout the growing season. They instead concentrated on crops such as wheat and other grains, which required more episodic investments of labor at the times of planting and harvesting (R. Mitchell 1977: 130–31). These crop choices reinforced the tendency of German-American farmers to avoid slave ownership, because there was less economic motivation to utilize slavery when a constant labor supply was not needed (R. Mitchell 1977: 131; Rice 1995: 356).

The German-American residents in the Loudoun Valley, as in the Shenandoah, employed the local church as a central forum for social interaction, having established Reformed and Lutheran churches within the first couple years of settlement (Goodhart 1999: 121; Stevenson 1996: 17–19; Weatherly 1986: 11, 19). The Reformed congregation was organized early in Loudoun, with a church building constructed of log timbers, and the congregation likely used that building as a schoolhouse as well. Lutheran families comprised a significant proportion of the Loudoun population by 1765, and they too constructed their first church building from log timbers and also used it as a school (Weatherly 1986: 11–16, 75). Lutheran church services and school lessons in Loudoun were conducted in the German language at least until 1825. Such German-language schools primarily taught children the basics of reading, writing, and arithmetic through the primary grades only. While these schools contributed to a large extent to maintaining German traditions, anyone seeking secondary or higher levels of education would have to attend English-language schools in the region (Weatherly 1986: 16, 100; Wust 1969: 162).

The German settlement in Loudoun thus remained a relatively cohesive and close-knit community up through the antebellum years. The town of Lovettsville developed as a commercial center within this community between 1820 and 1835 (Weatherly 1986: 19–21). Joseph Martin's 1835 *Gazetteer of Virginia* described Lovettsville at that time as possessing four stores, two churches, two shoe factories, one cabinetmaker, one saddler, one tailor, and one tavern (Weatherly 1986: 21, citing Martin 1835). An Anglo-American author named Yardley Taylor published a travel memoir about Loudoun County in 1853 that condemned the residents of the German settlement for being overly frugal and living in "barely tolerable" log houses (Taylor 1999: 6). These settlers appear to have been committed to overcoming the economic duress that had motivated their immigration, and for them frugality and hard work had undoubtedly become a way of life and a point of pride (Weatherly 1986: 23).

The notable cohesiveness of this social identity of German immigrant families and their descendants in communities of the Shenandoah Valley, western Maryland, and northern Loudoun County was fostered by their adherence to a number of cultural practices. Among such traditions were their preferences for marrying within their own community and for settling in rural enclaves of other families of German heritage (Kercheval 1850: 50–51; Nolt 2000: 65–66). They continued speaking the German language in private and public settings, and they published books, newspapers, pamphlets, and certificates of birth and death in German. They observed a ritual calendar marked by holidays distinct from those of Anglo-Americans, and practiced a number of distinctive culinary traditions (Fischer and Kelly 2000: 114, 118–19; Nolt 2000: 65–66). German-Americans in this period and region also developed decorative art styles that were incorporated into the design of ornate certificates describing life events such as births, marriages, and deaths. These stylistic motifs were also utilized in the ornaments placed on homes, outbuildings, and locally made household wares (Fischer and Kelly 2000: 114, 118–19). In turn, German-Americans were often treated as a distinct group by outsiders such as Anglo-American residents of the region. Anglo-Americans often derided the community-oriented preferences of German-American families as parochial and backward (Nolt 2000: 65–66).

Among the most visible and central components of this group cohesion were retention of the German language and use of the Lutheran and Reformed congregations as religious, educational, and social centers for maintaining their network of community relationships. James Kemper, born in 1753 and a member of one of the German settlements in the Virginia Piedmont, described the slow erosion of these elements: "'They kept up their worship, both public and private, in the German language, and their schools also, till being, as it were, lost in the crowd, the first generation removed by death and all their public political matters transacted in English, their language was gradually lost in the second generation'" (quoted in Wust 1969: 94). Loss of the German language apparently occurred at a faster pace in communities located south of Loudoun in this region of Virginia. For example, a congregation in Staunton, in the southern reaches of the Shenandoah Valley, was described in the 1790s as lacking any desire "'to teach their children their native language'" (Wust 1969: 39). Adoption of the English language for church and school functions occurred more slowly in rural and Piedmont congregations outside town centers of the Shenandoah. The settlement in Loudoun County remained notably resilient, and congregations there attended sermons delivered in the German language through the 1830s (Wust 1969: 95, 139).

In addition to the general social pressures for settlers to adopt the English language, German-Americans found the ranks of their religious congregations subjected to erosive forces of denominational competition during this period. The Great Awakening, with its focus on intensive and emotional contemplation of the dangers of damnation and the promise of personal salvation, spread through Virginia in the 1740–1790 period (May 1976: 42–44, 51–53; Poland 1976: 41). As a result, the memberships of Methodist and Baptist congregations increased in the region, attracting members away from the Lutheran and Reformed congregations that had played such an important role in maintaining social ties among German-American neighbors (Longenecker 2002: 73–74; Poland 1976: 41–42; Wust 1969: 141).

The cohesiveness of a particular social group can also increase in response to external pressures. A primary example of such external dynamics is discriminatory treatment imposed upon the group by other members of society who seek to maintain a dominant position over them (Pollard 1994: 79–80; Spicer 1971: 797–98). Anglo-Americans in the late 1700s often subjected German-Americans to ridicule and discrimination, maligning them as "Palatine boors" who refused to become fully Anglicized (Butler 2000: 31–32; Stevenson 1996: 19).

Just as the ethnic cohesiveness of French Huguenot and Scots immigrants in America tended to fade during the eighteenth century, the distinctiveness of German ethnicity would decrease significantly by the late nineteenth century. That dissipation began in the early 1800s, as German families began to intermarry increasingly with families of various European-American heritages (Butler 2000: 22–23, 29–32). The history of the Demory family presents an example of such intermarriage.

The Demory name is not listed in any of the numerous dictionaries, encyclopedias, and other compilations of surnames found in most libraries. The closest I have found is the French surname of Demaree, which was likely anglicized into Demory over a number of generations (for example, E. C. Smith 1969: 197). I have not been able to ascertain the maiden names of the wives of John Demory, Sr., and Peter Demory. However, Peter and Mary gave a number of their children first names that were popular among German-American families in the region. For example, Catharina and Margaretha are two of the most popular names appearing in lists of the members of local Lutheran and Reformed churches attended primarily by German-Americans (Hiatt and Scott 1995; Mower and Mower 1993). Their son William married Rebecca Link, whose family was of German descent, and Mahlon married Sophia Van Camp, whose maiden name reflected her German heritage (G. Jones 1990; Link 2001: 83–84).

The information available from past land deeds, wills, estate inventories, tax records, and census rolls provides a rich view of the possible past inhabitants of the abandoned log house on the Demory site. I have provided detailed transcriptions and analysis of these original documentary sources in an earlier publication for those interested in exploring the underlying data for this study in greater detail (Fennell 2003a). Unfortunately, I have found no definitive documentary accounts—no "smoking guns" in writing—that indicate specifically who built the log house and who resided there over time. Yet, it looks very likely that someone other than the Demorys erected the log house and lived there for a number of years. When Peter's sons Mahlon and William established their own households in the area immediately surrounding their father's farm, by the time of the 1830 census, one of them very likely took up residence in the log house after evicting the former residents (Fennell 2003a: 170–71).

The Demorys' neighbors also bore surnames of German heritage, including the Nieswanner, Everhard, and Rhopp families (G. Jones 1990; Link 2001: 83–84). In the mid-1700s and later, families with the German-origin names of Bateman, Crim, Eamich, Everhart, Grubb, Nicewarner, Rupp, and Virts were residents of the eastern portions of the German settlement (Weatherly 1986: 9) as well as the Loudoun Valley on the western edge of the settlement. Barbara Derry, a close neighbor of the Demorys for many years, had the maiden name of Everhard, and her daughter Elizabeth married a member of the Virts family. Barbara's married name was actually Doerry, and she, her husband, and her children attended the St. James United Church of Christ in Lovettsville at the center of the German settlement for years, as did their neighbor Levi Prince, whose name was spelled Printz in the church records. Members of the Miller, Fischer, Conard, and Everhard families of the Loudoun Valley also attended that church (Mower and Mower 1993).

Similarly, Peter Demory's 1843 estate inventory listed promissory notes representing past investments with John and Jacob Crim, who had attended the New Jerusalem Lutheran Church in Lovettsville and were later buried in its cemetery (Hiatt and Scott 1995: 7). I have not located any local church records that list the Demory family as members of the congregation in this period. Peter and Mary were buried near their farm in a local church cemetery that was likely affiliated with a Lutheran, and later Methodist, congregation.

Hexerei Practices among German-Americans

The clay skull figure uncovered at the log house site on the Demorys' twenty-two-acre parcel can be explained to some extent as the product of certain African American beliefs and practices. However, one cannot account for all the attributes of that figure based upon African American cultural traditions. An alternative, and ultimately more persuasive, explanation focuses on aspects of a German-American folk religion. This analysis is based on evidence that provides direct historical links between traditions in Germany and comparable beliefs and practices at these locations in the New World.

Many individuals of German-American heritage exercised beliefs and practices, often called *hexerei, braucherei,* or *powwowing,* that were the product of a separate history and independent development than the African American traditions discussed in earlier chapters. The development of the alternative name of powwowing for these traditions provides another example of intergroup dynamics in which outsiders impose identity labels on a group. *Powwow* is a corruption of an Algonquian word for healing practices that Anglo-Americans coined and applied as a "savage" epithet to German-American folk religion beliefs (Reimensnyder 1982: 7). Nonetheless, in time many members of the German-American community adopted and used the term as well.

Under hexerei beliefs, crossed lines also invoked spiritual powers, and the skull figure from the Loudoun site would communicate a focus on death or fear of death. The name of the targeted person would be inscribed onto the object pursuant to these German-American beliefs, again providing an explanation for the MD (or HD) initials. An object with such imagery related to a targeted person could be buried in the ground to symbolize the demise of that individual (Fennell 2000: 299–302; E. Smith, Stewart, and Kyger 1964: 156).

Notably, this German-American tradition also provides an explanation for the RS initials inscribed on the skull figure. A palindrome square of *rotas* or *sator* was a prominent form of written charm within this belief system, as were inscriptions employing Latin initials, such as INRI, in geometric patterns (see fig. 6.2). This invocation was created by writing or inscribing a square of five-letter words in Latin:

R O T A S
O P E R A
T E N E T
A R E P O
S A T O R

This translates roughly as "the sower Arepo holds steady the wheels," thus invoking a creative force that controls the wheels of the cosmos and the vicissitudes of fortune (for example, Merrifield 1988: 142). The word *Arepo* does not invoke an established deity name. Such circumlocution is a frequent technique in religious invocations for personal protection, due to fears of hubris or blasphemy (Keane 1997: 51).

To emphasize the symmetrical quality of this magic square, the word *rotas* would often appear first and *sator* last in the inscription. Protective uses of this charm date back to the expansion of the late Roman Empire throughout western Europe and were included in German-American folk religion traditions in the nineteenth century (Fennell 2000: 301–2; Gunn 1969: 23–31; Kieckhefer 1990: 77–78; Olsan 2004: 60–65, 74). Among numerous examples are plaster inscriptions uncovered in households of the Roman cities of Pompeii, Italy (circa AD 79) and Cirencester, England (circa AD 300), and uses of the palindrome in fifteenth-century medical texts in Europe and on a parchment enclosed in the frame of a doorway of a German-American household in Allentown, Pennsylvania (circa AD 1921) (Gunn 1969: 17–29; Kieckhefer 1990: 77–78; Merrifield 1988: 142–43; Olsan 2004: 60–65; Shaner 1961: 62–63; see figs. 1.1 and 1.3). The RS initials on the clay figure likely represent an abbreviation of the rotas palindrome, set within a geometric inscription, to provide a further invocation of spiritual forces. This explanation of the purpose and use of the clay skull remains the most persuasive, because it best accounts for all of the attributes and the context of the artifact.

Is it useful to refer to hexerei (or powwowing) as a particularly German-American practice? The creation and use of objects to invoke spiritual powers can be expressive of a practitioner's social group identity. This will not always be the case, because particular religions often crosscut many social group identities. If a particular religious belief system is shared within a population that has the bounded characteristics of a social group, however, then such religious practices may be part of the key criteria that members of a social group associate with their sense of solidarity. Artifacts of such past religious beliefs may therefore provide a significant line of interpretative evidence indicating past group identities (Fennell 2000: 303–8; see also A. Cohen 1976: 102; Emberling 1997: 318–20; Wolf 1972: 150; Yinger 1994: 264).

Knowledge of these German-American folk religion beliefs was spread by word of mouth from practitioner to practitioner. Persons subscribing to this belief system often followed a tradition of teaching it to an apprentice who was of the opposite gender than the teacher (Reimensnyder 1982: 130; Yoder 1966: 38). Persons seeking the aid of powwow healers similarly learned details of these beliefs and practices as the healers performed the ritual invocations and prescribed specific remedies for the petitioners to use in the course of combating disease, injury, or misfortune (Kercheval 1850: 240, 245; Yoder 1966: 38). In addition to the dissemination of this belief system through such oral traditions, the corpus of these spiritual invocations and prescribed modes of creating charms was also recorded in writing and published among German-Americans in this region during the early nineteenth century (Yoder 1980).

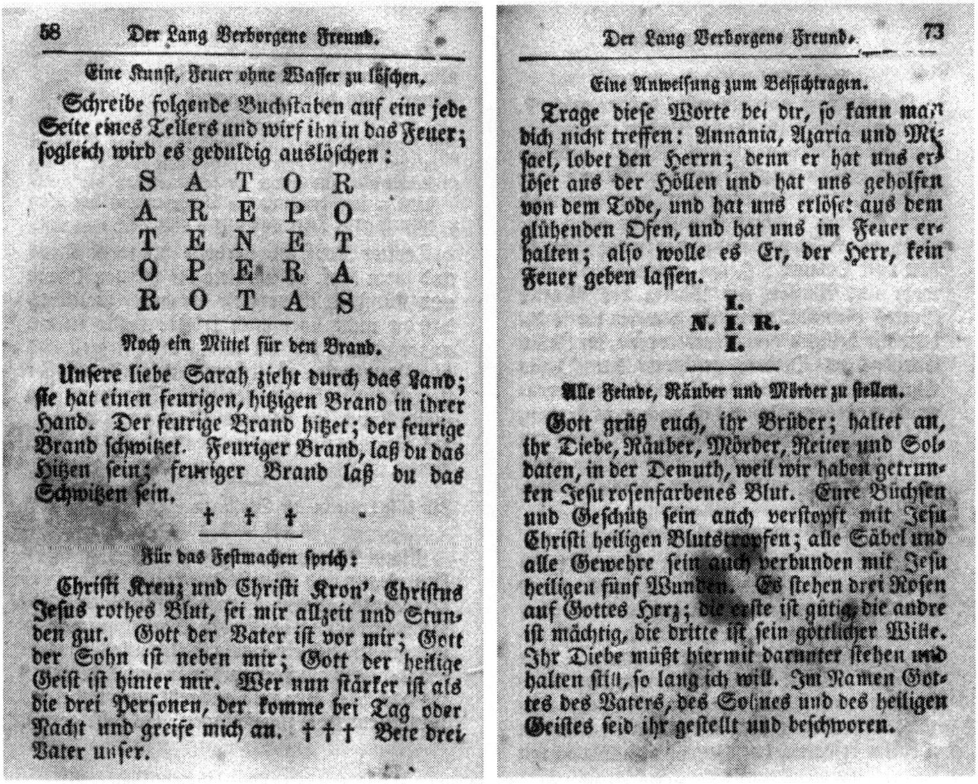

58　Der Lang Verborgene Freund.

Eine Kunst, Feuer ohne Wasser zu löschen.

Schreibe folgende Buchstaben auf eine jede Seite eines Tellers und wirf ihn in das Feuer; sogleich wird es geduldig auslöschen:

```
S A T O R
A R E P O
T E N E T
O P E R A
R O T A S
```

Noch ein Mittel für den Brand.

Unsere liebe Sarah zieht durch das Land; sie hat einen feurigen, hitzigen Brand in ihrer Hand. Der feurige Brand hitzet; der feurige Brand schwitzet. Feuriger Brand, laß du das Hitzen sein; feuriger Brand laß du das Schwitzen sein.

† † †

Für das Festmachen sprich:

Christi Kreuz und Christi Kron', Christus Jesus rothes Blut, sei mir allzeit und Stunden gut. Gott der Vater ist vor mir; Gott der Sohn ist neben mir; Gott der heilige Geist ist hinter mir. Wer nun stärker ist als die drei Personen, der komme bei Tag oder Nacht und greife mich an. † † † Bete drei Vater unser.

Der Lang Verborgene Freund.　73

Eine Anweisung zum Beschtragen.

Trage diese Worte bei dir, so kann man dich nicht treffen: Annania, Azaria und Misael, lobet den Herrn; denn er hat uns erlöset aus der Höllen und hat uns geholfen von dem Tode, und hat uns erlöse aus dem glühenden Ofen, und hat uns im Feuer erhalten; also wolle es Er, der Herr, kein Feuer geben lassen.

I.
N. I. R.
I.

Alle Feinde, Räuber und Mörder zu stellen.

Gott grüß euch, ihr Brüder; haltet an, ihr Diebe, Räuber, Mörder, Reiter und Soldaten, in der Demuth, weil wir haben getrunken Jesu rosenfarbenes Blut. Eure Büchsen und Geschütz sein auch verstopft mit Jesu Christi heiligen Blutstropfen; alle Säbel und alle Gewehre sein auch verbunden mit Jesu heiligen fünf Wunden. Es stehen drei Rosen auf Gottes Herz; die erste ist gütig, die andre ist mächtig, die dritte ist sein göttlicher Wille. Ihr Diebe müßt hiermit darunter stehen und halten still, so lang ich will. Im Namen Gottes des Vaters, des Sohnes und des heiligen Geistes seid ihr gestellt und beschworen.

Figure 6.1. Pages from the 1854 edition of Hohmann's text, showing sator-rotas palindrome and another geometric charm using Latin initials.

Johann Georg Hohmann was a practicing "powwow doctor" who emigrated to southeastern Pennsylvania from Germany in 1799. In 1819, he wrote a compilation in German of the charms, prayers, and prescribed rituals for performing spiritual invocations, which he entitled *Der Lang Verborgener Freund* (The Long-Hidden Friend) (C. Brown 1904: 89–95; Yoder 1980: 235–39; 1990: 99; see figs. 6.1, 6.2). He first published this compilation in 1820 through a small printing operation located in Reading, Pennsylvania, and it was later translated into English and reprinted in the 1850s and 1860s by other small presses located in southern Pennsylvania (C. Brown 1904: 95–96; Yoder 1980: 235–36; 1990: 99). Hohmann's seventy-page text presented uses of the rotas charm for protection in combating malign forces and witchcraft, along with numerous other charms that utilized the initials of key Latin phrases arranged in geometric patterns (fig. 6.1). His small book became a valuable resource used by persons who subscribed to these beliefs

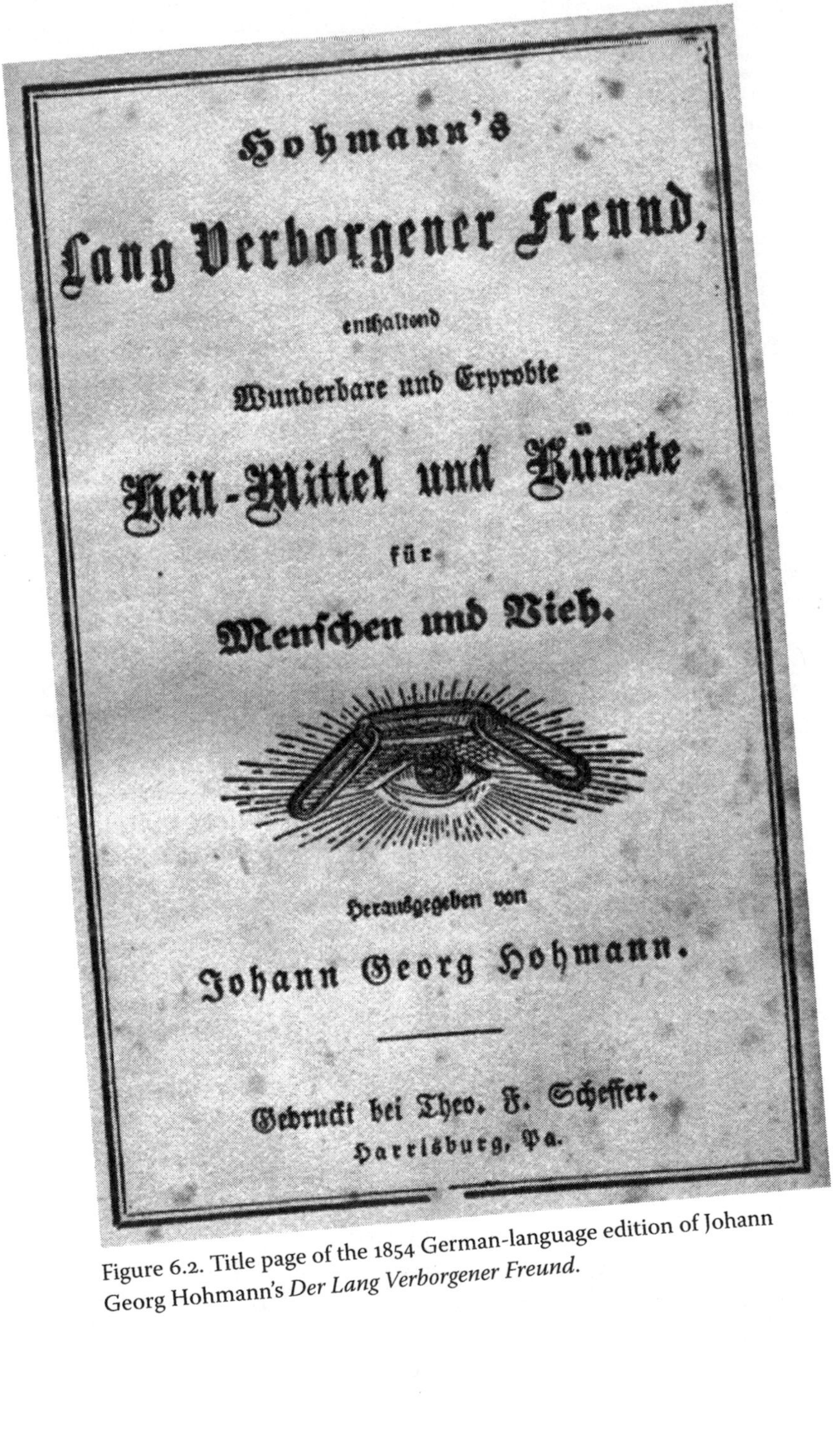

Hohmann's

Lang Verborgener Freund,

enthaltend

Wunderbare und Erprobte

Heil-Mittel und Künste

für

Menschen und Vieh.

Herausgegeben von

Johann Georg Hohmann.

Gedruckt bei Theo. F. Scheffer.

Harrisburg, Pa.

Figure 6.2. Title page of the 1854 German-language edition of Johann Georg Hohmann's *Der Lang Verborgener Freund*.

throughout the surrounding region (C. Brown 1904: 90–91, 126–33; Yoder 1990: 99; compare Wrenshall 1902).

It is interesting that Hohmann recorded many invocation phrases in his first edition using the original Latin spellings, whereas the remainder of his text was in German (fig. 6.1). One might wonder why Hohmann did not render the rotas palindrome in German. Yet, the use of an alternative linguistic code such as Latin in the expression of spiritual invocations is a frequent phenomenon and is used to "signal a special frame of interpretation" and mystical purpose (Keane 1997: 52).

These German-American folk religion practices had direct historical links with cultural practices in Germany. For example, Hohmann and another author of a German-American charm book, G. F. Helfenstein, were both born in Germany and emigrated to America as adults in the eighteenth century (Yoder 1980: 236, 241). Moreover, historical studies of popular culture traditions in the districts of Germany in the fifteenth through nineteenth centuries demonstrate a robust array of comparable folk religion beliefs (for example, Bever 1983: 112–13, 312–17; Davis 1982: 329–31; Dixon 1996: 120–28; Midelfort 1972: 23; 1982: 184–87; Rowlands 1996; Rublack 1992: 159–62).

The rotas palindrome was used extensively within German folk religion invocations for centuries leading up to the time of emigrations to America (Gunn 1969: 4). Similar Latin phrases and references to the Holy Trinity and the wounds of Christ were incorporated into spiritual supplications for healing and protection that have been recorded from at least the fifteenth century onward. Historian Gerald Strauss provides a detailed description of these beliefs and practices as recorded by an administrative official in the district of Wiesbaden, Germany, in 1594:

> "All the people hereabouts engage in superstitious practices with familiar and unfamiliar words, names, and rhymes, especially with the name of God, the Holy Trinity, certain angels, the Virgin Mary, the twelve Apostles, the Three Kings, numerous saints, the wounds of Christ, his seven words on the Cross, verses from the New Testament. . . . These are spoken secretly or openly, they are written on scraps of paper, swallowed . . . or worn as charms. They also make strange signs, crosses, gestures; they do things with herbs, roots, branches of special trees; they have their particular days, hours, and places for everything, and in all their deeds and words they make much use of the number three. And all this is done to work harm on others or to do good, to make things better or worse, or bring good or bad luck to their fellow men." (Strauss 1975: 62–63, quoting Hessisches Hauptstaatsarchiv Wiesbaden, Abt. 137, no. 1, f. 9)

Contrary to Keith Thomas' (1971) thesis, neither the Protestant Reformation nor the development of Enlightenment ideologies eliminated such folk religion beliefs in that region (Dixon 1996: 128; Fennell 2000: 289; Tambiah 1990: 19–23; Yoder 1990: 95). These customs remained popular in the districts of Germany through at least the nineteenth century (for example, Behringer 1997: 65–67, 84–89; Johnson 1996: 184–85; Scribner 1987: 7–14).

Thomas' (1971) influential analysis of European history in *Religion and the Decline of Magic* provides a primary intellectual basis for a tendency among researchers to assume that European settlers in the American colonies would not have practiced conjuration or divination practices. He argued that an increasingly rationalized Christian religion fully displaced systems of folk magic in European cultures over the last few centuries. Thomas (1971: 223) found that folk magic, pre-Reformation Christianity, and so-called pagan philosophies all shared basic attributes: "The universe was peopled by a hierarchy of spirits, and thought to manifest all kinds of occult influences and sympathies. The cosmos was an organic unity in which every part bore a sympathetic relationship to the rest. Even colours, letters and numbers were endowed with magical properties." Thomas contended, however, that folk magic and pagan philosophies, if not Catholicism, were swept away by the tides of the Reformation. This religious movement introduced a new worldview of separated spiritual and physical realms, and it declared illusory a panoply of intermediate spirits and intercessory saints. Enlightenment philosophies developed in near parallel, emphasizing for the academic and intellectual sectors of these societies a distinct separation of spirit and mind from nature, cause, and effect (641–68).

A primary flaw in Thomas' argument is seen in the ample evidence that many members of European ethnic groups continued to practice folk religions during and after the Reformation and Enlightenment (for example, Tambiah 1990: 19–23). This occurred even though the Reformation sought to sweep away the complex cosmology of Catholicism, its legions of hierarchical spirits and intercessory saints, and the practice of supplication to so many guardian spirits (for example, Yoder 1990: 95). Both the Reformation and Enlightenment humanism are based on the assumption that the divine is separate from the natural, physical world in which humans live out their lives. Ironically, the internal logic of those religious and intellectual movements likely facilitated the *persistence* of beliefs in folk magic.

Enlightenment humanism would draw a sharp line between the phenomena of mind and spirit versus the phenomenal world of nature and the physical trappings of humankind's daily existence. Thus, invisible forces such as gravity and the invisible forces of nonpersonified spiritual power would be articulated in parallel developments (Wagner 1986: 111). This parallel resulted because divine power was reconceptualized in fifteenth-century Catholicism and in the sixteenth-century Reformation as something that existed separate from the personified presence of God or Christ. One could access divine power without invoking the physical presence of a creator or Messiah. Conversely, one could seek to inflict malevolence by invoking a free-floating pool of evil power (also God's creation) without invoking the physical presence of a personified Satan (Fennell 2000: 288–90).

Rather than obviate widespread customs of folk magic and conjuration in Europe, this trajectory of the Reformation and Enlightenment simply drove them underground, making them less visible to the ecclesiastical, judicial, and academic segments of European societies (Scribner 1987: 44; Yoder 1990: 95). Moreover, those new religious and intellectual ideologies did not supplant the logic of folk magic, and instead facilitated those formulations by articulating the existence of nonpersonified forces that could be accessed by any person. Religion scholar Albert Raboteau (1980: 287–88) argues further that "Christianity, especially on the popular level, has a certain tendency to appropriate and baptize magical lore from other traditions. In an important sense, conjure and Christianity were not so much antithetical as complementary."

Social Networks and Interpersonal Conflicts

If the inscribed figure of a skull uncovered at the Demory site in Loudoun County was the product of German-American hexerei beliefs, who might have created it? A related question is the identity of the persons who built or occupied the log house in which the skull figure was uncovered. Architectural evidence concerning the design and construction techniques employed in building this house show that it was constructed in accordance with distinctive German-American traditions that were popular in this region during the late 1700s and early 1800s.

Walking around the outside and interior of the small log house on the old Demory property, I was immediately impressed by both its resilience and elegance of design (see fig. 2.1). The main structure was erected with practically no hardware. The builders had dug a level area into the sloping hillside and laid out the rectangular box of the foundation wall. They had stacked twenty- to forty-pound pieces of local rock, hefting them into place and creating a careful progression of close-fitting shapes, without any mortar. The foundation walls rose up at least two feet wide at all points, so that they could carry not only the thick logs of the house walls, but also the ends of similar, hand-hewn "sleeper" joists that suspended the floor over the underlying dirt. On the eastern, upslope side, the foundation wall is no more than a foot tall, but it increases in height as it extends downhill, stretching out like a flat-topped wedge to a few feet in height on the west side. A cube-shaped pier of the same rockwork was placed roughly in the center of the enclosed house floor, on which the builders erected a central chimney of coarse bricks.

On this foundation they built a house one-and-a-half stories tall, one room deep, and two rooms wide, constructed of thick timbers cut from the surrounding woods. These timbers are hand-hewn on all sides, and are typically twelve inches tall and six to eight inches wide. The builders smoothed the surfaces of the logs without the use of a saw, instead making skilled use of a drawing knife, adze, or other finishing tool. Then a series of sill beams was positioned horizontally along the length of each foundation wall, creating the base beams over which successive timbers would rise in alignment. The builders joined these layers of carved logs at the corners of the house with a joint often referred to as a V notch. No hardware—not a spike, nail, peg, or bracket—was used to reinforce these joints. Securing the timbers together by cutting them into interlocking shapes at the corners created small vertical spaces between the logs along the course of the wall. The builders filled those spaces with small pieces of the local stone—a technique called chinking—and likely covered that with clay from the subsoil lying just a foot or so beneath the ground cover. Additional plaster was smoothed over the interior sides of the walls.

The house is twenty feet long and fourteen feet wide, with an eighteen-inch-square chimney placed off-center, approximately six feet in from the south facade and eight feet in from the west facade (fig. 6.3). It is oriented on a west-facing mountain slope, roughly along the cardinal directions, with its long side running east to west. The design did not include a fireplace; instead, the central brick chimney served two stoves placed in adjacent rooms of the first floor. An off-center front door on the south facade is matched by an off-center rear doorway on the north side of the house. Just inside that north doorway is a collapsed box stair, leading to the half-story loft area above. A partition wall for this stair extends out to the chimney stack on the ground floor, separating a slightly larger room on the west side of the ground floor from a smaller room on the east side, which contains the stair (fig. 6.3). The surviving floorboards were cut with a straight saw and ride on top of the hand-hewn sleeper joists, which run north-south with their ends resting on the stone foundation, just inside the baselines of the timber walls.

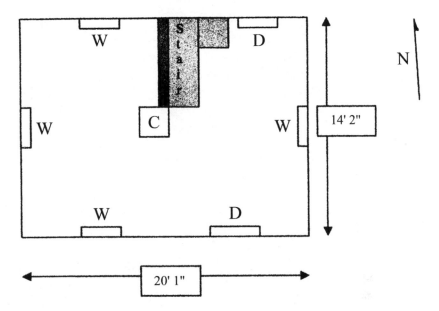

Figure 6.3. Floor plan of the Demory site house, with doors (D), windows (W), and chimney (C) marked. (Image by the author)

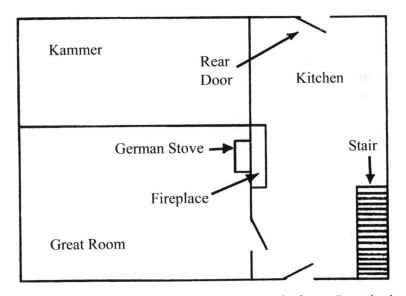

Figure 6.4. Floor plan of a typical German-American log house. (Image by the author)

Evidence of the existence of past social relationships based on ethnic identities can provide valuable data on the possible dynamics of past interactions between builders of this house and other households, craftspeople, or merchants in the area. The stylistic shaping of material culture, including the architectural styles and construction methods used in building dwellings, can function as an overt form of information exchange, broadcasting statements of group affiliation (for example, Wobst 1977: 327–28). Put another way, the design and construction choices exhibited in houses can "embody their creators and become for the period of their existence active images of their creators' wishes" (Glassie 1987: 231; see also Barrick 1986: 15).

Some residents of the Loudoun Valley today speak of the many old log houses in the region as representing rather shabby specimens of dwellings when compared to the alternatives of frame, brick, and clapboard houses. They express a bias that could be heard during the colonial and antebellum periods as well. For example, Yardley Taylor traveled through the Loudoun County area in the late 1840s and early 1850s, and published a memoir of his travels and thoughts about the character of the region in 1853. He noted that the Loudoun Valley and other portions of the northwestern region of the county "were originally settled by Germans, principally from Pennsylvania, and many of their descendants remain" in the area (Taylor 1999: 6). Observing the generally frugal disposition of these residents, he issued his disapproving judgment that "[t]his class of population seldom goes to much expense in building houses" and "[m]any old log houses that are barely tolerable, are in use by persons abundantly able to build better ones" (Taylor 1999: 6). When examined from a less biased perspective, however, one instead gains a great appreciation for the skill and industry that created those homes.

An extensive array of architectural history studies address the sources of design and construction methods used in many forms of log house construction in the American colonial and antebellum periods. From these studies emerge a number of fairly consistent trends in log house designs that are directly relevant to the traditions likely applied in the building of the Demory house. Distinctive patterns of stylistic preferences in house designs and construction techniques have been associated with German immigrants in the Pennsylvania and Virginia regions in the late 1700s and early 1800s (for example, Bucher 1962; Glassie 1965, 1968, 2000; Jordan 1980; Kniffen 1965; Kniffen and Glassie 1966; Lay 1982; Weaver 1986).

Although these trends were observable and significant, one cannot identify a particular ethnic group as having rigidly employed some unique and singular criterion in their design and construction techniques. For example, identifying a house as the product of Scots-Irish or German builders based only on the specific corner-notching technique or on chimney placement remains speculative due to close affinities in construction practices between these groups (Weslager 1969: 212, 239; see also Glassie 1978: 398; Wells 1998: 401–2). These similarities may have developed as the intragroup homogeneity of particular immigrant communities gave way to frequent intergroup borrowing as different settler populations interacted in the colonies (Weslager 1969: 241). Similar borrowing could have occurred among free African Americans and the German and Scots-Irish settlers as well, and African Americans were known to build various types of log houses by the late eighteenth century (Weslager 1969: 245; compare Horning 1999: 130). Nonetheless, a distinctive pattern of notable and repeated combinations of multiple design elements was observable in German-American building in certain areas and time periods.

A form of the basic "hall-and-parlor" plan was the most common design known to have been used in the middle and southern regions of the districts of Germany from which many people emigrated in the seventeenth through nineteenth centuries. This plan consisted of two rooms, called the Küche and Stube, with the latter functioning as a stove room within the house and being the design element most frequently associated with this German architectural tradition (Weaver 1986: 253). This house plan typically included a central chimney, with a hearth opening into the Küche and a stove opening into the Stube. A smaller room called the Kammer was often located on an upper story in German houses and served as the equivalent of the English sleeping chamber. Alternatively, some houses had a Kammer partitioned off the back of the Stube on the ground floor (259–60). In a typical German-American version of this design tradition, depicted in figure 6.4, the Stube was often called the Schtuppe or great room, and the Küche was called the Kich or kitchen (for example, Bucher 1962: 14–15; Weaver 1986: 254–58).

Edward Chappell's (1986: 28) study of the distribution of German log house construction in the Shenandoah Valley found a coherent German-American style of domestic architecture that began to dissipate around 1800. Like the rest of the Virginia backcountry, this area was settled in the middle and late eighteenth century by German, Scots-Irish, and English immigrants and their descendants. The traditional German log house forms in this area included a central chimney, a Stube, and a Küche. Front and rear doorways to the house opened into the Küche, which was located to the right of the central chimney in 80 percent of the traditional German houses examined by Chappell. An enclosed box stair led from the Küche to the second-story sleeping chamber (28–30; see fig. 6.4).

Based on these patterns of architectural features and construction techniques, Chappell identified a distinctively German house style and stated that the "shared characteristics of the buildings represent an architectural vocabulary that was one aspect of a transported cultural heritage" (37). He contends that both German and Swiss immigrants to this region maintained a "cohesive ethnic front" and "a strong cultural identity" (40). This assisted them in sustaining close social relationships within their groups that aided each family's ability to succeed in their new settlement. In addition, this ethnic identity was reinforced by external influences, with Anglo-Americans in the region also viewing the German and Swiss immigrants as separate and distinct groups (40–42).

However, this distinctness was not to last. Chappell (42) found that the German-American house tradition began to evolve in the late 1700s in the Shenandoah Valley region. German immigrants experienced pressures from Anglo-Americans to assimilate to broader lines of social and political relationships in this region. Some houses were built in this period with hybrid designs combining a traditional German plan in the interior with the more symmetrical exterior facade of the Anglo-American "I" house design. After 1800, the traditional German design was largely abandoned, and families of German heritage began building houses that more fully incorporated the "I" house style, which contains a central passage (Chappell 1986: 42–43; Glassie 1968: 74–75).

Chappell found that the changes in German families' choices of house styles were not passive expressions of a changing worldview. Instead, these changes reflected active, instrumental expressions of their shifting social relationships and new social identities in nineteenth-century Virginia. House design was actively used as part of a strategy for creating and maintaining those new social relationships by signaling affiliations through the type of house design one chose and lived in. Rather than continuing to use the symbolic expression of house designs to mark ethnic boundaries (Wobst 1977: 327–28), these German families used house designs after 1800 to signal assimilation with a broader array of socioeconomic groups in their area. They accordingly began to diminish their focus on a previous ethnic group affiliation. This instrumental process involved dynamics similar to those seen in the changing stylistic patterns of African and African American group affiliations discussed in earlier chapters.

The Demory house structure exhibits many features consistent with a German-American architectural design and construction method. It has a two-room plan on the first floor with a chimney placed roughly in the center. The overall dimensions of typical German-American two-room houses found in the surrounding region range from twenty to thirty feet in length, and sixteen to eighteen feet in length. The Demory house dimensions of approximately twenty feet by fourteen feet are consistent with that range. The cross-notch technique used at the old Demory house was a basic V notch, which continued to be popular among German settlers in this region in the late eighteenth century (for example, Kniffen and Glassie 1966: 59–60). The Demory house lacks a plate for rafters, which are fastened instead onto the topmost log of the side walls. Anglo-American builders more frequently supported rafters with an underlying plate that was set on the uppermost wall logs (Fennell 2003a: 210; Kniffen and Glassie 1966: 59–60).

The floor plan of the Demory house is also consistent with known German-American designs in the region (compare figs. 6.3 and 6.4). The front of the house faced south, providing the benefit of sun exposure at this northern latitude. There are two rooms on the main floor, one slightly larger than the other, and a central chimney that served two stoves, one placed on the great room side and another on the kitchen side. Additional sleeping spaces were located in the upper floor, reached by an L-shaped box stair at the rear of the kitchen (fig. 6.3). On the first floor, a partition wall extended out from the rear wall along this box stair and ended where it met the chimney. Another partition wall, with a doorway opening built into it, likely extended back from the front wall to the chimney to meet up with this rear partition, separating the kitchen and great room.

This floor plan is also generally consistent with the basic hall-and-parlor plan popular among Anglo-Americans and Scots-Irish in this region and time period. However, one of the more distinctive features of many German-American house designs in this area and time span was the use of a central chimney with a stove in the Stube (parlor) and large hearth in the Küche (hall or kitchen) (fig. 6.4). This pattern was modified in later German-American home designs to utilize stoves in both rooms. Anglo-American and Scots-Irish houses occasionally used central chimneys but were rarely known to use two stoves with no fireplace (for example, W. Roberts 1986: 269; Weaver 1986: 258).

Based on the patterns of architectural features in the Demory house, it is persuasive to conclude that this structure was built by someone knowledgeable of the building traditions and techniques used by German-Americans in this region during the late eighteenth and early nineteenth centuries. The documentary evidence indicates that the Demory family included persons of German heritage and that they were in close social interaction with German-American neighbors. The Demorys may themselves have known the customs of design and building techniques utilized in constructing this house, or they may have learned those skills from neighbors. Another possibility is that the Demorys subleased the land to a German-American family who built the house and then vacated the premises when the Demorys took occupancy.

What would the use of such a German-American design communicate to persons residing in, visiting, or walking by this house? As discussed earlier in this chapter, the German settlement in Loudoun County remained a cohesive and resilient ethnic enclave for a few decades longer than did comparable settlements in the Shenandoah Valley. Yet, in both areas the distinctive design motifs of the German house plan were adopted and modified by neighboring settlers of Scots-Irish, Anglo-American, and African American heritage as well. Similarly, German-American immigrants began innovating and varying their primary design features as they adjusted to new settings and interacted with other groups.

As Chappell (1986: 37) demonstrated, up through the end of the eighteenth century a distinctive German-American house design existed that was emblematic of that group's heritage and communicated a group identity for immigrants who utilized that shared heritage in forming local social networks. We see here examples of the operations of a habitus and of the dynamic interactions of individual innovations and shared cultural traditions, as discussed at a more general level in chapter 3. In early stages of settlement, German-Americans likely employed this consistent, emblematic style in an unconscious and routinized application of learned customs. In time, it was likely utilized consciously to signal a household's affiliation with the shared experiences and linguistic and cultural heritage of German-American immigrants. The design choice would also signal the residents' desire to create and maintain social and economic relationships with their German-American neighbors. Among other values associated with this stylistic choice was a perceived preference for an industrious and frugal approach to the operation of agrarian households that focused their resources more on productive capabilities than on domestic extravagance.

This emblematic quality of the German-American house design started to erode by the early 1800s. Ambiguous forms began to appear as persons of German heritage innovated on the design features of the older, emblematic composition. Such innovations were likely motivated by practical contingencies of their new settlement settings as well as by interactions with other social groups, such as Scots-Irish and Anglo-American neighbors, who employed different techniques of design and construction. Stylistic ambiguity and the erosion of a consistent, emblematic design motif also arose as members of those other social groups adopted many of the features of the German-American design for their own use. In doing so, they diminished the previous association of that style with persons of German heritage alone. These builders of ambiguous design forms, both within the communities of German-American immigrants and without, were not adrift in compositional incompetence. Rather, they likely employed ambiguity to signal their openness to forming new affiliations in a setting of shifting social networks (see, for example, Bowser 2000: 239–40).

Considering the evidence from sources such as census lists, church records, land deeds, leases, and the patterns of regional architectural traditions, we return to the questions of who built the log house on a twenty-two-acre parcel purchased by the Demorys and of who created the skull figure. Three primary interpretations emerge from the available evidence. I will refer to these alternative scenarios as family construction and discord, Bateman's revenge, and Emory's curse.

FAMILY CONSTRUCTION AND DISCORD

Peter Demory appears to have taken responsibility for renting a 120-acre parcel, called Near's lease, from the Fairfax family starting in the 1790s. In approximately 1804, he purchased a large tract of land situated on the Loudoun Valley floor, on which he resided until his death. By the time of his demise, that main farmstead had grown to 146 acres in size. He did not purchase the twenty-two-acre parcel, which was a subset of Near's lease, until 1811 (Fennell 2003a: 56–57). However, it is possible that he initially lived on the twenty-two-acre parcel and that his family, including persons of German-American heritage on his wife's side, built the log house there and lived in it until they had constructed a new home on the larger parcel downslope. If so, he would have built the house purely in the status of a renter. He may have vacated the log house to take up residence on the 146-acre parcel after 1804, and then purchased the 22-acre parcel a few years later to reclaim the resources his family had developed there.

It is possible that a member of Peter Demory's family created the clay figure as well. While unlikely, internal family conflicts could have been sufficiently severe to motivate another family member to target Mary, Mahlon, Margaretha, or Harry with such a malevolent expression (compare Henretta 1978: 22). In addition, Phillip and Barbara Doerry owned an upland parcel of land bordering the location of the log house. Conflicts may have arisen among the neighboring families, and a member of the Demory household could have created the clay figure to target a member of the Doerry family. Under the beliefs of hexerei, one buried the material component of a curse to symbolize the demise of the targeted person (Fennell 2000: 299). Therefore, burial of the object under the Demory house floor would still be consistent with efforts to target an outsider. This possibility appears unlikely, however, as I have yet to find evidence of a member of the Doerry family with a first initial of M or H during this period.

BATEMAN'S REVENGE

Census records show that a person named Thomas Bateman and his family resided next to the property on which Peter Demory lived at the time of the 1810 census (Fennell 2003a: 167). At that time, the Demory family likely lived on the larger tract of land located downhill from the old log house. Peter had continued to pay rent to the Fairfax family for use of Near's lease up through the time of his 1811 purchase of the smaller, twenty-two-acre parcel. The Bateman family is not mentioned in deed papers as having been neighboring landowners near the Demorys, and they may instead have sublet from the Demorys the land on which the log house stands. The Batemans could have been the builders of the log house. The Bateman family disappears from the census lists of Loudoun County residents after 1810 (Fennell 2003a: 167–77). Given these facts, one could infer that they may have been forced to vacate their farm and the log house sometime shortly after Peter purchased the twenty-two-acre parcel in 1811.

The surname Bateman is an anglicized version of a German name and a variant of the German surname Bethmann (G. Jones 1990: 73, 80; Reaney 1991: 31). It is possible that members of this family were knowledgeable about German-American building techniques, and that they applied those skills and stylistic preferences in constructing the log house. It is also possible that a member of the Bateman family was a practitioner of the German-American folk religion beliefs that included the rotas charm, and that this person created the clay skull figure to retaliate against one of the Demorys for this eviction.

EMORY'S CURSE

It was not until 1830 that Mahlon and William Demory appeared for the first time on the census rolls as heads of their own households, residing in dwellings adjacent to Peter and Mary's farm. In 1820, William Emory and his family were next-door neighbors to Peter and Mary. After that time, the Emory family does not appear again on the census lists as residents of Loudoun County (Fennell 2003a: 167–77). Here too, the Emory family may have been renting the land and log house from the Demorys and been forced to vacate sometime before 1830 when Mahlon and William took up residence on parcels surrounding their parents' farm.

One should ask whether "William Emory" was simply a mistaken recording of William Demory's name in the 1820 census. William Emory does not appear as a head of household in Loudoun County in 1810 or in the decennial census lists for 1830–1850. He was recorded in the 1820 census as being more than forty-five years of age. In the terminology of the 1820 census ledger, his household included one male under ten years of age, one male sixteen to twenty-five years of age, one female under ten years of age, one female sixteen to twenty-five years of age, and no enslaved persons. William Demory, born in 1790, would not have been more than forty-five years of age in 1820. His wife at that time, Mary Long, was twenty-six years old in 1820, close to fitting the category of the female of sixteen to twenty-five years recorded for the Emory household. William and Mary Demory's son Amos would fit the category of a male child under ten years of age that was recorded for the Emory household. However, William and Mary had no daughter who would fit the category of a child under ten years of age, and one cannot readily match another member of the Demory family with the male of sixteen to twenty-five years in age listed as residing in the Emory household (Fennell 2003a: 169–71). Given these multiple points of divergence, it is unlikely that William Emory's residence was actually the poorly recorded household of William Demory.

The Emory name is an English surname in many instances, but can also be an anglicized version of the German surnames Emmer or Emmerich (G. Jones 1990: 116; Reaney 1991: 155). Families named Emery, Emmerich, and Emich were members of the local German-American church denominations in northern Loudoun County in the late 1700s (Hiatt 1995; Hiatt and Scott 1995; Mower and Mower 1993). Thus, a member of William Emory's family could have been a practitioner of the German-American customs of hexerei and could have created the clay figure to retaliate against Mary, Mahlon, or Margaretha Demory.

Expressions Instrumental and Emblematic

What type of stylistic expression would an object like the Loudoun skull figure represent? Applying the theoretical framework outlined in previous chapters, would this object appear to have functioned as an emblematic or instrumental stylistic expression? Although it is designed with a rich symbolic composition, such folk religion objects could not easily serve as emblematic expressions. Designs shaped to harm a particular individual were likely not displayed with any appreciable visibility even within a small, cohesive group. The person who created the object may have displayed it to companions for a short period before burying it out of view, and such communications could have reinforced these individuals' subscription to a shared meaning system of hexerei and related cultural associations. The low visibility resulted from the malevolent intent of the expression, which made it far more of an instrumental and assertive form than emblematic form of stylistic communication.

However, the same belief system was also expressed in many forms of benevolent, protective, and benign invocations of spiritual forces to ward off disease, injury, and accidents. Objects designed with such protective symbolism could often be displayed in visible ways in intragroup and intergroup settings, and could serve as relatively emblematic expressions of a group's identity (Fennell 2000: 306–8). Indeed, Hohmann's *Der Lang Verborgener Freund* depicted many such symbolic motifs for use in healing and protective invocations, and a person's ownership and display of that book may have served as a signal of group identity within German-American enclaves. But what group identity would have been communicated?

The degree to which the stylistic motifs of hexerei would be read as indicators of German-American community identity would depend upon the viewing audience and the social setting. Persons of German heritage no doubt varied in their beliefs, with some subscribing to these customs, some tolerating them, and others condemning them. Within such a group, particular beliefs and practices would serve as emblematic expressions of the collectivity primarily if those beliefs were part of the key ascriptive criteria for membership in the social group (see, for example, Emberling 1997: 318–20; Wolf 1972: 150). Thus, one can imagine past small-scale groupings of practitioners and believers of hexerei for whom such expressions could be emblematic. In contrast, there no doubt existed larger-scale social networks of neighboring German-American farmers for whom such folk religion beliefs would not be emblematic. This would result if only some community members were practitioners and subscription to hexerei did not serve as a key criterion for membership in that larger social network.

If outsiders associated symbols of hexerei with some German-Americans, they might then broaden that association to encompass all German-American residents in the area. Outsiders often paint with broad brushstrokes in a manner designed to characterize another social group in an unflattering way. The Anglo-Americans who derisively referred to German immigrant families as "Palatine boors" might be expected to make the limited use of folk religion symbols by a number of German-American individuals the basis for a broad-brush indictment of an entire community of German-American settlers. However, no virulent campaigns of religious persecution or witchcraft accusations were ever targeted against the German-American communities in this region and time period.

On a more general level, private expressions of symbolism such as conjuration or hexerei can be divided into two analytic categories with regard to the creation or maintenance of social group boundaries. As discussed in chapter 3, one category includes artifacts that communicated intergroup messages of an ethnic group's social and political boundaries. In some contexts, this category includes artifacts that openly communicated religious beliefs in essentially benevolent, benign, or protective powers. The second category includes artifacts that communicated messages involving the possession or exercise of power in a manner that was malevolent or otherwise threatening to others. These artifacts likely involved information that was communicated only within the group that created them or was communicated only in covert manners, and the meaning of such material compositions was likely not meant to be communicated to outsiders. Such artifacts may still have played a role in maintaining ethnic boundedness within the group that created them, as secrecy and shared beliefs create their own bonds.

What other functions of individual and assertive expression might conjuration practices have served in intragroup settings? Such religious beliefs and practices provided a means of explaining misfortune and evil outcomes as the result of the individual conduct and intentions of others, rather than as mere happenstance or fate (Briggs 1996: 61; Krige 1982: 263; Marwick 1982: 462–63; Young 1997: 20–24). Conjuration practices thus provided a means for self-initiative, resistance, and retaliation against the conduct and desires of perceived adversaries (Leone and Fry 1999: 384; McKee 1995: 41; Wilkie 1997: 83–84).

Raboteau (1980: 286) described these social functions within communities of enslaved Africans and African Americans in a manner equally applicable to the beliefs and practices of European-Americans in New World locations of the same time periods:

[C]onjure served as a perfect vehicle for expressing and alleviating anger, jealousy, and sheer ill will among slaves. When unable to settle disputes openly, the slaves turned to the secret system of conjure. Primarily, conjure was a method of control: first, the control which comes from knowledge—being able to explain crucial phenomena, such as illness, misfortune and evil; second, the control which comes from the capacity to act effectively . . . ; third, a means of control over the future through reading the "signs"; fourth, an aid to social control because it supplied a system whereby conflict, otherwise stifled, could be aired.

Even in situations where a targeted person discovered a conjuration object directed at him or her with malevolent intent, and took responsive action, the action and reaction provided a means of social ventilation of a growing interpersonal dispute (Wilkie 1997: 89). These functions likely applied even when malevolent conjuration practices were targeted against persons who were members of other ethnic groups. Such conduct would not signal ethnic boundaries, but rather would undercut them, as a manifestation of interpersonal conflicts that were being addressed with a knowledge system and basic mode of expression recognizable to members of multiple ethnic groups (Wilkie 1997: 84).

Myriad European and African cultures independently developed various modes of instrumental symbolism for invoking spiritual forces for protection, healing, and aggression. In addition to people of German heritage, those of English, French, Dutch, Irish, Scots, Spanish, and Portuguese cultures, to name just a few, engaged in comparable beliefs and practices. An analyst would be short-sighted simply to assume that the instrumental symbolism of one social group would have been incomprehensible to someone from another culture. The multivalence of such symbolism provided opportunities for intergroup communications, even when the conveyed meanings remained to be negotiated. In settings of asymmetrical power relations between groups, such communications could lead to increased tensions and conflict. In circumstances of relatively cooperative power relations, such communications could help build new social networks over time, through a process I describe in the next chapter as ethnogenic bricolage.

7

Creolization, Hybridity, and Ethnogenic Bricolage

By focusing on the spectrum of emblematic and instrumental expressions of core symbols, this study makes two contributions to studies of diasporas. First, it establishes that the artifacts of African American religious practices found in North American sites did not represent merely the shreds and tatters of past African cultures. Rather, those artifacts represented the continuing use and development of private ritual undertakings that were vital components of those cultures even when practiced within dominant belief systems in west and west central Africa. Such points of correspondence are highlighted by analyzing those artifacts through the application of a detailed ethnohistorical analogy and an associated predictive model. The rich cultural heritage of instrumental traditions within European-American groups, such as immigrants from the Palatine region of Germany, is also evident.

Second, this study has revealed the interplay of disparate instrumental symbols in the creation of new emblematic expressions in locations such as Haiti and Brazil. This process of creation is illuminated by focusing on the points of contrast between developments in North America and the dynamics evident in the Caribbean and South America. These examples illustrate larger-scale mechanisms of symbolic communication and social ordering. The interpretative approach outlined here provides a vehicle for examining the ways in which social group memberships shift over time and space. These changes become manifest as individuals decrease their expression of a previous group identity in their material culture, increase their expression of individually assertive and creative styles, and in turn create and adopt new group identities. Individual exercises of creativity and instrumental symbolic expression provide the ingredients for the formulation of new emblematic symbols. The expression of those new emblematic configurations can then enhance the cohesiveness of new social networks in which those individuals participate. I define this process as ethnogenic bricolage.

I have refrained from referring to this blending of communicative forms as an operation of creolization. Recent symposia have addressed the question of whether concepts of creolization represent an emerging paradigm for the analysis of culture. No consensus has formed even as to a definition for this term as applied in archaeological or folklore studies (see, for example, Baron 2003; Dawdy 2000). Considering the varied uses of the terms *creole* and *creolization,* one might be compelled to ask, "How feasible is dialogue in the abstract when the concrete term itself is so unstable?" (Allen 2002: 48). Some studies of creolization in material culture tend to focus on a limited mixing of new "lexicons" with old "grammars," without analyzing the internal logic of such grammars and how they might change as well (Singleton 1995: 133; 2006: 266). Other creolization studies emphasize the importance of the dominant status of one group over another in past social settings (Gundaker 2000: 125–26).

Archaeologists borrowed the creolization concept from linguistic analysis. This concept of creolization differed from an earlier, largely demographic reference to colonial populations born in New World settings (Mintz 1996: 301–2). As used in linguistics, creolization and pidginization are theoretical constructs for processes that typically involve different cultural groups in contact. Concepts of creolization and pidginization usually posit that such populations engage in a purposeful simplification of communicative forms in a process of accommodation within a context of asymmetrical power relations between the groups (Bickerton 1999; Hymes 1971; Kapchan and Strong 1999; McWhorter 1997; Polomé 1980). Concepts of syncretism or acculturation also usually view one cultural system as dominant and imposing itself upon subordinated systems (Apter 1991: 236–42; Droogers 1989: 16–18; Shaw and Stewart 1994: 6–7).

The histories of diasporas examined in this book certainly played out in a context of European colonial interests exercising power over the members of numerous African cultures. Yet, when one shifts to the question of how members of those African cultures created new social networks in the plantations of the New World, answers are not to be found by looking solely at the exercise of European power. What internal engines of cultural creativity helped animate the development of new social networks within these diasporas?

The simplification and abbreviation of instrumental expressions of core symbols occurred in an internal process that was initially independent of intercultural contact. This is a communicative operation that occurs within the expressive range of core symbols within any coherent, shared meaning system. Yet, that abbreviation and increasing multivalence yields an instrumental expression that will be useful beyond its initial employment in private rituals for individual interests. Such abbreviation also produces multivalent expressions that can aid those social actors in their later attempts to build new relationships with persons from other cultures in contact settings. For persons abducted from different regions of Africa and brought together on New World terrain, that interaction usually involved individuals from groups in comparably subjugated positions, rather than an asymmetry of power relations between them.

This was not a matter of conservative grammars seeking new lexicons or of the subjugated making accommodations to their oppressors. Instead, those African and African American social actors creatively blended multivalent features of their disparate cultural systems to generate new symbolic repertoires to aid in the formation and consolidation of their new social networks. Viewing an ethnicity as a socially constructed concept of group identity, this process is more aptly characterized as ethnogenic bricolage.

I use this term to incorporate key facets of Claude Lévi-Strauss' (1966) concept of "bricolage" and to apply those concepts to a different setting of intercultural interactions. Lévi-Strauss (1966: 17) conceptualized a "bricoleur" as a practical, innovative manipulator of cultural knowledge within the bounded frame of an isolated social group. Lévi-Strauss (17) emphasized that the bricoleur's "universe of instruments is closed and the rules of his game are always to make do with 'whatever is at hand,' that is to say with a set of tools and materials which is always finite and is also heterogeneous." Distinguishing bricolage from more deductive forms of western, "scientific knowledge," Lévi-Strauss (16–36) demonstrated that bricolage can generate equally valid cultural expressions and knowledge claims in a "science of the concrete." A bricoleur thus engaged in formulating cultural forms and expressions, such as myths, through rearrangements and combinations of the varied components of his or her group's "finite set" of past traditions and symbolic compositions (Hénaff 1998: 144–45; compare D. Brown 1990: 20–21).

Theoretical paradigms in anthropology and sociology have moved beyond the limitations of Lévi-Strauss' structuralist framework (see, for example, Geertz 1973; Giddens 1979). However, his concept of bricolage incorporates very useful facets that can be applied in new ways (Dumont 1985; Hebdige 1999: 102–6). When moved to a setting of intercultural negotiation, one can conceive of multiple bricoleurs confronting open sets of cultural materials from various interacting cultural groups. In a process of ethnogenic bricolage, individuals of different cultural heritages interact over time to formulate new social networks with new repertoires of key symbols, communicative domains, and cultural practices. Those new symbols are created and developed over time in large part through engagements with the multiple elements of abbreviated, multivalent symbols from each of the contributing cultural groups (Fennell 2003b).

Jean Comaroff's (1985: 11, 196–99) excellent study of the Tshidi people of South Africa outlined a form of "subversive bricolage." She conducted a historical and ethnographic study of an intercultural context in which colonial power was imposed by Europeans over the Barolong boo Ratshidi (the Tshidi). The Tshidi people comprise a culture group governed by a Tswana chiefdom located in the borderland between Botswana and South Africa (see fig. 1.2). Comaroff's (1985: 194–251) analysis of changes in Tshidi culture over time demonstrated the ways in which members of that group succeeded in breaking down the facets of key symbols of European Christianity and recombining those components to create new forms of symbolic communication and cultural practice in opposition to the colonial regime. Such innovations over time "are at once both expressive and pragmatic, for they aim to change the real world by inducing transformations in the world of symbol and rite" (198).

Comaroff's application of a concept of bricolage thus differed from that formulated by Lévi-Strauss, who had articulated a creative process for a cultural actor within a single, closed cultural system (Hénaff 1998: 144–45). Comaroff revealed how such a creative process plays out in intercultural settings, with open sets of cultural elements that are susceptible to manipulation and change over time. Examining a colonial setting with two cultural groups possessing very different levels of power, she found a *subversive* bricolage at work among the Tshidi.

Examining New World contexts, we certainly see comparable incidents of subversive bricolage, as followers of Haitian Vodun, Brazilian Macumba, and Cuban Santería subverted Christian symbols in the creation of new symbolic motifs that summarized key aspects of their new cultural traditions. Afro-Christian traditions in North America entailed similar dynamics. However, we also see an increased number of interacting and contributing cultures, including several lines of African cultural heritages, indigenous cultures, and European influences. These New World contexts show a dynamism in which such multiple cultural traditions were being reconfigured to form new social networks—new, socially constructed ethnicities—and related domains of symbolism, ritual, and practice. In these New World examples, a multiplicity of groups of African and indigenous heritage, interacting on fairly even levels of social power, were engaged in a process more aptly described by the terms of *ethnogenic* bricolage.

I advocate such a specific label for this process because of the recent malaise in social theorists' deployment of the concepts of creolization and hybridity. Michel-Rolph Trouillot (1998: 8) captured the sentiments of many anthropologists and historians when he observed that "[c]reolization is a miracle begging for analysis." Unfortunately, the utility of this analytic concept has been significantly eroded by its ubiquitous and varied employment. Many sociocultural theorists have adopted the terms creolization and hybridity as interchangeable labels for virtually all moments of cultural creativity (for example, Hannerz 1987; Hutnyk 2005).

This universalizing tendency has followed a trend among many social theorists to focus on individuals as the primary agents of all cultural operations. Such analysts have increasingly abandoned any focus on concepts of stable and coherent cultural systems as phenomena that shape individual perception and conduct. Instead, each individual is viewed as the primary domain of cultural agency, subscribing to and negotiating among multiple social networks simultaneously. Single actors are viewed as the constantly engaged operators of hybridity and creolization across those multiple networks. In this perspective, any given culture is constantly in flux as it is negotiated and reconfigured among the individuals who subscribe to and perform it (for example, Baron and Cara 2003; Hannerz 1987; Hutnyk 2005). In essence, the interdependence of individual agents and social structures, as articulated by theorists such as Pierre Bourdieu (1977) and Anthony Giddens (1979), has been replaced by some analysts with a greater focus on individual agency and a disregard of stable structures.

The weakness in an almost universal invocation of the ideas of hybridity and creolization is that it is "too sweeping" and undefined to yield constructive dialogue among researchers, social analysts, and community members (Trouillot 1998: 34–36; see also Khan 2004: 169; Szwed 2003: 14–17). Historians and archaeologists focus on subjects with broad temporal and geographic scales. They therefore tend to see the impacts both of periods of stable social structures and episodes of change and innovation. For a social anthropologist studying a contemporary urban setting for a much shorter time period, creolization might be viewed as one individual's daily, transient selections from the cultural palettes of multiple social networks. In contrast, historians typically view creolization as involving the interactions of multiple cultures and their structures of beliefs and practices. This divergence in perspectives is in part a direct result of the difference in temporal and social scales of the subjects under study.

Within studies of African diasporas, Sidney Mintz and Richard Price (1976) advocated the use of a creolization model patterned after the grammar and lexicon approaches in linguistics. This framework is superior to more universalized concepts of hybridity, in that it provides a more specific definition of the analytic methods to be employed. Researchers utilizing this approach should not assume that there existed some form of "pan-African" grammar in an abstract and unconscious form. Instead, they should utilize the expanded historical studies of the African cultures impacted by the transatlantic slave trade to articulate more specifically the features of a "grammar" associated with each of those particular cultures (Hall 2005: 169–70; Singleton 2006: 266; Trouillot 1998: 21).

The analysis presented in this book advances this goal. I have worked to articulate significant features of the cultural belief systems and repertoires of symbolic communication that can be said to have made up part of the distinct cultural "grammars" of social groups such as the BaKongo and Yoruba. We must then ask how such specific grammars would change over time and be applied in new settings. I have formulated a methodology for this next, challenging step, based on the formulation of particular ethnohistorical analogies and associated predictive models. This approach enables us to see the workings of specific engines of cultural change, such as the ethnogenic bricolage that played out in particular cultures in the New World. By applying this methodology to the histories of additional African cultures and their diasporas, I hope that other researchers can reveal comparable insights in new domains.

Bibliography

Adams, Eric. 1994. "Religion and Freedom: Artifacts Indicate That African Culture Persisted Even in Slavery." *African-American Archaeology* 11: 1–2.

Agorsah, Kofi. 1996. "The Archaeology of the African Diaspora." *African Archaeological Review* 13 (4): 221–24.

Ahmad, Yahya. 2006. "The Scope and Definitions of Heritage: From Tangible to Intangible." *International Journal of Heritage Studies* 12 (3): 292–300.

Alexander, J. 2001. "Islam, Archaeology and Slavery in Africa." *World Archaeology* 33 (1): 44–60.

Allen, Carolyn. 2002. "Creole: The Problem of Definition." In *Questioning Creole: Creolisation Discourses in Caribbean Culture: In Honour of Kamau Brathwaite*, edited by Verene A. Shepherd and Glen L. Richards, 47–63. Kingston, Jamaica: Ian Randle.

Apter, Andrew. 1991. "Herskovits's Heritage: Rethinking Syncretism in the African Diaspora." *Diaspora* 1 (3): 235–60.

Asante, Molefi Kete. 1993. "Racism, Consciousness, and Afrocentricity." In *Lure and Loathing: Essays on Race, Identity, and the Ambivalence of Assimilation*, edited by Gerald Early, 127–43. New York: Penguin.

Ascher, Robert. 1961. "Analogy in Archaeological Interpretation." *Southwestern Journal of Anthropology* 17: 317–25.

Ayorinde, Christine. 2000. "*Regla de Ocha-Ifá* and the Construction of Cuban Identity." In *Identity in the Shadow of Slavery*, edited by Paul E. Lovejoy, 72–85. London: Continuum.

———. 2004. "Santería in Cuba: Tradition and Transformation." In *The Yoruba Diaspora in the Atlantic World*, edited by Toyin Falola and Matt D. Childs, 209–30. Bloomington: Indiana University Press.

Bacon, Alicia M., and Leonora Herron. 1896. "Conjuring and Conjure-Doctors in the Southern United States." *Journal of American Folklore* 9: 143–47.

Baerreis, David A. 1961. "The Ethnohistorical Approach and Archaeology." *Ethnohistory* 8 (1): 49–77.

Balandier, Georges. 1968. *Daily Life in the Kingdom of the Kongo: From the Sixteenth to the Eighteenth Century*. Translated by H. Weaver. London: George Allen and Unwin.

Balandier, Georges, and Jacques Maquet. 1974. *Dictionary of Black African Civilization*. New York: Leon Amiel.

Ballard, Eoghan C. 2005. "Ndoki Bueno Ndoki Malo: Historic and Contemporary Kongo Religion in the African Diaspora." PhD diss., University of Pennsylvania.

Banks, Marcus. 1996. *Ethnicity: Anthropological Constructions*. London: Routledge.

Barnes, Sandra T. 1989. "Introduction: The Many Faces of Ogun." In *Africa's Ogun:*

Old World and New, edited by Sandra T. Barnes, 1–26. Bloomington: Indiana University Press.

Barnes, Sandra T., and Paula G. Ben-Amos. 1989. "Ogun, the Empire Builder." In *Africa's Ogun: Old World and New*, edited by Sandra T. Barnes, 39–64. Bloomington: Indiana University Press.

Baron, Robert. 2003. "Amalgams and Mosaics, Syncretisms and Reinterpretations: Reading Herskovits and Contemporary Creolists for Metaphors of Creolization." *Journal of American Folklore* 116 (459): 88–115.

Baron, Robert, and Ana C. Cara. 2003. "Introduction: Creolization and Folklore—Cultural Creativity in Process." *Journal of American Folklore* 116 (459): 4–8.

Barrett, Leonard. 1977. "African Religion in the Americas: The 'Islands in Between.'" In *African Religions: A Symposium*, edited by Newell S. Booth, Jr., 183–215. New York: NOK Publishers.

Barrett, Stanley R. 1991. "Issues and Perspectives on Religion and Society." In *Religion and Society in Nigeria: Historical and Sociological Perspectives*, edited by Jacob K. Olupona and Toyin Falola, 3–30. Ibadan, Nigeria: Spectrum Books.

Barrick, Mac E. 1986. "The Log House as Cultural Symbol." *Material Culture* 18 (1): 1–19.

Barth, Fredrik. 1998a. Introduction to *Ethnic Groups and Boundaries: The Social Organization of Culture Difference*, edited by Fredrik Barth, 9–38. Prospect Heights, Ill.: Waveland Press.

———. 1998b. "Pathan Identity and Its Maintenance." *In Ethnic Groups and Boundaries: The Social Organization of Culture Difference*, edited by Fredrik Barth, 117–34. Prospect Heights, Ill.: Waveland Press.

———. 2000. "Boundaries and Connections." In *Signifying Identities: Anthropological Perspectives on Boundaries and Contested Values*, edited by Andrew P. Cohen, 15–36. London: Routledge.

Bassani, Ezio. 1983. "A Note on Kongo High-Status Caps in Old European Collections." *Res* 5 (Spring): 74–84.

———. 2000. *African Art and Artefacts in European Collections, 1400–1800*. Edited by Malcolm McLeod. London: British Museum Press.

Bastide, Roger. 1978. *The African Religions of Brazil: Toward a Sociology of the Interpretation of Civilizations*. Translated by Helen Sebba. Baltimore: Johns Hopkins University Press.

Beaudry, Mary C., Lauren J. Cook, and Stephen A. Mrozowski. 1991. "Artifacts and Active Voices: Material Culture as Social Discourse." In *The Archaeology of Inequality*, edited by Randall H. McGuire and Robert Paynter, 150–91. Oxford: Blackwell Publishers.

Behringer, Wolfgang. 1997. *Witchcraft Persecutions in Bavaria: Popular Magic, Religious Zealotry and Reasons of State in Early Modern Europe*. Translated by J. C. Grayson and David Lederer. Cambridge, U.K.: Cambridge University Press.

Bell, Michael E. 1980. "Pattern, Structure, and Logic in African-American Hoodoo Performance." PhD diss., Indiana University.

Bentley, G. Carter. 1987. "Ethnicity and Practice." *Comparative Studies in Society and History* 29 (1): 24–55.

———. 1991. "Response to Yelvington." *Comparative Studies in Society and History* 33 (1): 169–75.

Berlin, Ira. 1996. "From Creole to African: Atlantic Creoles and the Origins of African-American Society in Mainland North America." *William & Mary Quarterly,* 3rd ser., 53 (2): 251–88.

———. 1998. *Many Thousands Gone: The First Two Centuries of Slavery in North America.* Cambridge, Mass.: Harvard University Press.

Bever, Edward W. 1983. "Witchcraft in Early Modern Wuerttemberg." PhD diss., Princeton University.

Bickerton, Derek. 1999. "Pidgins and Language Mixture." In *Creole Genesis, Attitudes and Discourse,* edited by John R. Rickford and Suzanne Romaine, 31–44. Amsterdam: John Benjamins.

Binford, Lewis R. 1967. "Smudge Pit and Hide Smoking: The Use of Analogy in Archaeological Reasoning." *American Antiquity* 32: 1–12.

Blassingame, John W. 1972. *The Slave Community: Plantation Life in the Antebellum South.* New York: Oxford University Press.

Bourdieu, Pierre. 1977. *Outline of a Theory of Practice.* Cambridge, U.K.: Cambridge University Press.

Bowser, Brenda J. 2000. "From Pottery to Politics: An Ethnoarchaeological Study of Political Factionalism, Ethnicity, and Domestic Pottery Style in the Ecuadorian Amazon." *Journal of Archaeological Method and Theory* 7 (3): 219–48.

Brandon, George. 1993. *Santeria from Africa to the New World: The Dead Sell Memories.* Bloomington: Indiana University Press.

Briggs, Robin. 1996. "Many Reasons Why: Witchcraft and the Problem of Multiple Explanation." In *Witchcraft in Early Modern Europe: Studies in Culture and Belief,* edited by Jonathan Barry, Marianne Hester, and Gareth Roberts, 49–63. Cambridge, U.K.: Cambridge University Press.

Broadhead, Susan H. 1979. "Beyond Decline: The Kingdom of the Kongo in the Eighteenth and Nineteenth Centuries." *International Journal of African Historical Studies* 12 (4): 615–50.

Brown, Carleton F. 1904. "The Long-Hidden Friend." *Journal of American Folklore* 17: 89–152.

Brown, David F. 1990. "Conjure/Doctors: An Exploration of a Black Discourse in America, Antebellum to 1940." *Folklore Forum* 23 (1/2): 3–46.

Brown, Karen M. 1976. "The 'Veve' of Haitian Vodou: A Structural Analysis of Visual Imagery." PhD diss., Temple University, Philadelphia.

Brown, Kenneth L. 1994. "Material Culture and Community Structure: The Slave and Tenant Community of Levi Jordan's Plantation, 1848–1892." In *Working toward Freedom: Slave Society and Domestic Economy in the American South,* edited by Larry E. Hudson, Jr., 95–118. Rochester, N.Y.: University of Rochester Press.

———. 2001. "Interwoven Traditions: Archaeology at the Conjurer's Cabin and African American Cemetery at the Jordan and Frogmore Plantations." In *Places of Cultural Memory: African Reflections on the American Landscape*, 99–114. Washington, D.C.: National Park Service.

———. 2004. "Ethnographic Analogy, Archaeology, and the African Diaspora: Perspectives from a Tenant Community." *Historical Archaeology* 38 (1): 79–89.

Brown, Kenneth L., and Doreen C. Cooper. 1990. "Structural Continuity in an African-American Slave and Tenant Community." *Historical Archaeology* 24 (4): 7–19.

Brown, Kristine N., and Kenneth L. Brown. 1998. "Archaeology and Spirituality: The Conjurer/Midwife and the Praise House/Church at the Levi Jordan Plantation." Paper presented at the Society for Historical Archaeology Annual Conference, Atlanta, January, 9.

Brown, Ras Michael. 2004. "'Walk in the Feenda': West-Central Africans and the Forest in the South Carolina–Georgia Lowcountry." In *Central Africans and Cultural Transformations in the American Diaspora*, edited by Linda M. Heywood, 289–317. Cambridge, U.K.: Cambridge University Press.

Bruner, Edward M. 1993. "Epilogue: Creative Persona and the Problem of Authenticity." In *Creativity/Anthropology*, edited by Smadar Lavie, Kirin Narayan, and Renato Rosaldo, 321–34. Ithaca, N.Y.: Cornell University Press.

Bucher, Robert C. 1962. "The Continental Log House." *Pennsylvania Folklife* 12 (4): 14–19.

Bullen, A. K., and R. P. Bullen. 1945. "Black Lucy's Garden." *Bulletin of the Massachusetts Archeological Society* 6 (2): 17–28.

Bury, Shirley. 1991. *Jewellery, 1789–1910: The International Era*. Woodbridge, UK: Antique Collectors' Club.

Butler, Jon. 1990. *Awash in a Sea of Faith: Christianizing the American People*. Cambridge, Mass.: Harvard University Press.

———. 2000. *Becoming America: The Revolution before 1776*. Cambridge, Mass.: Harvard University Press.

Cabrera, Lydia. 1979. *Reglas de Congo: Palo Monte Mayombe*. Miami: Peninsular Printing.

Cantwell, Anne-Marie, and Diana diZerega Wall. 2001. *Unearthing Gotham: The Archaeology of New York City*. New Haven, Conn.: Yale University Press.

Carmack, Robert M. 1972. "Ethnohistory: A Review of Its Development, Definitions, Methods, and Aims." *Annual Review of Anthropology* 1: 227–46.

Chamberlin, Taylor M. 2003. *Where Did They Stand? The May 1861 Vote on Secession in Loudoun County, Virginia, and Post-War Claims against the Government*. Waterford, Va.: Waterford Foundation.

Chappell, Edward A. 1986. "Acculturation in the Shenandoah Valley: Rhenish Houses of the Massanutten Settlement." In *Common Places: Readings in American Vernacular Architecture*, edited by Dell Upton and John M. Vlach, 27–57. Athens: University of Georgia Press.

Childs, Matt D., and Toyin Falola. 2004. "The Yoruba Diaspora in the Atlantic World:

Methodology and Research." In *The Yoruba Diaspora in the Atlantic World*, edited by Toyin Falola and Matt D. Childs, 1–14. Bloomington: Indiana University Press.

Chireau, Yvonne P. 2003. *Black Magic: Religion and the African American Conjuring Tradition*. Berkeley: University of California Press.

Cirlot, Juan E. 1962. *A Dictionary of Symbols*. Translated by Jack Sage. New York: Philosophical Library Press.

Cohen, Abner. 1976. *Two-Dimensional Man: An Essay on the Anthropology of Power and Symbolism in Complex Society*. Berkeley: University of California Press.

Cohen, Andrew P., ed. 2000. *Signifying Identities: Anthropological Perspectives on Boundaries and Contested Values*. London: Routledge.

Comaroff, Jean. 1985. *Body of Power, Spirit of Resistance: The Culture and History of a South African People*. Chicago: University of Chicago Press.

Comaroff, John, and Jean Comaroff. 2001. "On Personhood: An Anthropological Perspective from Africa." *Social Identities* 7 (2): 267–83.

Costin, Cathy L. 1996. "Exploring the Relationship between Gender and Craft in Complex Societies: Methodological and Theoretical Issues of Gender Attribution." In *Gender and Archaeology*, edited by Rita P. Wright, 111–40. Philadelphia: University of Pennsylvania Press.

Csikszentmihalyi, Mihaly, and Eugene Rochberg-Halton. 1981. *The Meanings of Things: Domestic Symbols and the Self*. Cambridge, U.K.: Cambridge University Press.

Curtin, Philip D. 1969. *The Atlantic Slave Trade: A Census*. Madison: University of Wisconsin Press.

Cuthrell-Curry, Mary. 2000. "African-Derived Religion in the African-American Community in the United States." In *African Spirituality: Forms, Meanings, and Expressions*, edited by Jacob K. Olupona, 450–66. New York: Crossroad.

David, Nicholas, Judy Sterner, and Kodzo Gavua. 1988. "Why Pots Are Decorated." *Current Anthropology* 29 (3): 365–89.

Davidson, James M. 2004. "Rituals Captured in Context and Time: Charm Use in North Dallas Freedman's Town (1869–1907), Dallas, Texas." *Historical Archaeology* 38 (2): 22–54.

Davis, Natalie Z. 1982. "From 'Popular Religion' to Religious Cultures." In *Reformation Europe: A Guide to Research*, edited by Steven Osmont, 321–41. St. Louis: Center for Reformation Research.

Dawdy, Shannon L. 2000. Preface to Symposium on "Creolization." *Historical Archaeology* 34 (3): 1–4.

Deagan, Kathleen A. 2002. *Artifacts of the Spanish Colonies of Florida and the Caribbean, 1500–1800*. Vol. 2, *Portable Personal Possessions*. Washington, D.C.: Smithsonian Institution Press.

DeBoer, Warren R., and James A. Moore. 1982. "The Measurement and Meaning of Stylistic Diversity." *Nawpa Pacha* 20: 147–62.

DeCorse, Christopher R. 1999. "Oceans Apart: Africanist Perspective on Diaspora

Archaeology." In *I, Too, Am America: Archaeological Studies of African-American Life*, edited by Theresa A. Singleton, 132–55. Charlottesville: University Press of Virginia.

———, ed. 2001. *West Africa during the Atlantic Slave Trade: Archaeological Perspectives*. New York: Leicester University Press.

Deetz, James. 1995. "Cultural Dimensions of Ethnicity in the Archaeological Record." Keynote address presented at the 28th Annual Meeting of the Society for Historical Archaeology, Washington, D.C., January.

———. 1996. *In Small Things Forgotten: An Archaeology of Early American Life*. Rev. and exp. ed. New York: Anchor Books.

Deetz, James, and Patricia Scott Deetz. 2000. *The Times of Their Lives: Life, Love and Death in Plymouth Colony*. New York: W. H. Freeman.

de Heusch, Luc. 1989. "Kongo in Haiti: A New Approach to Religious Syncretism." *Man*, new ser., 24 (2): 290–303.

Denbow, James. 1999. "Heart and Soul: Glimpses of Ideology and Cosmology in the Iconography of Tombstones from the Loango Coast of Central America." *Journal of American Folklore* 112 (445): 404–23.

De Vos, George. 1975. "Ethnic Pluralism: Conflict and Accommodation." In *Ethnic Identity: Cultural Continuities and Change*, edited by George De Vos and Lola Romanucci-Ross, 5–41. Palo Alto, Calif.: Mayfield.

Dietler, Michael, and Ingrid Herbich. 1998. "Habitus, Techniques, Style: An Integrated Approach to the Social Understanding of Material Culture and Boundaries." In *The Archaeology of Social Boundaries*, edited by Miriam T. Stark, 232–63. Washington, D.C.: Smithsonian Institution Press.

Dixon, C. Scott. 1996. "Popular Beliefs and the Reformation in Brandenburg-Ansbach." In *Popular Religion in Germany and Central Europe, 1400–1800*, edited by Bob Scribner and Trevor Johnson, 119–39. New York: St. Martin's.

Dobres, Marcia-Anne, and John E. Robb. 2000. "Agency in Archaeology: Paradigm or Platitude?" In *Agency in Archaeology*, edited by Marcia-Anne Dobres and John E. Robb, 3–17. London: Routledge.

Douglas, Mary. 1975. *Implicit Meanings: Essays in Anthropology*. London: Routledge and Kegan Paul.

———. 1996. *Natural Symbols: Explorations in Cosmology*. London: Routledge.

Douglas, Mary, and Baron Isherwood. 1979. *The World of Goods*. New York: Basic Books.

Drewal, Henry J. 1989. "Ife: Origins of Art and Civilization." In *Yoruba: Nine Centuries of African Art and Thought*, edited by Allen Wardwell, 45–74. New York: Center for African Art.

Drewal, Henry J., John Pemberton III, and Rowland Abiodun. 1989. "The Yoruba World." In *Yoruba: Nine Centuries of African Art and Thought*, edited by Allen Wardwell, 13–42. New York: Center for African Art.

Droogers, André. 1989. "Syncretism: The Problem of Definition, the Definition of the Problem." In *Dialogue and Syncretism: An Interdisciplinary Approach*, edited by Jerald Gort, Hendrik Vroom, Rein Fernhout, and Anton Wessels, 7–25. Grand Rapids: Wm. B. Eerdmans.

Duany, Jorge. 1985. "Ethnicity in the Spanish Caribbean: Notes on the Consolidation of Creole Identity in Cuba and Puerto Rico, 1762–1868." *Ethnic Groups* 6: 99–123.

Dumont, Jean-Paul. 1985. "Who Are the *Bricoleurs?*" *American Journal of Semiotics* 3 (3): 29–48.

Eltis, David. 2000. *The Rise of African Slavery in the Americas.* Cambridge, U.K.: Cambridge University Press.

———. 2001. "The Volume and Structure of the Transatlantic Slave Trade: A Reassessment." *William & Mary Quarterly*, 3rd ser., 58 (1): 17–46.

Elworthy, Frederick T. 1895. *The Evil Eye: An Account of This Ancient and Widespread Superstition.* London: John Murray.

———. 1900. *Horns of Honour and Other Studies in the By-Ways of Archaeology.* London: John Murray.

Emberling, Geoff. 1997. "Ethnicity in Complex Societies: Archaeological Perspectives." *Journal of Archaeological Research* 5 (4): 295–344.

Eriksen, Thomas H. 1993. *Ethnicity and Nationalism: Anthropological Perspectives.* London: Pluto Press.

Fabian, Johannes. 1985. "Religious Pluralism: An Ethnographic Approach." In *Theoretical Explorations in African Religion,* edited by Wim van Binsbergen and Matthew Schoffeleers, 138–63. London: KPI.

Fairbanks, Charles. 1974. "The Kingsley Slave Cabins in Duval County, Florida, 1968." *Conference on Historic Sites Archaeology Papers* 7: 62–93.

Fales, Martha G. 1995. *Jewelry in America, 1600–1900.* Woodbridge, UK: Antique Collectors' Club.

Fennell, Christopher C. 2000. "Conjuring Boundaries: Inferring Past Identities from Religious Artifacts." *International Journal of Historical Archaeology* 4 (4): 281–313.

———. 2003a. "Consuming Mosaics: Mass-Produced Goods and Contours of Choice in the Upper Potomac Region." PhD diss., University of Virginia.

———. 2003b. "Group Identity, Individual Creativity and Symbolic Generation in a BaKongo Diaspora." *International Journal of Historical Archaeology* 7 (1): 1–31.

Ferguson, Leland G. 1992. *Uncommon Ground: Archaeology and Early African America.* Washington, D.C.: Smithsonian Institution Press.

———. 1998. "Early African-American Pottery in South Carolina: A Complicated Plainware." Paper presented at the 63rd Annual Meeting of the Society of American Archaeology, Seattle, Washington, March 25.

———. 1999. "'The Cross Is a Magic Sign': Marks on Eighteenth-Century Bowls from South Carolina." In *I, Too, Am America: Archaeological Studies of African-American Life,* edited by Theresa A. Singleton, 116–31. Charlottesville: University Press of Virginia.

Fett, Sharla M. 2002. *Working Cures: Healing, Health and Power on Southern Slave Plantations.* Chapel Hill: University of North Carolina Press.

Firth, Raymond. 1973. *Symbols: Public and Private.* Ithaca, N.Y.: Cornell University Press.

Fischer, David H., and James C. Kelly. 2000. *Bound Away: Virginia and the Westward Movement.* Charlottesville: University Press of Virginia.

Fogel, Edwin M. 1915. *Beliefs and Superstitions of the Pennsylvania Germans.* Philadelphia: American Germanica Press.

Fogleman, Aaron S. 1996. *Hopeful Journeys: German Immigration, Settlement, and Political Culture in Colonial America, 1717–1775.* Philadelphia: University of Pennsylvania Press.

Franklin, Maria. 1997. "Out of Site, Out of Mind: The Archaeology of an Enslaved Virginian Household, ca. 1740–1778." PhD diss., University of California, Berkeley.

Franklin, Maria, and Garrett Fesler. 1999. "The Exploration of Ethnicity and the Historical Archaeological Record." In *Historical Archaeology, Identity Formation, and the Interpretation of Ethnicity,* edited by Maria Franklin and Garrett Fesler, 1–10. Williamsburg, Va.: Colonial Williamsburg Foundation.

Franklin, Maria, and Larry McKee. 2004. "African Diaspora Archaeologies: Present Insights and Expanding Discourses." In "Transcending the Boundaries, Transforming the Discipline: African Diaspora Archaeologies in the New Millennium," edited by Maria Franklin and Larry McKee. Special issue, *Historical Archaeology* 38 (1): 1–9.

Frazier, E. Franklin. 1966a. *The Negro Church: The Negro in America.* New York: Academic Press.

———. 1966b. *The Negro Family in the United States.* Chicago: Academic Press.

Friedman, Jonathan. 1989. "Culture, Identity and World Process." In *Domination and Resistance,* edited by Daniel Miller, Michael Rowlands, and Christopher Tilley, 246–60. London: Routledge.

———. 1994. Introduction to *Consumption and Identity,* edited by Jonathan Friedman, 1–22. Amsterdam: Harwood Academic Publishers.

Fu-Kiau, Kimbwandènde Kia Bunseki. 2001. *African Cosmology of the Bântu-Kôngo: Tying the Spiritual Knot; Principles of Life and Living.* 2nd ed. Brooklyn, N.Y.: Athelia Henrietta Press/Orunmila.

Galke, Laura J. 2000. "Did the Gods of Africa Die? A Re-examination of a Carroll House Crystal Assemblage." *North American Archaeologist* 21 (1): 19–33.

Geertz, Clifford. 1973. *The Interpretation of Cultures.* New York: Basic Books.

Gell, Alfred. 1998. *Art and Agency: An Anthropological Theory.* Oxford: Clarendon Press.

Genovese, Eugene. 1976. *Roll, Jordan, Roll: The World the Slaves Made.* New York: Vintage.

Georgia Writers' Project, Works Project Administration. 1940. *Drums and Shad-*

ows: Survival Studies among the Georgia Coastal Negroes. Athens: University of Georgia Press.

Gibson, Gordon D., and Cecilia R. McGurk. 1977. "High-Status Caps of the Kongo and Mbundu Peoples." *Textile Museum Journal* 4 (4): 71–96.

Giddens, Anthony. 1979. *Central Problems in Social Theory: Action, Structure and Contradiction in Social Analysis.* Berkeley: University of California Press.

Glassie, Henry. 1965. "The Pennsylvania Barn in the South." *Pennsylvania Folklife* 15 (2): 8–19.

———. 1968. *Pattern in the Material Folk Culture of the Eastern United States.* Philadelphia: University of Pennsylvania Press.

———. 1978. "The Types of Southern Mountain Cabins." In *The Study of American Folklore,* edited by Jan H. Brunvand, 391–420. New York: W. W. Norton.

———. 1987. "Vernacular Architecture and Society." In *Mirror and Metaphor: Material and Social Constructions of Reality,* edited by Daniel W. Ingersoll, Jr., and Gordon Bronitsky, 230–45. Lanham, Md.: University Press of America.

———. 2000. *Vernacular Architecture.* Bloomington: Indiana University Press.

Gomez, Michael A. 1998. *Exchanging Our Country Marks: The Transformation of African Identities in the Colonial and Antebellum South.* Chapel Hill: University of North Carolina Press.

González-Wippler, Migene. 1989. *Santería: The Religion.* St. Paul: Llewellyn Publications.

Goodhart, Briscoe. 1999. "The German Settlement: Early History of This Interesting Section of Loudoun County." In *Loudoun County Virginia Families and History,* edited and compiled by Jim Presgraves, 120–26. Wytheville, Va.: Wordsprint. (Originally published circa 1896.)

Goucher, Candice. 1999. "African-Caribbean Metal Technology: Forging Cultural Survivals in the Atlantic World." In *African Sites Archaeology in the Caribbean,* edited by Jay B. Haviser, 143–56. Princeton, N.J.: Markus Wiener Publishers.

Griffin, Patrick. 2001. *The People with No Name: Ireland's Ulster Scots, America's Scots Irish, and the Creation of a British Atlantic World, 1689–1764.* Princeton, N.J.: Princeton University Press.

Gundaker, Grey. 1998. *Signs of Diaspora, Diaspora of Signs: Literacies, Creolization, and Vernacular Practices in African America.* New York: Oxford University Press.

———. 2000. "Creolization, Complexity and Time." *Historical Archaeology* 34 (3): 124–33.

Gunn, Charles D. 1969. "The Sator-Arepo Palindrome: A New Inquiry into the Composition of an Ancient Word Square." PhD diss., Yale University.

Hahn, Steven. 1985. "The 'Unmaking' of the Southern Yeomanry: The Transformation of the Georgia Upcountry, 1860–1890." In *The Countryside in the Age of Capitalist Transformation,* edited by Steven Hahn and Jonathan Prude, 179–203. Chapel Hill: University of North Carolina Press.

Hall, Gwendolyn M. 1992. *Africans in Colonial Louisiana: The Development of Afro-Creole Culture in the Eighteenth Century.* Baton Rouge: Louisiana State University Press.

———. 2005. *Slavery and African Ethnicities in the Americas: Restoring the Links.* Chapel Hill: University of North Carolina Press.

Hand, Wayland D., ed. 1964. *The Frank C. Brown Collection of North Carolina Folklore,* vol. 7. Durham, N.C.: Duke University Press.

Handler, Jerome S. 2000. "Slave Medicine and Obeah in Barbados, circa 1650 to 1834." *New West Indian Guide* 74: 57–80.

Handler, Jerome S., and Frederick W. Lange. 1978. *Plantation Slavery in Barbados: An Archaeological and Historical Investigation.* Cambridge, Mass.: Harvard University Press.

Handler, Richard. 1994. "Is 'Identity' a Useful Cross-cultural Concept?" In *Commemorations: The Politics of National Identity,* edited by J. R. Gillis, 27–40. Princeton, N.J.: Princeton University Press.

Hannerz, Ulf. 1987. "The World in Creolisation." *Africa: Journal of the International African Institute* 57 (4): 546–59.

Hansmann, Liselotte, and Lenz Kriss-Rettenbeck. 1966. *Amulett und Talisman: Erscheinungsform und Geschichte.* Munich: Callwey.

Harding, Vincent. 1997. "Religion and Resistance among Antebellum Slaves, 1800–1860." In *African-American Religion: Interpretive Essays in History and Culture,* edited by Timothy E. Fulop and Albert J. Raboteau, 108–30. New York: Routledge.

Head, James W. 1908. *History and Comprehensive Description of Loudoun County, Virginia.* Leesburg, Va.: Park View Press.

Heath, Barbara J. 1999. *Hidden Lives: The Archaeology of Slave Life at Thomas Jefferson's Poplar Forest.* Charlottesville: University Press of Virginia.

Heath, Barbara J., Randy Lichtenberger, Keith Adams, Lori Lee, and Elizabeth Paull. 2004. "Poplar Forest Archaeology: Studies in African American Life; Excavations and Analysis of Site A, Southeast Terrace and Site B, Southeast Curtilage, June 2003–June 2004." Report to the Public Welfare Foundation, June 15, 2004. Forest, Va.: Corporation of Jefferson's Poplar Forest.

Hebdige, Dick. 1999. *Subculture: The Meaning of Style.* London: Routledge.

Hegmon, Michelle. 1992. "Archaeological Research on Style." *Annual Review of Anthropology* 21: 517–36.

———. 1998. "Technology, Style, and Social Practices: Archaeological Approaches." In *The Archaeology of Social Boundaries,* edited by Miriam T. Stark, 264–79. Washington, D.C.: Smithsonian Institution Press.

Hénaff, Marcel. 1998. *Claude Lévi-Strauss and the Making of Structural Anthropology.* Translated by Mary Baker. Minneapolis: University of Minnesota Press.

Henretta, James A. 1978. "Families and Farms: Mentalité in Pre-Industrial America." *William and Mary Quarterly,* 3rd ser., 35 (1): 3–32.

Herskovits, Melville. 1941. *The Myth of the Negro Past.* New York: Academic Press.

Hiatt, Marty. 1995. *Early Church Records of Loudoun County, Virginia, 1745–1800.* Westminster, Md.: Family Line Publications.

Hiatt, Marty, and Craig R. Scott. 1995. *New Jerusalem Lutheran Church Cemetery, Established 1765.* Lovettsville, Va.: New Jerusalem Church.

Hildburgh, W. L. 1906. "Notes on Spanish Amulets." *Folklore* 17 (4): 454–71.

Hilton, Anne. 1985. *The Kingdom of the Kongo.* Oxford: Clarendon Press.

Hinks, Peter. 1975. *Nineteenth Century Jewellery.* London: Faber and Faber.

Hodder, Ian. 2000. "Agency and Individuals in Long-Term Processes." In *Agency in Archaeology,* edited by Marcia-Anne Dobres and John E. Robb, 21–33. London: Routledge.

Hohmann, Johann Georg. 1854. *Der Lang Verborgener Freund.* Harrisburg: Theo. F. Scheffer.

Holloway, Joseph E. 1990. "The Origins of African-American Culture." In *Africanisms in American Culture,* edited by Joseph E. Holloway, 1–18. Bloomington: Indiana University Press.

Horning, Audrey J. 1999. "In Search of 'Hollow Ethnicity': Archaeological Explorations of Rural Mountain Settlement." In *Historical Archaeology, Identity Formation, and the Interpretation of Ethnicity,* edited by Maria Franklin and Garrett Fesler, 121–37. Williamsburg, Va.: Colonial Williamsburg Foundation.

Howard, Philip A. 1998. *Changing History: Afro-Cuban Cabildos and Societies of Color in the Nineteenth Century.* Baton Rouge: Louisiana State University Press.

Howson, Jean E. 1990. "Social Relations and Material Culture: A Critique of the Archaeology of Plantation Slavery." *Historical Archaeology* 24 (4): 78–91.

Hutnyk, John. 2005. "Hybridity." *Ethnic and Racial Studies* 28 (1): 79–102.

Hyatt, Harry M. 1965. *Folk-Lore from Adams County, Illinois.* Hannibal, Mo.: Western Printing and Lithographing.

Hymes, Dell, ed. 1971. *Pidginization and Creolization of Languages.* London: Cambridge University Press.

ICPSR [Inter-University Consortium for Political and Social Research]. 1992. *Historical, Demographic, Economic and Social Data: The United States, 1790–1970.* Ann Arbor, Mich.: ICPSR.

Israel, Fred L., ed. 1968. *1897 Sears Roebuck Catalogue.* New York: Chelsea House.

Jacobson-Widding, Anita. 1979. *Red-White-Black as a Mode of Thought: A Study of Triadic Classification by Colours in the Ritual Symbolism and Cognitive Thought of the Peoples of the Lower Congo.* Stockholm: Uppsala University. Distributed by Almquist and Wiksell, Stockholm.

———. 1991. "The Encounter with the Water Mirror." In *Body and Space: Symbolic Models of Unity and Division in African Cosmology and Experience,* edited by Anita Jacobson-Widding, 177–216. Stockholm: Uppsala University. Distributed by Almquist and Wiksell, Stockholm.

Jamieson, Ross W. 1995. "Material Culture and Social Death: African-American Burial Practices." *Historical Archaeology* 29 (4): 39–58.

Janzen, John M. 1972. "Laman's Kongo Ethnography: Observations on Sources,

Methodology, and Theory." *Africa: Journal of the International African Institute* 42 (4): 316–28.

———. 1977. "The Tradition of Renewal in Kongo Religion." In *African Religions: A Symposium*, edited by Newell S. Booth, Jr., 69–116. New York: NOK Publishers.

Janzen, John M., and Wyatt MacGaffey. 1974. *An Anthology of Kongo Religion: Primary Texts from Lower Zaire*. Publications in Anthropology No. 5. Lawrence: University of Kansas.

Johnson, Trevor. 1996. "Blood, Tears and Xavier-Water: Jesuit Missionaries and Popular Religion in the Eighteenth-Century Upper Palatinate." In *Popular Religion in Germany and Central Europe, 1400–1800*, edited by Bob Scribner and Trevor Johnson, 183–202. New York: St. Martin's.

Jones, George F. 1990. *German-American Names*. Baltimore: Genealogical Publishing.

Jones, Lynn. 2000. "Crystals and Conjuring at the Charles Carroll House, Annapolis, Maryland." *African-American Archaeology* 27: 1–2, 10–11.

Jones, Siân. 1997. *The Archaeology of Ethnicity*. London: Routledge.

Jordan, Terry G. 1980. "Alpine, Alemannic and American Log Architecture." *Annals of the Association of American Geographers* 70 (2): 154–80.

Joseph, J. W., Theresa M. Hamby, and Catherine S. Long. 2004. "Historical Archaeology in Georgia." University of Georgia, Laboratory of Archaeology Series, Report No. 39. Georgia Archaeological Research Design Paper No. 14. Stone Mountain, Ga.: New South Associates.

Kapchan, Deborah A., and Pauline T. Strong. 1999. "The Metaphor of Hybridity." *Journal of American Folklore* 112 (445): 239–53.

Keane, Webb. 1997. "Religious Language." *Annual Review of Anthropology* 26: 47–71.

Keller, Kenneth W. 1990. "What Is Distinctive about the Scotch-Irish?" In *Appalachian Frontiers: Settlement, Society and Development in the Preindustrial Era*, edited by Robert D. Mitchell, 69–86. Lexington: University of Kentucky Press.

Kelly, Marsha C., and Roger E. Kelly. 1980. "Approaches to Ethnic Identification in Historical Archaeology." In *Archaeological Perspectives on Ethnicity in America*, edited by Robert L. Schuyler, 133–44. Farmingdale, N.Y.: Baywood.

Kercheval, Samuel. 1850. *A History of the Valley of Virginia*. Woodstock, Va.: J. Gatewood.

Kessel, Elizabeth A. 1990. "Germans in the Making of Frederick County, Maryland, 1730–1800." In *Appalachian Frontiers: Settlement, Society and Development in the Preindustrial Era*, edited by Robert D. Mitchell, 87–104. Lexington: University of Kentucky Press.

Khan, Aisha. 2004. "Sacred Subversions? Syncretic Creoles, the Indo-Caribbean, and 'Culture's In-between.'" *Radical History Review* 89: 165–84.

Kieckhefer, Richard. 1990. *Magic in the Middle Ages*. Cambridge, U.K.: Cambridge University Press.

Klein, Herbert. 1986. *African Slavery in Latin America and the Caribbean.* New York: Oxford University Press.

Klingelhofer, Eric. 1987. "Aspects of Early Afro-American Material Culture: Artifacts from the Slave Quarters at Garrison Plantation, Maryland." *Historical Archaeology* 21 (2): 112–19.

Kniffen, Fred. 1965. "Folk Housing: Key to Diffusion." *Annals of the Association of American Geographers* 55 (4): 549–77.

Kniffen, Fred, and Henry Glassie. 1966. "Building in Wood in the Eastern United States: A Time-Place Perspective." *Geographical Review* 56 (1): 40–66.

Krige, J. D. 1982. "The Social Functions of Witchcraft." In *Witchcraft and Sorcery,* edited by Max Marwick, 263–75. London: Penguin.

Kulikoff, Allan. 2000. *From British Peasants to Colonial American Farmers.* Chapel Hill: University of North Carolina Press.

Laguerre, Michel S. 1980. *Voodoo Heritage.* Beverly Hills, Calif.: Sage.

Laman, Karl E. 1953. *The Kongo I.* Studies Ethnographica Upsaliensia IV. Uppsala, Sweden: Almqvist and Wiksells.

———. 1957. *The Kongo II.* Studies Ethnographica Upsaliensia IV. Uppsala, Sweden: Almqvist and Wiksells.

———. 1962. *The Kongo III.* Studies Ethnographica Upsaliensia IV. Uppsala, Sweden: Almqvist and Wiksells.

———. 1968. *The Kongo IV.* Studies Ethnographica Upsaliensia IV. Uppsala, Sweden: Almqvist and Wiksells.

La Rosa Corzo, Gabino. 2003. *Runaway Slave Settlements in Cuba: Resistance and Repression.* Translated by Mary Todd. Chapel Hill: University of North Carolina Press.

Lay, K. Edward. 1982. "European Antecedents of Seventeenth and Eighteenth Century Germanic and Scots-Irish Architecture in America." *Pennsylvania Folklife* 32 (1): 2–43.

Leone, Mark P. 2005. *The Archaeology of Liberty in an American Capital: Excavations in Annapolis.* Berkeley: University of California Press.

Leone, Mark P., and Gladys-Marie Fry. 1999. "Conjuring in the Big House Kitchen: An Interpretation of African American Belief Systems Based on the Uses of Archaeology and Folklore Sources." *Journal of American Folklore* 112 (445): 372–403.

Levine, Lawrence W. 1977. *Black Culture and Black Consciousness: Afro-American Folk Thought from Slavery to Freedom.* New York: Oxford University Press.

Lévi-Strauss, Claude. 1966. *Savage Mind.* Chicago: University of Chicago Press.

Lightbrown, Ronald W. 1992. *Mediaeval European Jewellery.* London: Trustees of the Victoria and Albert Museum.

Link, Paxon. 2001. *The Link Family.* Bowie, Md.: Heritage Books.

Logan, George C. 1995. "African Religion in America." In *Invisible America: Unearthing Our Hidden History,* edited by Mark P. Leone and Neil L. Silberman, 154–55. New York: Henry Holt.

Long, Carolyn M. 2001. *Spiritual Merchants: Religion, Magic, and Commerce*. Knoxville: University of Tennessee Press.

Long, Charles H. 1997. "Perspectives for a Study of African-American Religion in the United States." In *African-American Religion: Interpretive Essays in History and Culture*, edited by Timothy E. Fulop and Albert J. Raboteau, 22–35. New York: Routledge.

Longenecker, Stephen L. 2002. *Shenandoah Religion: Outsiders and the Mainstream, 1716–1865*. Waco, Texas: Baylor University Press.

Lovejoy, Paul E. 1989. "The Impact of the Atlantic Slave Trade on Africa: A Review of the Literature." *Journal of African History* 30 (3): 365–94.

———. 1997. "The African Diaspora: Revisionist Interpretations of Ethnicity, Culture and Religion under Slavery." *Studies in the World History of Slavery, Abolition and Emancipation* 2 (1): 1–22.

———. 2000. "Identifying Enslaved Africans in the African Diaspora." In *Identity in the Shadow of Slavery*, edited by Paul E. Lovejoy, 1–29. London: Continuum.

———. 2003. "Ethnic Designations of the Slave Trade and the Reconstruction of the History of Trans-Atlantic Slavery." In *Trans-Atlantic Dimensions of Ethnicity in the African Diaspora*, edited by Paul E. Lovejoy and David V. Trotman, 9–42. London: Continuum.

Lowenthal, David. 1996. *Possessed by the Past: The Heritage Crusade and the Spoils of History*. New York: Free Press.

———. 1997. "History and Memory." *Public Historian* 19 (2): 30–39.

MacGaffey, Wyatt. 1970a. *Custom and Government in the Lower Congo*. Berkeley: University of California Press.

———. 1970b. "The Religious Commissions of the BaKongo." *Man*, new ser., 5 (1): 27–38.

———. 1986. *Religion and Society in Central Africa: The BaKongo of Lower Zaire*. Chicago: University of Chicago Press.

———. 1988a. "Complexity, Astonishment and Power: The Visual Vocabulary of Kongo Minkisi." *Journal of Southern African Studies* 14 (2): 188–203.

———. 1988b. "BaKongo Cosmology." *The World & I*, Sept. 1988: 512–21.

———. 1991. *Art and Healing of the BaKongo, Commented by Themselves: Minkisi from the Laman Collection*. Stockholm: Folkens Museum-Etnografiska. Distributed in North America by Indiana University Press, Bloomington.

———. 1993. "The Eyes of Understanding: Kongo Minkisi." In *Astonishment and Power*, edited by Sylvia H. Williams and David C. Driskell, 21–106. Washington, D.C.: Smithsonian Institution Press.

———. 2000a. Art and Spirituality. In *African Spirituality: Forms, Meanings, and Expressions*, edited by Jacob K. Olupona, 223–56. New York: Crossroad.

———. 2000b. *Kongo Political Culture: The Conceptual Challenge of the Particular*. Bloomington: Indiana University Press.

———. 2000c. "The Kongo Peoples." In *In the Presence of Spirits: African Art from the*

National Museum of Ethnology, Lisbon, edited by Frank Herreman, 35–59. New York: Museum for African Art.

———. 2004. "Twins, Simbi Spirits, and Lwas in Kongo and Haiti." In *Central Africans and Cultural Transformations in the American Diaspora*, edited by Linda M. Heywood, 211–26. Cambridge, U.K.: Cambridge University Press.

MacGaffey, Wyatt, and Clifford R. Barnett. 1962. *Cuba: Its People, Its Society, Its Culture*. New Haven, Conn.: Human Relations Area Files Press.

Maloney, Clarence. 1976. Introduction to *The Evil Eye*, edited by Clarence Maloney, v–xvi. New York: Columbia University Press.

Martin, Joseph. 1835. *A New and Comprehensive Gazetteer of Virginia and the District of Columbia*. Charlottesville: Moseley and Pompkins.

Marwick, Max. 1982. "Witchcraft and the Epistemology of Science." In *Witchcraft and Sorcery*, edited by Max Marwick, 460–68. London: Penguin.

Mathers, Clay, Timothy Darvill, and Barbara J. Little. 2005. "Introduction: Archaeological Value in a World Context." In *Heritage of Value, Archaeology of Renown: Reshaping Archaeological Assessment and Significance*, edited by Clay Mathers, Timothy Darvill, and Barbara J. Little, 1–18. Gainesville: University Press of Florida.

Matibag, Eugenio. 1996. *Afro-Cuban Religious Experience*. Gainesville: University Press of Florida.

May, Henry F. 1976. *The Enlightenment in America*. Oxford: Oxford University Press.

Mbiti, John. 1970. *Concepts of God in Africa*. London: SPCK Press.

———. 1990. *African Religions and Philosophy*. Oxford: Heinemann Press.

McCusker, John J. 2001. *Comparing the Purchasing Power of Money in the United States (or Colonies) from 1665 to Any Other Year Including the Present*. Economic History Services. Available online at http://www.measuringworth.com/calculators /ppowerus.

McKee, Larry. 1995. "The Earth Is Their Witness." *The Sciences* 35 (2): 36–41.

McWhorter, John H. 1997. *Towards a New Model of Creole Genesis*. New York: Peter Lang.

Merrifield, Ralph. 1988. *The Archaeology of Ritual and Magic*. New York: New Amsterdam Books.

Metraux, Alfred. 1972. *Voodoo in Haiti*. New York: Schocken.

Midelfort, H. C. Erik. 1972. *Witch Hunting in Southwestern Germany, 1562–1684: The Social and Intellectual Foundations*. Stanford, Calif.: Stanford University Press.

———. 1982. "Witchcraft, Magic, and the Occult." In *Reformation Europe: A Guide to Research*, edited by Steven Osmont, 183–209. St. Louis: Center for Reformation Research.

Miller, Daniel. 1987. *Material Culture and Mass Consumption*. Oxford: Basil Blackwell.

Miller, Joseph C. 1976. "The Slave Trade in Congo and Angola." In *The African Di-*

aspora: Interpretive Essays, edited by Martin L. Kilson and Robert I. Rotberg, 75–113. Cambridge, Mass.: Harvard University Press.

———. 2002. "Central Africa during the Era of the Slave Trade, circa 1490s-1850s." In *Central Africans and Cultural Transformations in the American Diaspora,* edited by Linda M. Heywood, 21–69. Cambridge, U.K.: Cambridge University Press.

Mintz, Sidney W. 1996. "Enduring Substances, Trying Theories: The Caribbean Region as Oikoumene." *Journal of the Royal Anthropological Institute* 2 (2): 289–311.

Mintz, Sidney W., and Richard Price. 1976. *An Anthropological Approach to the Afro-American Past: A Caribbean Perspective.* ISHI Occasional Papers in Social Change, vol. 2. Philadelphia: Institute for the Study of Human Issues.

Mitchell, Peter. 2005. *African Connections: An Archaeological Perspective on Africa and the Wider World.* Walnut Creek, Calif.: AltaMira Press.

Mitchell, Robert D. 1977. *Commercialism and Frontier: Perspectives on the Early Shenandoah Valley.* Charlottesville: University Press of Virginia.

———. 1990. "Introduction: Revisionism and Regionalism." In *Appalachian Frontiers: Settlement, Society and Development in the Preindustrial Era,* edited by Robert D. Mitchell, 1–22. Lexington: University Press of Kentucky.

Mogobe, Ramose. 1988. "The Ontology of Invisible Beings." *Boleswa: Occasional Papers in Theology and Religion, African Spirituality* 1 (2): 1–24.

Moltmann, Günter. 1985. "The Pattern of German Emigration to the United States in the Nineteenth Century." In *America and the Germans: An Assessment of a Three-Hundred-Year History,* vol. 1, edited by Frank Trommler and Joseph McVeigh, 14–24. Philadelphia: University of Pennsylvania Press.

Morgan, Philip D. 1998. *Slave Counterpoint: Black Culture in the Eighteenth-Century Chesapeake and Lowcountry.* Chapel Hill: University of North Carolina Press.

Morris, Brian. 1994. *Anthropology of the Self: The Individual in Cultural Perspective.* London: Pluto Press.

Mörz, Stefan. 2002. "The Palatinate: The Elector and the Mermaid." *German History* 20 (3): 332–53.

Moss, Leonard W., and Stephen C. Cappannari. 1976. "*Mal'occio, Ayin ha ra, Oculus fascinus, Judenblick*: The Evil Eye Hovers Above." In *The Evil Eye,* edited by Clarence Maloney, 1–15. New York: Columbia University Press.

Mouer, L. Daniel, Mary E. Hodges, Stephen R. Potter, Susan L. Renaud, Ivor Noël Hume, Dennis J. Pogue, Martha W. McCartney, and Thomas E. Davidson. 1999. "Colonoware Pottery, Chesapeake Pipes, and 'Uncritical Assumptions.'" In *I, Too, Am America: Archaeological Studies of African-American Life,* edited by Theresa A. Singleton, 83–115. Charlottesville: University Press of Virginia.

Mower, Jerry, and Tedi Mower, trans. 1993. *St. James United Church of Christ Church Register (Reformed Church), Loudoun County, Virginia, ca. 1789–1823.* Apollo, Pa.: Closson.

Mulira, Jessie G. 1990. "The Case of Voodoo in New Orleans." In *Africanisms in*

American Culture, edited by Joseph E. Holloway, 34–68. Bloomington: Indiana University Press.

Murphy, Joseph M. 1993. *Santería: African Spirits in America*. Boston: Beacon Press.

Neuwirth, Jessica L., and Matthew Cochran. 2000. "Archaeology in the East Wing of the Brice House, Annapolis, Maryland." Report on file at the Department of Anthropology, University of Maryland, College Park.

Noël Hume, Ivor. 1970. *A Guide to Artifacts of Colonial America*. New York: Alfred A. Knopf.

Nolt, Steven M. 2000. "The Quest for American Kinship: Liberty, Ethnicity, and Ecumenism among Pennsylvania German Lutherans, 1817–1842." *Journal of American Ethnic History* 19 (2): 64–91.

Nwokeji, G. U. 2001. "African Conceptions of Gender and the Slave Traffic." *William & Mary Quarterly*, 3rd ser., 58 (1): 47–68.

Olmos, Margarite F., and Lizabeth Paravisini-Gebert. 2003. *Creole Religions of the Caribbean: An Introduction from Vodou and Santería to Obeah and Espiritismo*. New York: New York University Press.

Olsan, Lea T. 2004. "Charms in Medieval History." In *Charms and Charming in Europe*, edited by Jonathan Roper, 59–88. New York: Palgrave Macmillan.

Orser, Charles E., Jr. 1989. "On Plantations and Patterns." *Historical Archeology* 23 (2): 28–40.

———. 1994. "The Archaeology of African-American Slave Religions in the Antebellum South." *Cambridge Archaeological Journal* 4 (1): 33–45.

———. 1996. *A Historical Archaeology of the Modern World*. New York: Plenum Press.

Orser, Charles E., Jr., and Pedro P. Funari. 2001. "Archaeology and Slave Resistance and Rebellion." *World Archaeology* 33 (1): 61–72.

Ortner, Sherry B. "On Key Symbols." 1973. *American Anthropologist* 75 (5): 1338–46.

Otterness, Philip. 2004. *Becoming German: The 1709 Palatine Migration to New York*. Ithaca, N.Y.: Cornell University Press.

Palmer, Colin A. 1995. "From Africa to the Americas: Ethnicity in the Early Black Communities of the Americas." *Journal of World History* 6 (2): 223–36.

Patten, Drake. 1992. "Mankala and Minkisi: Possible Evidence of African American Folk Beliefs and Practices." *African-American Archaeology* 6: 5–7.

Paynter, Robert. 2000a. "Historical and Anthropological Archaeology: Forging Alliances." *Journal of Archaeological Research* 8 (1): 1–37.

———. 2000b. "Historical Archaeology and the Post-Columbian World of North America." *Journal of Archaeological Research* 8 (3): 169–217.

Perdue, Charles L., Thomas E. Barden, and Robert K. Phillips. 1976. *Weevils in the Wheat: Interviews with Ex-Slaves*. Charlottesville: University Press of Virginia.

Perdue, Martin C. 1985. "The Log-Cabin in American Art and Architecture, 1840–1890." M.A. thesis, School of Architecture, University of Virginia.

Perry, Warren, and Robert Paynter. 1999. "Artifacts, Ethnicity, and the Archaeology of African Americans." In *I, Too, Am America: Archaeological Studies of African-American Life*, edited by Theresa A. Singleton, 299–310. Charlottesville: University Press of Virginia.

Poland, Charles P., Jr. 1976. *From Frontier to Suburbia*. Marceline, Mo.: Walsworth.

Pollard, Helen P. 1994. "Ethnicity and Political Control in a Complex Society: The Tarascan State of Prehispanic Mexico." In *Factional Competition and Political Development in the New World*, edited by Elizabeth M. Brumfiel and John W. Fox, 79–88. Cambridge, U.K.: Cambridge University Press.

Polomé, Edgar. 1980. "Creolization Processes and Diachronic Linguistics." In *Theoretical Orientations in Creole Studies*, edited by Albert Valdman and Arnold Highfield, 185–202. New York: Academic Press.

Posnansky, Merrick. 1972. "Archaeology, Ritual and Religion." In *The Historical Study of African Religion*, edited by Terence O. Ranger and Isaria N. Kimambo, 29–44. London: Heinemann.

———. 1999. "West Africanist Reflections on African-American Archaeology." In *I, Too, Am America: Archaeological Studies of African-American Life*, edited by Theresa A. Singleton, 21–37. Charlottesville: University Press of Virginia.

Powdermaker, Hortense. 1939. *After Freedom: A Cultural Study in the Deep South*. New York: Viking Press.

Puckett, Newbell N. 1926. *Folk Beliefs of the Southern Negro*. Chapel Hill: University of North Carolina Press.

Raboteau, Albert J. 1980. *Slave Religion: The Invisible Institution in the Antebellum South*. Oxford: Oxford University Press.

Rawick, George P. 1978. "Some Notes on a Social Analysis of Slavery: A Critique and Assessment of 'The Slave Community.'" In *Revisiting Blassingame's "The Slave Community": The Scholars Respond*, edited by Al-Tony Gilmore, 17–26. Westport, Conn.: Greenwood Press.

Reaney, P. H. 1991. *A Dictionary of English Surnames*. London: Routledge.

Reid, Andrew M., and Paul J. Lane, eds. 2004. *African Historical Archaeologies*. New York: Kluwer Academic/Plenum.

Reimensnyder, Barbara L. 1982. *Powwowing in Union County: A Study of Pennsylvania German Folk Medicine in Context*. New York: AMS Press.

Rice, James D. 1995. "Old Appalachia's Path to Interdependency: Economic Development and the Creation of Community in Western Maryland, 1730–1850." *Appalachian Journal* 22 (4): 348–75.

Richardson, David. 1989. "Slave Exports from West and West-Central Africa, 1700–1810: New Estimates of Volume and Distribution." *Journal of African History* 30: 1–22.

Rietstap, Johannes B. 1953. *General Illustrated Armorial by V. & H. Rolland*, vols. 1–6. Lyon, France: Sauvegarde Historique.

Rigaud, Milo. 1985. *Secrets of Voodoo*. Translated by R. B. Cross. San Francisco: City Lights Books.

Rivera, Ray. 2005. "Annapolis House Yields Clues to Hoodoo Mysteries." *Washington Post*, July 6, sec. B, p. 1.

Roberts, John M. 1976. "Belief in the Evil Eye in World Perspective." In *The Evil Eye*, edited by Clarence Maloney, 221–78. New York: Columbia University Press.

Roberts, Warren E. 1986. "German American Log Buildings of Dubois County, Indiana." *Winterthur Portfolio* 21 (4): 265–74.

Roeber, A. G. 1993. *Palatines, Liberty, and Property: German Lutherans in Colonial British America*. Baltimore: Johns Hopkins University Press.

Roosens, Eugeen E. 1989. *Creating Ethnicity: The Process of Ethnogenesis*. London: Sage.

Rorty, Richard. 1979. *Philosophy and the Mirror of Nature*. Princeton, N.J.: Princeton University Press.

Rosaldo, Renato, Samar Lavie, and Kirin Narayan. 1993. "Introduction: Creativity in Anthropology." In *Creativity/Anthropology*, edited by Samar Lavie, Kirin Narayan, and Renato Rosaldo, 1–8. Ithaca, N.Y.: Cornell University Press.

Rowlands, Alison. 1996. "Witchcraft and Popular Religion in Early Modern Rothenburg ob der Tauber." In *Popular Religion in Germany and Central Europe, 1400–1800*, edited by Bob Scribner and Trevor Johnson, 101–18. New York: St. Martin's.

Rublack, Hans-Christoph. 1992. "Success and Failure of the Reformation: Popular 'Apologies' from the Seventeenth and Eighteenth Centuries." In *Germania Illustrata: Essays on Early Modern Germany Presented to Gerald Strauss*, edited by Andrew C. Fix and Susan C. Karant-Nunn, 141–65. Kirksville, Miss.: Sixteenth Century Journal Publishers.

Ruffin, Edmund. 1992. *Agriculture, Geology, and Society in Antebellum South Carolina: The Private Diary of Edmund Ruffin, 1843*. Edited with an Introduction by William M. Mathew. Athens: University of Georgia Press.

Ruppel, Timothy, Jessica Neuwirth, Mark P. Leone, and Gladys-Marie Fry. 2003. "Hidden in View: African Spiritual Spaces in North American Landscapes." *Antiquity* 77 (296): 321–35.

Russell, Aaron E. 1997. "Material Culture and African-American Spirituality at the Hermitage." *Historical Archaeology* 31 (2): 63–80.

Sackett, James R. 1985. "Style and Ethnicity in the Kalahari: A Reply to Wiessner." *American Antiquity* 50 (1): 154–59.

Sacks, Stephen. 1979. *On Metaphor*. Chicago: University of Chicago Press.

Salamone, Frank A. 1991. "Ethnic Identities and Religion." In *Religion and Society in Nigeria: Historical and Sociological Perspectives*, edited by Jacob K. Olupona and Toyin Falola, 45–65. Ibadan, Nigeria: Spectrum Books.

Samford, Patricia. 1996. "The Archaeology of African-American Slavery and Material Culture." *William and Mary Quarterly*, 3rd ser., 53 (1): 87–114.

Sapir, Edward. 1949. "Cultural Anthropology and Psychiatry." In *Selected Writings of Edward Sapir*, edited by David G. Mandelbaum, 509–21. Berkeley: University of California Press.

Schmidt, Peter R. 1995. "Using Archaeology to Remake History in Africa." In *Making Alternative Histories: The Practice of Archaeology and History in Non-Western Settings*, edited by Peter R. Schmidt and Thomas C. Patterson, 119–47. Santa Fe: School of American Research Press.

Schneider, David M. 1980. *American Kinship: A Cultural Account*. Chicago: University of Chicago Press.

Schuyler, Robert L. 1974. "Sandy Ground: Archeological Sampling in a Black Community in Metropolitan New York." *Conference of Historic Sites Archaeology Papers* 7: 13–52.

Scribner, Robert W. 1987. *Popular Culture and Popular Movements in Reformation Germany*. London: Hambledon.

Segal, Daniel A., and Richard Handler. 1995. "U.S. Multiculturalism and the Concept of Culture." *Identities* 1 (4): 391–407.

Shackel, Paul A. 2000. "Craft to Wage Labor: Agency and Resistance in American Historical Archaeology." In *Agency in Archaeology*, edited by Marcia-Anne Dobres and John E. Robb, 232–46. London: Routledge.

———. 2001. "Public Memory and the Search for Power in American Historical Archaeology." *American Anthropologist* 103 (3): 655–70.

Shaner, Richard H. 1961. "Living Occult Practices in Dutch Pennsylvania." *Pennsylvania Folklife* 12 (3): 62–63.

Shanks, Michael, and Christopher Tilley. 1992. *Re-Constructing Archaeology: Theory and Practice*. London: Routledge.

Shaw, Rosalind, and Charles Stewart. 1994. "Introduction: Problematizing Syncretism." In *Syncretism/Anti-Syncretism: The Politics of Religious Synthesis*, edited by Rosalind Shaw and Charles Stewart, 1–26. London: Routledge.

Shorter, Aylward. 1972. "Symbolism, Ritual and History: An Examination of the Work of Victor Turner." In *The Historical Study of African Religion*, edited by Terence O. Ranger and Isaria N. Kimambo, 139–49. London: Heinemann.

Sider, Gerald M. 1986. *Culture and Class in Anthropology and History*. Cambridge, U.K.: Cambridge University Press.

Singleton, Theresa A. 1991. "The Archaeology of Slave Life." In *Before Freedom Came: African-American Life in the Antebellum South*, edited by Edward D. C. Campbell, Jr., and Kym S. Rice, 155–75. Charlottesville: University Press of Virginia.

———. 1995. "The Archaeology of Slavery in North America." *Annual Review of Anthropology* 24: 119–40.

———. 1999. "An Introduction to African-American Archaeology." In *I, Too, Am America: Archaeological Studies of African-American Life*, edited by Theresa A. Singleton, 1–17. Charlottesville: University Press of Virginia.

———. 2001. "An Americanist Perspective on African Archaeology: Toward an Archaeology of the Black Atlantic." In *West Africa during the Atlantic Slave Trade: Archaeological Perspectives*, edited by Christopher R. DeCorse, 179–84. New York: Leicester University Press.

———. 2006. "African Diaspora Archaeology in Dialogue." In *Afro-Atlantic Dialogues: Anthropology in the Diaspora*, edited by Kevin A. Yelvington, 249–87. Santa Fe: School of American Research Press.

Singleton, Theresa A., and Mark D. Bograd. 1995. *The Archaeology of the African Diaspora in the Americas. Guides to the Archaeological Literature of the Immigrant Experience in America*, No. 2. Tucson: Society for Historical Archaeology.

Smith, Elmer, John Stewart, and M. E. Kyger. 1964. *The Pennsylvania Germans of the Shenandoah Valley*. Allentown, Pa.: Schlecter's Printing.

Smith, Elsdon C. 1969. *American Surnames*. Philadelphia: Chilton.

Smith, Laurajane. 2005. "Archaeological Significance and the Governance of Identity in Cultural Heritage Management." In *Heritage of Value, Archaeology of Renown: Reshaping Archaeological Assessment and Significance*, edited by Clay Mathers, Timothy Darvill, and Barbara J. Little, 77–88. Gainesville: University Press of Florida.

Sobel, Mechal. 1987. *The World They Made Together: Black and White Values in Eighteenth-Century Virginia*. Princeton, N.J.: Princeton University Press.

Spicer, Edward H. 1971. "Persistent Cultural Systems." *Science*, new ser., 174 (4011): 795–800.

Stafford, Thomas A. 1942. *Christian Symbolism in the Evangelical Churches*. New York: Abingdon-Chokesbury.

Stahl, Ann B. 1993. "Concepts of Time and Approaches to Analogical Reasoning in Historical Perspective." *American Antiquity* 58 (2): 235–60.

Steiner, Roland. 1901. "Observations on the Practice of Conjuring in Georgia." *Journal of American Folklife* 14: 173–80.

Sterner, Judy. 1989. "Who Is Signalling Whom? Ceramic Style, Ethnicity and Taphonomy among the Sirak Bulahay." *Antiquity* 63: 451–59.

Stevenson, Brenda E. 1996. *Life in Black and White: Family and Community in the Slave South*. New York: Oxford University Press.

Steward, Julian H. 1942. "The Direct Historical Approach in Archaeology." *American Antiquity* 7 (4): 337–43.

Stine, Linda F., Melanie A. Cabak, and Mark D. Groover. 1996. "Blue Beads as African-American Cultural Symbols." *Historical Archaeology* 30 (3): 49–75.

Strauss, Gerald. 1975. "Success and Failure in the German Reformation." *Past and Present* 67: 30–63.

Stuckey, Sterling. 1987. *Slave Culture: Nationalist Theory and the Foundations of Black America*. New York: Oxford University Press.

Sturm, Fred G. 1977. "Afro-Brazilian Cults." In *African Religions: A Symposium*, edited by Newell S. Booth, Jr., 217–39. New York: NOK Publishers.

Sweet, James H. 2003. *Recreating Africa: Culture, Kinship, and Religion in the African-Portuguese World, 1441–1770*. Chapel Hill: University of North Carolina Press.

———. 2004. "'Not a Thing for White Men to See': Central African Divination in Seventeenth-Century Brazil." In *Enslaving Connections: Changing Cultures of Africa and Brazil during the Era of Slavery*, edited by José C. Curto and Paul E. Lovejoy, 139–48. Amherst, N.Y.: Humanity Books.

Szwed, John, F. 2003. "Metaphors of Incommensurability." *Journal of American Folklore* 116 (459): 9–18.

Tait, Hugh, ed. 1986. *Jewelry: 7000 Years*. New York: Harry N. Abrams.

Tambiah, Stanley J. 1990. *Magic, Science, Religion and the Scope of Rationality*. Cambridge, U.K.: Cambridge University Press.

Taylor, Yardley. 1999. "Memoir of Loudoun County." In *Loudoun County Virginia Families and History*, edited and compiled by Jim Presgraves, 3–29. Wytheville, Va.: Wordsprint. (Originally published in 1853.)

Thomas, Brian W. 1995. "Source Criticism and the Interpretation of African-American Sites." *Southeastern Archaeology* 14 (2): 149–57.

———. 2001. "African-American Tradition and Community in the Antebellum South." In *The Archaeology of Traditions: Agency and History before and after Columbus*, edited by Timothy Pauketat, 17–33. Gainesville: University Press of Florida.

Thomas, Keith. 1971. *Religion and the Decline of Magic*. New York: Charles Scribner's Sons.

Thompson, Robert F. 1983. *Flash of the Spirit: African and Afro-American Art and Philosophy*. New York: Random House.

———. 1990. "Kongo Influences on African-American Artistic Culture." In *Africanisms in American Culture*, edited by Joseph E. Holloway, 148–84. Bloomington: Indiana University Press.

———. 1993. *Face of the Gods: Art and Altars of Africa and African Americas*. New York: The Museum for African Art.

———. 1997. "Translating the World into Generousness." *Res* 32 (Autumn): 19–36.

———. 1998. "Bighearted Power: Kongo Presence in the Landscape and Art of Black America." In *Keep Your Head to the Sky: Interpreting African American Home Ground*, edited by Grey Gundaker, 37–64. Charlottesville: University Press of Virginia.

Thompson, Robert F., and Joseph Cornet. 1981. *The Four Moments of the Sun: Kongo Art in Two Worlds*. Washington, D.C.: National Gallery of Art.

Thornton, John K. 1977. "Demography and History in the Kingdom of the Kongo, 1550–1750." *Journal of African History* 18 (4): 507–30.

———. 1983. *The Kingdom of the Kongo: Civil War and Transition, 1641–1718*. Madison: University of Wisconsin Press.

———. 1998. *Africa and Africans in the Making of the Atlantic World, 1400–1800*. 2nd ed. Cambridge, U.K.: Cambridge University Press.

———. 2002. "Religious and Ceremonial Life in the Kongo and Mbundu Areas, 1500–1700." In *Central Africans and Cultural Transformations in the American*

Diaspora, edited by Linda M. Heywood, 71–90. Cambridge, U.K.: Cambridge University Press.

Thorpe, S. A. 1991. *African Traditional Religions*. Pretoria: University of South Africa.

Tilley, Christopher. 1999. *Metaphor and Material Culture*. Oxford: Blackwell Publishers.

Trigger, Bruce G. 1995. "Expanding Middle-Range Theory." *Antiquity* 69: 449–58.

Trouillot, Michel-Rolph. 1995. *Silencing the Past: Power and the Production of History*. Boston: Beacon Press.

———. 1998. "Culture on the Edges: Creolization in the Plantation Context." *Plantation Society in the Americas* 5 (1): 8–28.

Turner, Victor. 1967. *The Forest of Symbols: Aspects of Ndembu Ritual*. Ithaca, N.Y.: Cornell University Press.

———. 1973. "Symbols in African Ritual." *Science* 179 (4078) (March 16): 1100–05.

UNESCO [United Nations Educational, Scientific, and Cultural Organization]. 1993. *Resolution 27C/3.13 of the General Conference*. Paris: UNESCO.

———. 2003. *Convention for the Safeguarding of the Intangible Cultural Heritage*. Paris: UNESCO.

———. 2006a. *The Slave Route Project*. Paris: UNESCO.

———. 2006b. *Report of Expert Meeting on Community Involvement in Safeguarding Intangible Cultural Heritage: Towards the Implementation of the 2003 Convention*. Paris: UNESCO and the Asia/Pacific Cultural Centre for UNESCO.

USGS [United States Geological Survey]. 1960. *Soil Survey for Loudoun County, Virginia*. Washington, D.C.: U.S. Government Printing Office.

Vanhee, Hein. 2004. "Central African Popular Christianity and the Making of Haitian Vodou Religion." In *Central Africans and Cultural Transformations in the American Diaspora*, edited by Linda M. Heywood, 243–64. Cambridge, U.K.: Cambridge University Press.

Vansina, Jan. 1962. "Ethnohistory in Africa." *Ethnohistory* 9 (2): 126–36.

———. 1966. *Kingdoms of the Savanna*. Madison: University of Wisconsin Press.

Van Wing, J. 1941. "Bakongo Magic." *Journal of the Royal Anthropological Institute of Great Britain and Ireland* 71 (1): 85–98.

Wagner, Roy. 1975. *The Invention of Culture*. Chicago: University of Chicago Press.

———. 1986. *Symbols That Stand for Themselves*. Chicago: University of Chicago Press.

Walsh, Lorena S. 2001. "The Chesapeake Slave Trade: Regional Patterns, African Origins, and Some Implications." *William & Mary Quarterly*, 3rd ser., 58 (1): 139–70.

Weatherly, Yetive R. 1986. *Lovettsville: The German Settlement*. Lovettsville, Va.: Lovettsville Museum.

Weaver, William W. 1986. "The Pennsylvania German House: European Antecedents and New World Forms." *Winterthur Portfolio* 21 (4): 243–64.

Webber, F. R. 1971. *Church Symbolism: An Explanation of the More Important Symbols of the Old Testament and New Testament, the Primitive, the Medieval, and the Modern Church*. Detroit: Gale Research.

Weber, Frederick P. 1971. *Aspects of Death and Correlated Aspects of Life in Art, Epigram and Poetry: Contributions towards an Anthology and an Iconography of the Subject*. College Park, Md.: McGrath.

Wedel, Johan. 2004. *Santería Healing: A Journey into the Afro-Cuban World of Divinities, Spirits, and Sorcery*. Gainesville: University Press of Florida.

Weik, Terry. 1997. "Archaeology of Maroon Societies in the Americas: Resistance, Cultural Continuity, and Transformation in the African Diaspora." *Historical Archaeology* 31 (2): 81–92.

Wells, Camille. 1998. "The Multistoried House: Twentieth-Century Encounters with the Domestic Architecture of Colonial Virginia." *Virginia Magazine of History and Biography* 106 (4): 353–418.

Weslager, Clinton A. 1969. *The Log Cabin in America*. New Brunswick, N.J.: Rutgers University Press.

Whitten, Norman E., Jr. 1962. "Contemporary Patterns of Malign Occultism among Negroes in North Carolina." *Journal of American Folklore* 75: 311–25.

Wiessner, Polly. 1983. "Style and Social Information in Kalahari San Projectile Points." *American Antiquity* 48 (2): 253–76.

———. 1984. "Reconsidering the Behavioral Basis for Style: A Case Study among the Kalahari San." *Journal of Anthropological Archaeology* 3 (3): 190–234.

———. 1985. "Style or Isochrestic Variation? A Reply to Sackett." *American Antiquity* 50 (1): 160–66.

———. 1990. "Is There a Unity to Style?" In *The Uses of Style in Archaeology*, edited by Margaret Conkey and Christine Hastorf, 105–12. Cambridge, U.K.: Cambridge University Press.

Wilkie, Laurie A. 1995. "Magic and Empowerment on the Plantation: An Archaeological Consideration of African-American World View." *Southeastern Archaeology* 14 (2): 136–48.

———. 1997. "Secret and Sacred: Contextualizing the Artifacts of African-American Magic and Religion." *Historical Archaeology* 31 (4): 81–106.

———. 2000. *Creating Freedom: Material Culture and African American Identity at Oakley Plantation, Louisiana, 1840–1950*. Baton Rouge: Louisiana State University Press.

Williams, Harrison. 1938. *Legends of Loudoun*. Richmond: Garrett and Massie.

Wills, David W. 1997. "The Central Themes of American Religious History: Pluralism, Puritanism, and the Encounter of Black and White." In *African-American Religion: Interpretive Essays in History and Culture*, edited by Timothy E. Fulop and Albert J. Raboteau, 8–20. New York: Routledge.

Winston, Anne. 1993. "Tracing the Origins of the Rosary: German Vernacular Texts." *Speculum* 68 (3): 619–36.

Wobst, H. Martin. 1977. "Stylistic Behavior and Information Exchange." In *Papers for the Director: Research Essays in Honor of James B. Griffin*, edited by Charles E. Cleland, 317–42. Anthropological Papers, No. 61. Ann Arbor: University of Michigan.

———. 2000. "Agency in (Spite of) Material Culture." In *Agency in Archaeology*, edited by Marcia-Anne Dobres and John E. Robb, 40–50. London: Routledge.

Wolf, Eric R. 1972. "The Virgin of Guadalupe: A Mexican National Symbol." In *Reader in Comparative Religion: An Anthropological Approach*, edited by William A. Lessa and Evon Z. Vogt, 149–53. New York: Harper and Row.

———. 1982. *Europe and the People without History*. Berkeley: University of California Press.

Wrenshall, Leticia H. 1902. "Incantations and Popular Healing in Maryland and Pennsylvania." *Journal of American Folklore* 15 (5): 268–74.

Wust, Klaus. 1969. *The Virginia Germans*. Charlottesville: University Press of Virginia.

Wylie, Allison. 1985. "The Reaction against Analogy." In *Advances in Archaeological Method and Theory*, vol. 8, edited by Michael B. Schiffer, 63–111. New York: Academic Press.

Yelvington, Kevin A., ed. 2006. *Afro-Atlantic Dialogues: Anthropology in the Diaspora*. Santa Fe: School of American Research Press.

Yentsch, Anne. 1994. *A Chesapeake Family and Their Slaves: A Study in Historical Archaeology*. Cambridge, U.K.: Cambridge University Press.

Yentsch, Anne, and Mary C. Beaudry. 2001. "American Material Culture in Mind, Thought and Deed." In *Archaeological Theory Today*, edited by Ian Hodder, 214–40. Cambridge, U.K.: Polity Press.

Yinger, J. Milton. 1994. *Ethnicity: Source of Strength? Source of Conflict?* Albany: State University of New York Press.

Yoder, Don. 1953. *Pennsylvania German Immigrants, 1709–1786*. Baltimore: Genealogical Publishing.

———. 1965. "Official Religion versus Folk Religion." *Pennsylvania Folklife* 15 (2): 36–52.

———. 1966. "Twenty Questions on Powwowing." *Pennsylvania Folklife* 15 (4): 38–40.

———. 1980. "Hohman and Romanus: Origins and Diffusion of the Pennsylvania German Powwow Manual." In *American Folk Medicine*, edited by Wayland Hand, 235–48. Berkeley: University of California Press.

———. 1985. "The Pennsylvania Germans: Three Centuries of Identity Crisis." In *America and the Germans: An Assessment of a Three-Hundred-Year History*, vol. 1, edited by Frank Trommler and Joseph McVeigh, 41–65. Philadelphia: University of Pennsylvania Press.

———. 1990. *Discovering American Folklife: Studies in Ethnic, Religious and Regional Culture*. Ann Arbor: UMI Research Press.

Young, Amy L. 1996. "Archaeological Evidence of African-Style Ritual and Healing Practices in the Upland South." *Tennessee Anthropologist* 21 (2): 139–55.

———. 1997. "Risk Management Strategies among African-American Slaves at Locust Grove Plantation." *International Journal of Historical Archaeology* 1 (1): 5–37.

Zierden, Martha. 2002. "Frontier Society in South Carolina: An Example from Willtown (1690–1800)." In *Another's Country: Archaeological and Historical Perspectives on Cultural Interactions in the Southern Colonies,* edited by J. W. Joseph and Martha Zierden, 181–97. Tuscaloosa: University of Alabama Press.

Index

Pages with *f* denote figures and photographs.

Christopher C. Fennell is an assistant professor in the Department of Anthropology at the University of Illinois, Urbana–Champaign, where he is also an affiliate faculty member of the Center for African Studies and the African American Studies and Research Program. He has published articles on archaeology and African diaspora subjects in peer-reviewed journals such as the *International Journal of Historical Archaeology*. He also edits and publishes the *African Diaspora Archaeology Newsletter*.